Hearts Torn Asunder

Trauma in the
Civil War's Final Campaign
in North Carolina

Ernest A. Dollar Jr.

SB

Savas Beatie

California

Library of Congress Cataloging-in-Publication Data

Names: Dollar, Ernest A., Jr., author.
Title: Hearts Torn Asunder: Trauma in the Civil War's Final Campaign in
   North Carolina / Ernest A. Dollar, Jr.
Other titles: Trauma in the Civil War's Final Campaign in North Carolina
Description: El Dorado Hills : Savas Beatie, LLC, 2020. | Includes
   bibliographical references and index. | Summary: "This book explores the
   psychological experience of these soldiers and civilians during the end
   of the Civil War in North Carolina. Using letters, diaries, and accounts
   the book explores how deeply "hard war" hurt soldiers and civilians and
   shaped the memory of the war's end."— Provided by publisher.
Identifiers: LCCN 2020016119 | ISBN 9781611215120 (hardcover) |
   ISBN: 9781611215137 (ebook)
Subjects: LCSH: North Carolina—History—Civil War, 1861-1865— Campaigns |
   North Carolina—History—Civil War, 1861-1865—Psychological aspects. |
   North Carolina—History—Civil War, 1861-1865—Moral and ethical
   aspects. | United States—History—Civil War, 1861-1865—Psychological
   aspects. | Combat—Psychological aspects—History—19th century. |
   Sherman's March through the Carolinas—Psychological aspects. | North
   Carolina—Social conditions—History—19th century.
Classification: LCC E477.7 .D65 2020 | DDC 973.7/456—dc23
LC record available at https://lccn.loc.gov/2020016119

First edition, first printing

Savas Beatie
989 Governor Drive, Suite 102
El Dorado Hills, CA 95762
Phone: 916-941-6896 / (E-mail) sales@savasbeatie.com

Savas Beatie titles are available at special discounts for bulk purchases in the United States. Contact us for more details.

Proudly published, printed, and warehoused in the United States of America.

Dust jacket image: *North and South, 1865* (oil on canvas), Mayer, Constant (1832-1911) / Museum of Fine Arts, Houston, Texas, USA / © Museum of Fine Arts, Houston / Museum purchase with funds provided by "One Great Night in November, 2011," and the Alice Pratt Brown Museum Fund; and Nancy and Richard D. Kinder in honor of Emily Ballew Neff / Bridgeman Images.

To those who have felt war

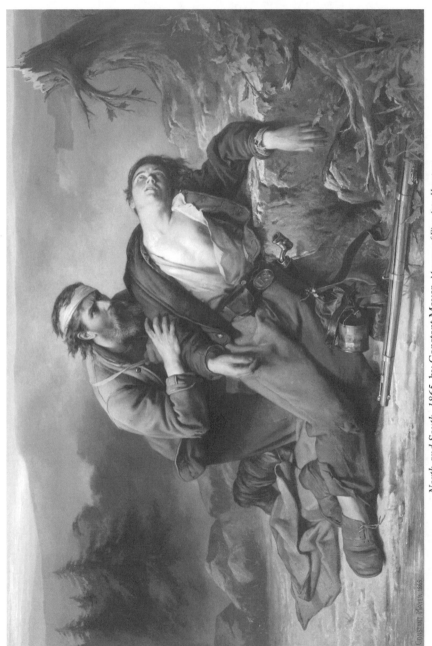

North and South, 1865, by Constant Mayer. *Museum of Fine Arts, Houston*

Table of Contents

MAP

LIST OF ILLUSTRATIONS

LIST OF ABBREVIATIONS

AU	Special Collections and Archives, Auburn University, Auburn, AL
AHSL	Library and Archives Room, Atlanta Historical Society Library, Atlanta, GA
ADAH	Alabama Department of Archive and History, Montgomery, AL
ALPLM	Abraham Lincoln Presidential Library and Museum, Springfield, IL
BL-UMI	Bentley Historical Library, University of Michigan, Ann Arbor, MI
B&L	Johnson &. Buel, eds. Battles and Leaders of the Civil War
BP	Bennett Place State Historic Site, Durham, NC
BUA	Rare Books and Special Collections, St. Bonaventure University Archives, Bonaventure, NY
CSU	Special Collections, California State University. Long Beach
CV	Confederate Veteran Magazine
DU	Perkins Library, Duke University, Durham, NC
GDAH	Georgia Department of Archives and History, Morrow, GA
GHI	Gilder Lehrman Institute of American History Collection, New York, NY
GHM	Greensboro Historical Museum, Greensboro, NC
IHS	Indiana Historical Society, Indianapolis
INHS	Smith Memorial Library, Indiana Historical Society, Indianapolis
ILSHS	Illinois State Historical Society, Springfield
ISA	Iowa State Archives, Des Moines
ISUA	Special Collections and University Archives, Iowa State University, Ames
KCA	Special Collections, Knox College, Galesburg, IL
LOC	Library of Congress, Washington, D.C.
MLHC	Michigan Library and Historical Center, Lansing
MHP	Mordecai Historic Park, Raleigh, NC
MHS	Minnesota Historical Society, St. Paul
MSU	Special Collections, Michigan State University, East Lansing
NARA	National Archives Records Administration, Washington, D.C.
NCDAH	North Carolina Department of Archives and History, Raleigh

NYSL	New York State Library, New York
OR	U.S. War Department. The War of the Rebellion: A Compilation of the Official Records of the Union and Confederate Armies. 128 vols. Washington, DC
SHC/UNC	Southern Historical Collection, University of North Carolina, Chapel Hill
SHSW	State Historical Society of Wisconsin, Madison
SHSP	Southern Historical Society Papers, Richmond, VA
SMS	Kennan Library, St. Mary's School, Raleigh, NC
TSLA	Tennessee State Library and Archives, Nashville
UASC	W.S. Hoole Special Collection. University of Alabama, Tuscaloosa
UA	Special Collections, University of Arkansas, Fayetteville
UGA	Hargrett Rare Book and Manuscript Library, University of Georgia, Athens
UM	Department of Archives and Special Collections, University of Mississippi, Oxford
UNCW	Special Collections, Randall Library, University of North Carolina at Wilmington
UND	University Archives, University of Notre Dame, South Bend, Indiana
UI	Special Collections, University of Iowa, Iowa City
USC	South Caroliniana Library, University of South Carolina, Columbia
USMHI	Archives Branch, United States Military History Institute, Carlisle Barracks, Pennsylvania
UT	Briscoe Center for American History, University of Texas at Austin
UTK	Betsey B. Creekmore Special Collections and University Archives, University of Tennessee, Knoxville
VMHC	Virginia Museum of History and Culture, Richmond
VMI	Manuscript Collections, Virginia Military Institute, Lexington
WCHS	John Hay Center, Washington County Historical Society. Salem, Indiana
WFU	Z. Smith Reynolds Library, Wake Forrest University, Winston Salem, North Carolina
WPA	Works Progress Administration, Federal Writers Project, Slave Narratives
WS	Special Collections and Archives, Wright State University, Dayton, OH

ACKNOWLEDGMENTS

Few books are written without the help of others. I thank those who have lent their time, energy, and insights to help make this book possible. David Southern, Duke University Press, Dr. Jim Broomall, George Tyler Moore Center for the Study of the Civil War, Dr. Christopher Graham, American Civil War Museum, Diane Smith, Ryan Reed, and Ken McCoury, Bennett Place State Historic Site, and Jeremiah DeGennaro, Alamance Battleground Historic Site.

Those veteran scholars who provided valuable insight and historical resources and military experience that helped shaped the direction of this book likewise deserve thanks: Tom Magnuson, Maj. Dave Hunter (Ret.), Steve Rankin, and Col. Wade Sokolosky (Ret). Dr. Mark Bradley, U.S. Army Center of Military History, deserves special thanks for his advice and landmark books that provided a foundation upon which this work seeks to build on.

Thanks also to those generous people across the country who have provided valuable historical material over the past twenty years: Brenda McKean, Susy Barile, Paul Scott, Bob Ferrell, Bill Hancock, Ted Yeatman, M.J. Hall, David Waller, Pam Dickerson, George Reeves, Sue Scullion, Charles Druer, Percy Horton, Ben Hitchings, Krissy Gray, Felicia Abrams, and Cheri Szcodronski

A big thank you is also deserved to those who helped in refining the manuscript and provided enormous moral support, Joshua Sokal, Derek Adams, Laura Soldevilla, Steve Guthauser, and Libby Parins.

Thanks also go out to the many historic organizations that have provided me an opportunity to speak and present my developing thoughts on encompassed by this book.

Also many thanks to my publisher Theodore P. Savas of Savas Beatie and his staff, including editors Dr. Tom Schott and Joel Manuel, Lee Merideth, and the wonderful marketing team for their hard work to this book a reality.

And finally to my parents, Ernest And Foye Mae Dollar who believed in me enough to support me in any endeavor. The biggest acknowledgement belongs to my wife, Suzie, and our children, Elijah and Kilby, for their support and benevolence as I labored through this work for many years.

"So perish the memory of their faults!"

Cornelia Phillips Spencer looked out of the windows of her Chapel Hill home at the scars left by war. She saw blood-stained towels sway in the spring breeze above red mounds of dirt from newly dug Confederate graves. The once lush groves she explored as a girl now stood a wasteland after the Union army made them their camping ground. Her neighbors, too, looked different after the surrender. Women appeared as ghostly figures draped in mourning veils as they darted down streets searching for food or laudanum. Men wrung their hands and worried about their crops and the unfamiliar world in which they now found themselves. But for Cornelia the veterans who hobbled past her window most embodied the war's painful legacy.

War scarred Spencer and everyone she knew, especially those men who survived it. Spencer's own experience left her emotionally overwhelmed and physically drained. Her still raw emotions moved her to write a "true" account of the Civil War's last painful months, which she hoped would indict the triumphant Yankees. She focused on the cruelty of Major General William T. Sherman's Union army and the devastation Southerners suffered at its hands.

In 1866, Spencer published *The Last Ninety Days of the War*, the earliest history of the surrender in North Carolina. "[W]hen the history of the war at the South comes to be truthfully written," she wrote, "they will receive its records with incredulity; and when belief is compelled, will turn from them shuddering." She wanted to show how savage and immoral Sherman's war on them was. But in her desire for truth, Spencer reluctantly recorded episodes of Confederate immorality. One account she struggled to record was the surrender of Raleigh in 1865. Her version of events not only acknowledged the psychological damage suffered by

Rebel soldiers at war's end, but also the South's efforts to shape healing memories to mitigate the war's horrors.[1]

Spencer recounted the exploits of her neighbor, ex-Governor David L. Swain, who surrendered the state capitol on April 13. While waiting on the steps of the capitol for the Union army to arrive, Swain spied a group of Confederate cavalrymen looting a nearby jewelry store and confronted them. He recognized the men as members of Major General Joseph Wheeler's notorious cavalry, which he considered the "debris" of the Confederate army. The former governor warned them of the impending approach of Federal cavalry. "D[am]n Sherman and the town," barked one trooper, who admitted he "cared for neither." The confrontation grew into a shouting match until Major General Judson Kilpatrick's Federal horsemen turned onto the street. All but one of the Confederates mounted their horses and dashed off; the one who waited began firing as the Union column rode into range. The trooper then sped off but was soon captured and dragged before Kilpatrick, who questioned the captive about why he violated the city's surrender terms. Spencer claimed the young Confederate denied knowledge of any agreement, but the infuriated Kilpatrick ordered his immediate execution. She included a rumor that the nameless trooper had "asked for five minutes to write his wife." Kilpatrick denied the request, and the prisoner was marched off to pay for what Spencer called his "rash" and "wild act."[2]

Another eyewitness remembered the scene differently. An enslaved woman named Milly saw the attack and the trooper's capture. She identified the soldier as Robert Walsh of the 8th Texas Cavalry. When Kilpatrick asked Walsh why he fired at him, the Rebel horseman replied, "Cause I hate de Yankees an' I wush dat dey wus daid in a pile." This was an unfortunate reply, considering Kilpatrick had actually found several of his men dead, executed by the Texans over the past two months. But what struck Milly was the soldier's reaction to his death sentence. She remembered he laughed maniacally and thanked the general saying, "Kin[d] of you sir" and waved goodbye to the crowd as he was carried off to be hanged. Milly was haunted the rest of her life by the fact that he kept laughing until his neck broke.[3]

---

1 Cornelia Phillips Spencer, *The Last Ninety Days of the War in North Carolina* (New York, 1866), 46.

2 Ibid., 161.

3 Milly Henry, *Slave Narratives from the Federal Writers' Project, 1936-1938, North Carolina Narratives*, 17 vols., (Washington, DC, 1941), 11/1:403.

The sting of defeat made it difficult for Spencer and other Southerners to reconcile painful stories like Robert Walsh's. Memories of what happened in the war's final days tormented a society trying to recover from a deeply traumatic experience. Humiliated, ruined, and overwhelmed by grief, the South sought to provide solace for the broken soldiers and families staggering under the grief over lost loved ones. Spencer would be followed by writers who drifted away from recording truth, who mythologized the Confederacy and its warriors in order to remind the South that their cause had been just and its defenders noble. But the implosion of the Confederate army as it surrendered brought on much lawlessness and violence, and precious little exultation. Spencer admitted Walsh's moral lapse, but in her eyes the demoralized men's behavior was forgivable, because their deaths and ultimate defeat balanced any wrongs they might have committed. She blamed war for men's clouded minds, which led to their immoral deeds.

> What our soldiers did or did not do in those last dark days of confusion and utter demoralization, we record with sad and tender allowance. Wrong was done in many instances, and excesses committed; but we feel that the remembrance of their high and noble qualities will in the end survive all temporary blots and blurs. And for those who perished in the wrong-doing engendered by desperation and failure and want, their cause has perished with them. *So perish the memory of their faults!*[4]

This belief would forever shape the South's memory of its soldiers' roles in the war. But the victorious Northerners crafted their own history, which overlooked Union soldiers' cruelties and the moral cost of victory.

In the shadow of Walsh's dangling corpse, Brigadier General Newell Gleason marched into Raleigh with his hardened veterans of the 87th Indiana. Newell had fought with these men through the horrific battles of the war's Western Theater, most notably at Chickamauga in September 1863. There, amidst ferocious hand-to-hand fighting, Gleason and his men had helped save Major General William Rosecrans's Union army, but paid dearly. The regiment lost 61 of the 380 men who had gone into battle. Gleason's combat leadership earned him a promotion, but it also left him a changed man. He continued to lead his men in Sherman's Atlanta campaign in the spring of 1864, but his mental state steadily deteriorated. His men watched his transformation from a capable leader into a troubled man. Gleason grew "nervous," "excitable," and "erratic," with his moods

---

4 Spencer, *The Last Ninety Days*, 161-162.

swinging from melancholy and uncontrollable sobbing to jubilancy and incessant laughing. He would pull his fellow officers aside in camp and quietly confide to them his knowledge of a conspiracy within the brigade to ruin him.[5]

Gleason finally snapped when Sherman's army marched into South Carolina in January 1865. The usually strict disciplinarian surprised his men by ordering them to shoot livestock and urging them to "not leave a live thing in [S]outh Carolina." In the years after the war, Gleason's mental wounds left him depressed. Nightmares and an inability to concentrate plagued his deteriorating mental state and eventually led to his suicide in 1886. He was one of many Union soldiers whose mental health shaped the way he fought, the way he made war.[6]

Serving in the same brigade as Gleason, Captain Samson Jack North struggled with the awful sights swirling around him. Days before the Federals entered Raleigh, he declared himself "thoroughly disgusted" with the behavior of his fellow soldiers, noting that one man had been recently been publicly executed for rape and two others awaited trial for the same crime. His repulsion and shame led him to censor further details of the campaign to his wife because he considered them to be "a disgrace to the American Nation and her Armies." In fact, North believed the real story of Sherman's march would never be written, and if it were, it would be whitewashed. "I would to God they should never be chronicled in the annals of the nineteenth century but if chronicled only by American historians they will pander to public opinion sufficiently to gild them up and make them appear in less repulsive form."[7]

War's power to cause pain is unmatched in the human experience. The Civil War stands as a conflict whose intensity caused deeply profound changes in a generation, changes we are still struggling to fully understand a century and a half later. The power of the war's close deeply affected those who survived it, but comparatively little has been written about this experience. One reason for its relative obscurity is the fact of just how stressful these last days actually were. These traumas made a deep and lasting impact on the fragile physical and mental state of soldiers and civilians. The moral health of those involved became degraded, and

---

5 William F. Fox, *Regimental Losses in the American Civil War* (Albany, NY, 1889), 29; Eric Dean, *Shook Over Hell: Post-Traumatic Stress, Vietnam, and the Civil War* (Cambridge, 1997), 152-153.

6 Ibid.

7 S. Jack North to "Dear Mary," April 2, 1865, Bentley Library, University of Michigan Ann Arbor (BL-UMI).

good people did terrible things. The result was a complicated memory of the war's largest surrender, which many wished to forget.

This final campaign began on April 10, 1865, a day after the surrender at Appomattox Court House in Virginia. Over 120,000 Union and Confederate soldiers cut across North Carolina's heartland, bringing war with them: the final march of Sherman's army in its effort to destroy Southerners' ability and moral stamina to wage war. The demoralized but still dangerous Confederate Army of Tennessee, under General Joseph E. Johnston, struggled to organize and resist Union forces as they entered the state. Thousands of Rebel veterans streaming south from the surrender in Virginia added to the chaos. Distraught North Carolina civilians found themselves caught in the middle and suffered when these forces collided. The emotional intensity of the war's final weeks roiled the minds and tore the hearts of many already-troubled people.

This book examines the events of the war's close to show individuals' psychological, physical, and moral reactions to intense stress during moments of monumental change. To understand the impact of these events on survivors requires exploring how they expressed themselves, how they behaved, and how they remembered. Men and women are seen as, and some confess to, being overcome by deeply emotional, wildly irrational, and often uncontrollable reactions. Others came away from the experience guilt-ridden and wracked by troublesome memories. Closely observing individuals during this time reveals emotional and psychological stress disorder similarities to symptoms of modern stress injuries, specifically post-traumatic stress disorder (PTSD). Using this term to describe Civil War soldiers may be jarring at first, but understanding PTSD provides insight into how extreme stress dramatically affects both the bodies and minds of those at war. PTSD is no longer just a psychological diagnosis; neuroscience reveals how the stress of war changes the actual physical structure of the brain. It provides proof that stress causes damage that directly influences the emotions, behavior, and physical health of individuals. It played a central role in shaping how the war ended. PTSD left survivors, and the nation, conflicted about how to remember the surrender in North Carolina.[8]

Modern science has provided doctors with unprecedented tools to understand how war affects the mind and the body. Human brains deal with stress or fear by releasing a neurochemical cocktail of norepinephrine, cortisol, and serotonin. These redirect the brain's focus from the frontal lobe, which governs reasoning and

---

8 Dean, *Shook Over Hell*, 70.

logical thought, to the medulla oblongata, where the body's physical systems such as breathing, cardiovascular activity, and digestion are controlled. This shift from the "modern brain" to the primal or instinctual brain helps the body respond to a physical threat. This switch, often referred to as the "fight, freeze, or flight" response, generates energy and causes muscle tensing, rapid heartbeat, increased respiration, narrowed vision, and heightened hearing. It also decreases the brain response that controls judgment, impulses, and empathy. Ordinarily, these chemicals would dissipate after the threat dissolves, but sometimes the intensity of this change, or lingering hormones, can injure the brain. The chances of damage also increase with sustained or repeated trauma, such as extended combat. This leaves an individual's primal brain in control, and the body stuck in a heightened state of preparation in order to cope with fear. Sufferers can often have violent outbursts of intense rage, harmful self-medicating, uncontrollable weeping, wild mood swings, or emotional numbness. They can experience flashbacks of the traumatic event, nightmares, or insomnia. Physically, individuals exhibit heightened vigilance, headaches, fatigue, or rapid heart rate. They often complain of not being able to eat or concentrate. These symptoms can show up immediately post-trauma, or can manifest years later. Drug and alcohol abuse also may affect diagnosed individuals. Science has revealed that alcohol reproduces the numbing effect of the body's natural endorphins, which deal with pain during trauma. Some soldiers discovered that alcohol and other stimulants could mimic the effect of these natural opioids and sought constant self-medication. Comparing brain imaging of diagnosed individuals with PTSD provides proof of toxic stress' impact on behavior and health. Exploring the historic record with this knowledge provides important insights into soldiers of the Civil War and their connections to warriors across time.[9]

---

9 Diane M. Sommerville, "'Will They Ever Be Able to Forget?': Confederate Soldiers and Mental Illness in the Defeated South," in Stephen Berry, ed., *Weirding The War: Stories from The Civil War's Ragged Edges* (Athens, GA, 2011), 321-39; Cornelius W. Thomas, "Post-traumatic stress disorder: review of DSM criteria and functional neuroanatomy," *Marshall Journal of Medicine* (2018), 4:30-38; Manish Dwivedi, "Physiology and Anatomy of Stress," *Journal of Advanced Research in Ayurveda, Yoga, Unani, Siddha, Homeopathy* (2018), 2:23-26. *Diagnostic and Statistical Manual of Mental Disorders* (DSM-V), 5th ed., (Washington, DC, 2013), 271-280; R. Gregory Lande, "Felo De Se: Soldier Suicides in America's Civil War," *Military Medicine* (May 2011), 5:531-536; W. A. Achenbaum, J. D. Howell, and M. Parker, "Patterns of alcohol use and abuse among aging Civil War veterans, 1865-1920," *Bulletin of the New York Academy of Medicine* (January-February 1993), 69:69-85; David T. Courtwright, "The Hidden Epidemic: Opiate Addiction and Cocaine Use in the South, 1860-1920," *The Journal of Southern History* (1983),

Since the 1990s, historians have debated the appropriateness of applying modern diagnoses like PTSD to past generations and cultures. But thirty years of subsequent research has reshaped our understanding of how the human brain works, and has quickened our ability to recognize injuries to it. Scientific advancements, along with the growing body of research on veterans' lives, have reshaped the conversation about PTSD's application across time. But PTSD is another term in a long history of ways, starting in the ancient world, that man has struggled to articulate the psychological and physical effects of battle.[10]

From the world's first written story, the *Epic of Gilgamesh*, c. 1,800 BCE, hints of war trauma can be found in Gilgamesh's deep grief and survivor's guilt over the loss of a close comrade. Five hundred years later Assyrian soldiers fighting in Mesopotamia around 1,300 BCE heard and talked to the ghosts of people they had slain in battle. Soldiers in the Icelandic story *Gísla saga Súrssonar*, from 980 CE, also suffered reoccurring nightmares of battle. Historians exploring connections to soldiers across time have compared Homer's 8th century BCE tale of the Trojan War, *The Iliad*, with experiences of Vietnam veterans. Further evidence suggest the "father of medicine," Greek physician Hippocrates, understood the impact of war and described troubled soldiers in his work *The Doctrine of Critical Days*, an account probably written to train physicians to recognize the conditions of men suffering war trauma. Roman poet Lucretius, in *De Rerum Natura (On the Nature of Things)*, c. 50 BCE, describes the bodies of former soldiers who would "wrestle and groan with pains" while their minds were tortured as if "gnawed by fangs of panther or of lion fierce," and men who dreamt about fighting, lashing out as if in battle, and experiencing problems with their limbs. Accounts of troubled soldiers continue to be recorded into the Middle Ages. In 1388, French poet and historian Jean Froissart told of one veteran of the Hundred Years' War who couldn't sleep near

---

1:58-103; Joseph Volpicelli, Geetha Balaraman, Julie Hahn, Heather Wallace, and Donald Bux, "The role of uncontrollable trauma in the development of PTSD and alcohol addiction," *Alcohol, Research, & Health* (1999), 23:256-262.

10 Ala Young, *The Harmony of Illusions: Inventing Post-Traumatic Stress Disorder* (Princeton, NJ, 1995), 1-5; John Talbott, "Combat Trauma in the American Civil War," *History Today* (March 1996), 46:41–47; Gary W. Gallagher and Kathryn S. Meirer, "Coming to Terms with Civil War Military History," *Journal of the Civil War Era* (December 2014), 491-493; Yoav Di-Capua, "Trauma and Other Historians: An Introduction," *Historical Reflections/Réflexions Historiques* (December 2015), 41; Larry M. Logue and Peter Blanck, *Heavy Laden: Union Veterans, Psychological Illness* (Cambridge, 2018), 1-2; Tony Horwitz, "Did Civil War Soldiers Have PTSD?," *Smithsonian Magazine* (January 2015), www.smithsonianmag.com/history/ptsd-civil-wars-hidden-legacy-180953652/, accessed December 21, 2019.

his family because he would wake up at night and grab his sword to fight imaginary enemies.[11]

Ancient accounts have also documented the physical problems suffered by combat veterans. Herodotus recorded the experience of a Greek soldier in 490 BCE who inexplicably went blind during the battle of Marathon after the soldier next to him was killed. Advances in military medicine allowed doctors during Europe's late 18th century revolutionary wars to refine the connection between war and soldiers' health. German poet and writer Goethe described the changes he felt himself undergoing during the battle of Valmy in 1792:

> . . . as if you were in a very hot place, and at the same time impregnated with that heat until you blended completely with the element surrounding you. Your eyes can still see with the same acuity and sharpness, but it is as if the world had put on a reddish-brown hue that makes the objects and the situation still more scary. . . . I had the impression that everything was being consumed by this fire . . . this situation is one of the most unpleasant that you can experience.

The French whom Goethe fought noticed the stupefied condition of soldiers after suffering a bombardment. Doctors attributed this catatonic state to the concussion of shells, which they termed *"vent du boulet"* or "wind of the bullet." In 1798, French surgeon Phillippe Pinel crafted a diagnosis for soldiers he saw with heart problems of unidentified causes as "cardiorespiratory neurosis" and a general dazed state he called "idiotism." All of these mental and emotional conditions appeared in the American armies of the Civil War.[12]

After the outbreak of war in 1861, surgeons on both sides noticed similar cases of abnormal conditions in soldiers' bodies and minds. Most curious were inexplicable cardiac abnormalities they referred to as "soldier's heart." Doctors struggled to understand these conditions and their causes, and blamed weak character and poor moral fiber as causes for soldiers' mental and physical failings. But as more men reported to hospitals, surgeons felt compelled to take a closer look at these recurring disorders. Their wartime experiences with psychological

11 Walid Khalid Abdul-Hamid and Jamie Hacker Hughes, "Nothing New Under the Sun: Post-traumatic Stress Disorders in the Ancient World," *Early Science and Medicine Journal* (2014), 6:545-557.

12 Marc-Antonie Crocq and Louis Crocq, "Overview: Literature, History, and the DSM All Document PTSD," in Barbara Krasner, ed., *Returning Soldiers and PTSD* (New York, 2018), 129-145.

and psychophysiological changes in soldiers suggested a relationship, but doctors struggled to articulate symptoms and classify this widespread phenomenon. In June 1862, Union army Surgeon General William A. Hammond instituted new regulations for reporting sick and wounded in order to use this data to advance the study of battlefield medicine. *The Medical and Surgical History of the War of the Rebellion* (1870) provided numbers for diseases of the nervous system, such as insanity, nostalgia, headaches, paralysis, and sunstroke. This compendium also profiled afflictions of other major organs, such as the heart, lungs, and digestive systems. One of the first doctors to study the relationship between military service and physical changes was the Union army's Jacob M. Da Costa.

Da Costa had studied medicine across Europe and at the Jefferson Medical College in Philadelphia, where he became interested in current theories on somatic conditions. War eventually swept him into Federal service as an assistant surgeon at Philadelphia's Turner's Lane Hospital. There he critically evaluated soldiers suffering conditions that had no clear causes. In 1864, Da Costa published an outline of a disorder he had discerned in the soldiers, and fully detailed his observations in the 1871 paper, "On Irritable Heart: A Clinical Study of Functional Cardiac Disorder and its Consequences." He cited similar cases found among British soldiers during the Crimean War and speculated that Confederate soldiers had suffered the same afflictions. Irregular heart rhythms often caused headaches, giddiness, disturbed sleep, and dizziness, symptoms he attributed to "over-action and frequent excitement." Another doctor, I. H. Stearns, encountered similar symptoms in veterans with "unexplainable, constantly reoccurring symptoms" that caused sleeplessness, uneasiness, and a lack of concentration. The culprit, Stearns believed, was a soldier's irregular diet, excessive physical activity, exposure to climate, and mental strain. Stearns adopted the theories of British physician Dennis de Berdt Hovell, who hypothesized that soldiers suffered from a shakeup of the nervous system and dubbed the condition "post-bellum neurokinesis." As part of his diagnosis, Hovell sought to explain how military service affected morality. To him, veterans seemed to suffer "neurosis from moral shock," which he attributed to hard fighting and the drastic experience of soldiering. This was progressive thought, given previous beliefs that social, moral, and religious conditions affected mental instability.[13]

---

13 J. M. Da Costa, "On Irritable Heart: A Clinical Study of a Form of Functional Cardiac Disorder and Its Consequences," *The American Journal of Medical Science*, Isaac Hays, ed., (January 1871), 61:17-52; I. H Stearns, "A New Name for an old Veteran's Disease," *Medical*

A former Union medical inspector, Horace Porter, embraced Hovell's research and took it a step further. He surmised these factors permanently harmed the old soldiers. As the chief medical officer for the Grand Army of the Republic (GAR), Porter took careful note of the common long-term effects of the war on veterans' nervous systems. He endorsed the work of Stearns and Hovell and claimed the "neurokinesis of battle" and environmental factors such as diet, lack of sleep, disease, and prison life exacerbated the harmful conditions of soldiering. Critically, he linked the damaged nervous systems of veterans to the "hundreds of hours of the brain tension of expected danger." In the end, Porter believed war damaged the nervous systems of those who fought it.[14]

The study of soldiers continued as America fought its subsequent wars. Da Costa's and others' research laid the foundation for doctors treating neurological injuries on Europe's battlefields in World War I. Soldiers shook uncontrollably and experienced headaches, dizziness, hypersensitivity to noise, and amnesia, all symptoms of a diagnosis commonly called "shell shock." Building on this experience, the U.S. army established special psychiatric hospitals to treat the flood of mentally wounded soldiers during World War II. The term "combat fatigue" was generally applied to men suffering from depression, suicidal thoughts, depersonalization, schizophrenia, and psychotic behavior. The most enduring realization of this wartime experience for G.I.s was that "every man has his breaking point." The long-term assessment of these veterans suggested that at least 27 percent of them experienced some lifelong behaviors attributed to war trauma. Advances in the fields of psychology, psychiatry, and mental health science resulted in a new classification of service-related issues for Vietnam veterans. "Post-traumatic stress disorder" officially became a diagnosis in 1980, and was eventually added to the official list of mental conditions related to soldiers' exposure to extreme trauma. Researchers believe that between 15-30 percent of Vietnam veterans suffered full or partial effects of PTSD.[15]

Summary (May 1888), 49-50; Stearns, "Neurokinesis," *The Medical Bulletin: A Monthly Journal of Medicine and Surgery* (July 1888), 216-217.

14 Loague and Blanck, *Heavy Laden*, 122-123; Matthew J. Friedman, Paula P. Schnurr, and Annmarie McDonagh-Coyle, "Post-Traumatic Stress Disorder in the Military Veteran," *Psychiatric Clinics of North America* (June 1994) 17: 265-277; Brian Matthew Jordan, *Marching Home: Union Veterans and Their Unending Civil War* (New York, 2014), 127-128.

15 James Marten, *Sing Not War: The Lives of Union and Confederate Veterans in Gilded Age America* (Chapel Hill, NC, 2011), 90; Dean, *Shook Over Hell*, 37, 41.

In the shadow of the 1991 Gulf War, in which an estimated 12 percent suffered from chronic war-time stress, historian Eric Dean examined medical records of Civil War veterans in the Indiana Hospital for the Insane and found evidence of PTSD symptoms among the inmates. Fifteen years and two wars later, in 2006, Judith Pizarro, Roxanne Silver, and JoAnn Prause surveyed the medical records of 17,700 Union veterans to understand how the war affected their physical and mental health. Their research has shown that wartime service led to increased health issues such as cardiovascular disease, hypertension, and gastrointestinal disorders. Those most at risk were young enlistees or those who experienced prisoner of war (POW) camps. They discovered that the biggest indicators of long-term mental injuries were seen in veterans serving in high causality units. These men were 51 percent more likely to develop physical problems in postwar life.[16]

By 2018, Dora Costa expanded the research started by historian Robert Fogel, surveying and collecting data from pension records of nearly 70,000 U.S. army veterans to understand the health of soldiers before, during, and after war. Costa's study, *The Early Indicators of Later Work Levels, Disease, and Death*, provides the best evidence of how Northern soldiers, both black and white, dealt with the war's lasting effects. Compiling information from soldiers' pension files, and connecting it with unprecedented demographic, economic, and health data, confirms that different wartime experiences caused similar life-long problems. The "Early Indicators" study offers comprehensive evidence that most physical and mental issues suffered by veterans were a result of their war service with younger soldiers among the most vulnerable. This groundbreaking study of thousands of soldiers provided new insight into the long term impact of war.[17]

The physical and emotional damage of wartime stress helps explain the moral changes that played a role in how the war's final months were fought. By 1865, soldiers who suffered from years of toxic stress found their abilities to think

---

16 Marten, *Sing Not War*, 86, 106; Judith Pizarro, Roxanne Cohen Silver, and JoAnn Prause, "Physical and Mental Health Costs to Traumatic War Experiences Among Civil War Veterans," *Archives of General Psychiatry* (February 2006), 63:193.

17 Dora L. Costa, Heather DeSomer, Eric Hanss, Christopher Roudiez, Sven E. Wilson and Noelle Yetter, "Union Army veterans, all grown up," *Historical Methods: A Journal of Quantitative and Interdisciplinary History* (2017), 50:79-95; Dora L. Costa, Noelle Yetter, and Heather DeSomer, "Intergenerational transmission of paternal trauma among US Civil War ex-POWs," *Proceedings of the National Academy of Sciences*, Department of Veteran's Affairs, www.ptsd.va.gov/understand/common/common_veterans.asp., accessed January 21, 2019; Judith P. Pizarro, Roxanne C. Silver, and JoAnn Prause, "Physical and Mental Health Costs of Traumatic War Experiences Among Civil War Veterans," *Archives of General Psychiatry*, 193-194.

For many veterans, the hardening process began with their first experiences on the battlefield. The physical and emotional changes caused by combat and its aftermath stayed with them forever. Adolph Metzner of the 32nd Indiana, an amateur sketch artist, captured many scenes of death during the war, but none more grisly than two decapitated Confederates whose card game had been ended by a cannonball during the battle of Shiloh. *Library of Congress*

rationally and to make moral judgments difficult. Battlefield trauma kept the primal brain in charge while the frontal lobe modulating empathy and cognitive thought struggled for control. Veteran soldiers who showed signs of this stress were described as numb, detached, and practically devoid of emotion; a result of a process soldiers called "hardening." By the end of the war soldiers on both sides were "hardened" to the extreme. For William T. Sherman, emotionally numb soldiers were perfect for the kind of warfare he employed to break the South's spirit. But using these men to wage the largest and most successful psychological warfare operation came at a cost. In addition to destroying the Confederacy's infrastructure and economic resources, Sherman used them to terrorize Southern civilians in order to undercut their moral support for the war. He relied on his soldiers' redefined morals to win the war, and in its last months, Sherman pushed his strained men past their ethical boundaries. On April 2, 1865, William Craig wrote to his family in Illinois from Goldsboro, North Carolina, and described his war in cold, stark terms:

> The country that we have traveled over in the last 8 months is destroyed totally. Sherman told us to burn everything and you may depend there was nothing left. Neither stock of any

kind that we could eat we shot down and left them laying. Houses we burned and fencing and large cotton factories. . . . We burned the houses and the women and children standing outside crying. Neither clothes nor nothing to eat.[18]

This was from a man who had survived three wounds, two of which came within a month of each other in fighting outside Atlanta. Craig was a hardened veteran who fought this war with a mind shaped by it. He realized what the experience of warfare had done to him and his generation. "This rebellion will be the ruination of thousands of men. They have become hardened to everything. Neither cares for God nor man." Those men who were the most numbed drifted the furthest from their moral anchors and made the hardest war. One hardened Yankee chillingly described the Union army's feelings about war in the Carolinas: "Our army did not feel bound by the ordinary restraints of human warfare." But this moral transformation left Craig conflicted after the war, fighting another battle with alcohol that he struggled to win.[19]

Craig was like many of Sherman's veterans, who returned home and tried to explain their experiences to a society largely ignorant of the realities of war. Old soldiers realized they could not describe, nor completely rationalize to civilians, their war on Southern civilians or articulate how the war changed them. Many of the veterans themselves failed to find words to explain the changes in their own bodies and minds. The ferocity of the war they waged, and the true price paid for victory, rendered their campaigns unfathomable to those on the home front. Indiana soldier Jerome Carpenter echoed what many of his fellow Yankees thought about the march. "I wish I could give you something of an idea of the magnitude of this campaign, but I cannot, and can only say that the half will never be told." Soldiers like Solomon North were proud of victory, but ashamed of the war they had fought.[20]

18 David H. Marlow, "Modern War: The American Civil War," *Psychological and Psychosocial Consequences of Combat and Deployment with Special Emphasis on the Gulf War* (Santa Monica, CA, 2001), 19; William Craig to wife, April 3, 1865, "Civil War Letters of William Craig," Ohio State University Department of History, www.ehistory.osu.edu/exhibitions/letters/craig/default, accessed March 3, 2018.

19 Joseph T. Glatthaar, *The March to the Sea and Beyond: Sherman's Troops in the Savannah and Carolinas Campaigns* (New York, 1985), 140; Francis Marion McAdams, *Every-day Soldier Life: Or A History of the One Hundred and Thirteenth Ohio Infantry* (Columbus, OH, 1884), 147.

20 Victor D. Hanson, *The Soul of Battle: From Ancient Times to the Present Day, How Three Great Liberators Vanquished Tyranny* (New York, 1999), 178-179.

Most Union soldiers managed their stress and retained their concepts of right and wrong but measured them on the scale war provided. Some tolerated what they judged as immoral behavior, rationalizing it as a tool for victory, while others sickened at what they saw. Soldiers like Solomon North were guilt-ridden by a war that violated his judgment of right and wrong. The Northern public echoed his feelings as it tried to understand Sherman's final campaigns. With the veterans remaining quiet, the story of their final march through the Carolinas drifted into obscurity or, as North predicted, it was "gilded" to make it palatable for a Northern public longing to put the war behind them. But Southerners faced the same issues with morality as the war ended and memory began.[21]

Confederate soldiers struggled to fight the war amid increasingly painful conditions. Unlike their Northern counterparts, they faced the additional trauma of suffering the emotional distress of defeat. Fear of starvation, ruin, and the collapse of their world caused extreme stress that eroded soldiers' cognitive ability to fight the war in accordance with the morals espoused by an honor-bound society. This was especially true in the Army of Tennessee, where the stress from years of defeats and deaths of comrades eroded its members' concepts of duty, honor, and discipline. This moral breach caused thousands of men to abandon the cause, desert the army, or attack what remained of the Confederacy and its people. Those who suffered the greatest stress became the most violent as defeat drew closer. John Claiborne, a companion of the executed Robert Walsh in Raleigh, looked back and tried to understand what impelled his violent wartime behavior. These men were responsible for grisly executions of Union prisoners and slaves, and they terrorized Southern civilians. Claiborne sought to explain the temporary moral lapse that occurred during the war's finale: "We did some things that were not credible to our hearts, but they seemed necessary." But they were not going to talk about it. "We afterwards concluded never to refer to them, as for twenty years we would have been subject to the rope." The impact of stress had turned Rebel soldiers into the antithesis of the postwar heroes society made them out to be.

---

21 Jonathan R. Dettmer, Erika M. Kappes, and Patcho N. Santiago, "Shame and Moral Injury in an Operation Iraqi Freedom Combat Veteran," in Elspeth Cameron Ritchie, ed., *Posttraumatic Stress Disorder and Related Diseases in Combat Veterans* (Switzerland, 2015), 36; S. Jack North to "Dear Mary," April 2, 1865, Nina Ness, BL-UMI; Spencer, *The Last Ninety Days*, 46; Gerald F. Linderman, *Embattled Courage: The Experience of Combat in the American Civil War* (New York, 1987), 266.

These were the "blots and blurs" Southerners like Cornelia Spencer strove to erase in order to process defeat.[22]

Southern civilians also suffered their own trauma that shaped how they remembered the war's end. The arrival of both armies terrified North Carolinians and amplified the stress four years of war had caused them. This violent collision ignited a fear for survival and inflamed an already unstable home front. Suffering from want of subsistence, drowning in grief, and unsettled by an internal war, civilians staggered under the increased worry for their safety brought on by the arrival of the armies. Like soldiers, this stress had an impact on civilians' morality. In the war's final days, widespread looting by soldiers was fueled by civilians. As the Confederate army tried to feed and equip itself, men and women ransacked depots and warehouses and made off with vital supplies. The preoccupation with Sherman's "bummers" and the need to survive distracted them from supporting the Confederate war effort. This confirmed the success of the Union army's psychological warfare campaign on the hearts and minds of Southerners. The economic, ecological, and psychological damage caused by the contending armies caused toxic stress that injured many, especially women. Depression, weight loss, and addiction were seen in those struggling under the intensity of the war's final days. Wake County plantation owner Kimbrough Jones told relatives about the suffering his family had endured. The evidence of the damage on survivors was obvious. "Sherman's march through this county was marked by a course of utter destruction . . . I am afraid this generation will never be able to recover. This county suffered to an alarming extent." For years afterward, men and women arrived at the state's asylums suffering from what doctors simply termed "the war."[23]

To deal with traumatic defeat, Southerners crafted a memory of the war that supplemented its negative memories with positive, idealized ones. This cultural movement, known as the "Lost Cause," sought to redefine the South's rebellion as a heroic crusade by a virtuous people. The old Rebel soldiers thus became knights and defenders of an honorable people fighting for a just cause. The Lost Cause bound white Southerners together with the idea of noble warriors combating radical change. Many of them embraced the Lost Cause and used wreath laying, monument building, and worship of the Confederacy to regain control and

22 Linderman, *Embattled Courage*, 2; John M. Claiborne, "Secret Service for General Hood," *Confederate Veteran (CV)*, Vol. 9 (1901), 31.

23 Kimbrough Jones to "Cousin William," June 27, 1867, Crabtree Jones Collection, North Carolina Office of Archives and History, Raleigh (NCDAH).

superiority over their world. But the Lost Cause also served a deeply personal purpose for its supporters: it helped to ease their unhealed wounds and lingering grief. But accomplishing this required altering the narrative, especially that of the war's final days, in order to disguise the reality of how horrendous the war had been and what their defenders had done.

The most complicated experience at the war's end was that of black men and women. Removal of the extraordinary stress of 250 years of chattel slavery via emancipation was a radically dissimilar experience than that of whites. The sublimity of freedom is impossible to convey. Sadly, few period accounts by African Americans reflect their thoughts and feelings about the war's end and emancipation. It is only through white observers that their expressions of joy, celebration, and determination are recorded. It would not be until the mid-1930s, with the Works Progress Administration's effort to document black perspectives on the end of the war that firsthand information was gathered. The merits of these interviews of the formerly enslaved conducted by white writers have been debated extensively, yet they remain the most comprehensive and valuable tool to understand how slaves felt as slavery came to its violent end.

These accounts reveal the exaltation of emancipation but also the anxiety and fear that came with it. Slaves worried about the violent reaction by whites as freedom approached. As black men and women transformed from assets to liabilities, they were attacked by soldiers of both sides. Sarah Debro remembered Confederate cavalrymen executing slaves who admitted looking forward to freedom, while Union soldiers also killed blacks randomly. One Federal remembered that "some scoundrel went up to a negro not 75 yards from us, and with one whack of a bowie knife, cut the contraband's head 1/3 off, killing him." In addition to violence, African Americans suffered increased anxiety over starvation. With both armies consuming almost all available food, white masters were sure to feed themselves first and let their human chattel fend for themselves. The WPA narratives provide a glimpse of the deprivations suffered in the days after the surrender and the insecurity of freedom.[24]

The trauma of the war's close melded with the severe mental health issues caused by a lifetime of slavery. Five days after arriving in Raleigh, the Union army forced the North Carolina Insane Asylum to admit several freedmen with symptoms attributed to "the war." Doctors believed that mental health among

---

24 Sarah Debro, *Slave Narratives,* 11/2:325-326, 213-214; H. H. Orendorff, *Reminiscences of the Civil War from Diaries of Members of the 103rd Illinois Volunteer Infantry* (Chicago, 1904), 197.

black men and women improved after the war as evidenced by the decline of African American suicides, as opposed to those for whites, which increased in the postwar years. But there was a mental health crisis among the freedmen population that necessitated the construction of a dedicated asylum for African Americans. In 1877, North Carolina organized its third mental institution, the Asylum for Colored Insane in Goldsboro, to ease this growing problem. The generational trauma of the formerly enslaved and their descendants requires its own full treatment. One early examination of this area of study came in 2005, when Dr. Joy DeGruy linked 21st century issues facing African Americans to the experience of their 19th century ancestors in a diagnosis she termed "post-traumatic slavery syndrome."[25]

The final weeks of the war were a short but traumatic chapter in the survivors' lives. The moment of defeat and victory overwhelmed the hearts and minds of a worn people. It was a deeply transformative experience that left lasting scars for many and provided relief for others. Men and women expressed this change through their words, emotions, and actions. Exploring the final days of the American Civil War leads to an understanding of how stress influences the body and brain, and reveals a generation more troubled than we have thought. Besides the wrecked bodies and psyches of soldiers and civilians, the war's moral cost shaped how this dark chapter of it was remembered and forgotten.[26]

---

25 Admission rolls, Dorothea Dix Hospital Records, NCOAH.

26 Marten, *Sing Not War*, 10.

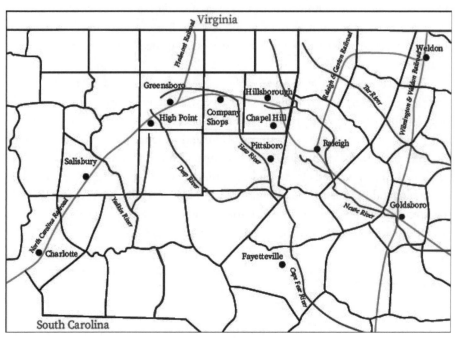

Central North Carolina, 1865. *Ernest Dollar*

Chapter 1

Confederate Soldiers:
"I don't believe they know right from wrong"

Lieutenant Robert M. Collins gazed into his flickering campfire trying to make peace with all he had seen and felt. Around him sat his fellow Texans, gaunt and solemn, deep in their own thoughts.

Their ears still rang from the battle they'd just fought at Bentonville days earlier, their third major bloodletting in less than four months. Ill-fated assaults in back-to-back battles at Franklin and Nashville in November and December 1864 had killed off half of the unit. One Rebel witness remembered that blood flowed "along the sewer by the pike like water" while another noted, "our men laid like Railroad ties and puddles of blood. It is hard for a person to realize a sight." One Texan felt overwhelmed as he wandered through a sea of graves after one of the battles. "The great many graves here. . . . This is one part of the war we have never seen before. The dead part. The graveyard." Generals were not immune to the carnage. One soldier saw a forlorn Maj. Gen. Benjamin Cheatham standing motionless wearing the saddest expression he had ever seen, "his grey eyes set with a fixed and vacant look, and his countenance wearing an expression of profound melancholy." Another officer simply admitted, "Take it all [together] the army may be said to be in bad condition."[1]

---

1 Larry J. Daniel, *Soldiering in the Army of Tennessee: A Portrait of Life in a Confederate Army* (Chapel Hill, NC, 1991), 160-162; John R. Lundberg, "Granbury's Texas Brigade, C.S.A.: The Color

Among the dead were 14 beloved Confederate generals. Of these, none was more crushing to the Texans than the loss of their commander, Hiram Granbury. With his death, "the heart of the grand army of Tennessee was broken," Lt. Collins thought. These veterans had experienced some of the worst combat of the war in the past months, and it had changed them. The loss of their leaders and the demoralizing collapse of the army cut deep wounds into men already scarred by war.[2]

Collins tried to explain how the waves of death and horrific fighting had traumatized them. "Reverses in recent battles, hardships and exposure, together with the hopelessness of our cause, rendered a majority of our soldiers a dangerous outfit, and subject to be led on into reckless excesses when led by shrewd designing men." The intensity of their recent experiences in battle overwhelmed Collins and his fellow soldiers, which made their next deployment an angry, violent endeavor.

What remained of the western Confederate army left Tupelo, Mississippi, in January 1865 to join Gen. Joe Johnston in North Carolina. On the way to Montgomery, commanders quickly realized the volatility of Granbury's Brigade and placed guards around its camp. But soldiers slipped past the sentries and roamed the streets of the city, threatening provost guards, hospital stewards, and anybody they considered "rats," men who had avoided field service. The boisterous crowd soon uncovered copious amounts of alcohol, which they quickly consumed with predictable effect. "[T]he boys took charge of the city and run it for their own account that night" Collins remembered. He admitted his fellow soldiers "are more liable to get drunk than anybody else," and the amount and voracity by which the men drank from the barrels led Collins to claim that violence had been a possibility, "if those demoralized soldiers had met with resistance that night there would have been music in the air."

Brigade of the Army," MA thesis, Texas Christian University, 2005, 319; Christopher Losson, *Tennessee's Forgotten Warrior: Frank Cheatham and His Confederate Division* (Knoxville, TN, 1989), 243. The Army of Tennessee lost more than 12,000 men in those two battles: 6,252 at Franklin, and an estimated 6,000 at Nashville.

2   Robert M. Collins, *Chapters from the Unwritten History of the War Between the States; Or, The Incidents in the Life of a Confederate Soldier in Camp, on the March, in the Great Battles, and in Prison* (St. Louis, 1893), 273. The toll on the Army of Tennessee's officer corps at Franklin alone totaled 18 killed, 38 wounded, 8 missing, and 1 captured. *The War of the Rebellion: A Compilation of the Official Records of the Union and Confederate Armies*, 128 vols. (Washington, DC, 1880-1901), Series 1, vol. 45, pgs. 684-686. Hereafter cited as *OR*. All references are to Series 1 unless otherwise noted.

Citizens of Columbus, Georgia, met the soldiers at their next stop hoping to calm the men with a grand welcome, band music, and stirring banners proclaiming, "Welcome to the Brave Defenders of our Homes and Fire-sides." The city set out its finest food on long tables around the train depot. Local men and women gave speeches as the soldiers ate, comparing the Confederates' heroic deeds to those of Caesar, Antony, and Napoleon. They had hoped to dissuade the soldiers from tearing up their town, but, said Collins, their efforts "fell as harmless and ineffective on the boys' ears." After gorging themselves, the men took their guns, marched by companies into Columbus, and filled its saloons and gambling houses. The drunken soldiers soon lost control and vandalized the town—"doing them up" in an "artistic manner." Traveling on toward Macon, the officers concluded that stopping in towns had been a bad idea and ordered the train to speed through at 40 miles per hour. Some desperate men jumped off anyway.[3]

The rail journey ended in Milledgeville, Georgia, where the men continued their trek overland. Here they confronted another shocking scene: the devastation marking the passage of Sherman's army. The ruined land and desperate people they met only deepened their depression. Collins noted the universal gloom, and recalled that the "evident early demise of our Confederacy was marked on everything." The devastation reignited the Rebels' anger. Passing through Augusta, Collins remembered that some of his erstwhile comrades worked the city over "pretty well." Another soldier, William E. Stanton, watched the behavior of his fellows with shame. He considered their journey to North Carolina to be one of the lowest points for the once-proud unit. "Granbury's Brig is counted the best brig in the army to fight and a set of thieves otherwise. Our Brig behaved shamefully all the way around from Tupelo Miss to Raleigh, N.C." Stanton blamed the absence of dead leaders for this lack of discipline: "I never seen men go do as our Brigade done after Maj Genl Cleburne and Granbury got killed there was not an officer who could do any thing with them." But waiting for them at the end of their journey was an officer who gave these troubled soldiers hope.[4]

General Joseph E. Johnston was an accomplished commander, much loved by his men but flawed by his obsession with his personal honor. Born in Farmville, Virginia, in 1807, he entered West Point and graduated in 1829 with classmate Robert E. Lee. Johnston demonstrated his bravery in combat with the U.S. Army

3 Ibid., 273-276.

4 Ibid., 282; Wm. E. Stanton to Mary G. Moody, March 30, 1865, William E. Stanton Letters, University of Texas Archives, Austin (UT).

during the Second Seminole and Mexican Wars. He rose to the rank of quartermaster general of the army but resigned his commission in 1861 to fight with the Confederacy. Johnston was the highest-ranking officer to do so and believed he deserved an equally high rank in the Southern army, but found himself jilted by President Jefferson Davis. The insult wounded his honor, an injury that poisoned their relationship during the war. Johnston's finest hour came with his leadership during the South's victory at First Manassas in July 1861. But in the following years, he was unable to repeat his success, his star slowly faded. Johnston's career and his honor suffered when Davis removed him from command of the Army of Tennessee for not stopping William T. Sherman's advance to Atlanta in May-July, 1864. Now, seven months later, Davis begrudgingly recalled "Old Joe" to rebuild the mutilated army he once commanded and launch another attempt to stop Sherman.[5]

Some soldiers now camped around Johnston at Smithfield knew the general well having served under him since Manassas, while others had fought for him in Mississippi and Georgia. Johnston won their respect because he saw to their welfare and refused to be reckless with their lives. Reluctant Confederate leaders reinstated Johnston because of his close relationship with his men. Alex Hall of the 3rd Alabama Cavalry believed that "[t]hings look pretty blue, to us who have seen the demoralization of our army. It is my opinion, and that of two thirds of the army, that this little Conf-fed is 'gone up.'" But he optimistically declared, "Joe Johnston Could might get a pretty good fight out of this army in the Spring. No one else can." A soldier in Manigault's Brigade who saw Johnston in Charlotte wrote of the three cheers soldiers gave him, and remarked, "He is as well loved in this army among the men, as an officer can be. They have every confidence in him, and that alone will benefit the army and the service."[6]

Johnston's return to command lifted some spirits, but many believed it had come too late. "Thank God he has been reinstated," wrote one army inspector, "and I hope [he] will be able to organize the army again, it is now a complete mob. I never have witnessed so much demoralization in my life." Another soldier, the 20th Alabama's John J. Huston, took heart that "Joe is again steerman of our 'Boat' & light hearts now compose her crew." Nonetheless, "despondency is an intruder

5　Craig L. Symonds, *Joseph E. Johnston: A Civil War Biography* (New York, 1992), 3-4.

6　Bradley. *This Astounding Close: The Road to Bennett Place* (Chapel Hill, NC, 2000), 8; George Blackwell to Father, Feb. 24, 1865, Civil War Soldiers' Letters, Alabama Department of Archives and History, Montgomery (ADAH).

Nothing was more important to Maj. Gen. Joseph E. Johnston than his men and his honor. By the spring of 1865 both were suffering. The stress of becoming the Confederacy's scapegoat for failure and the distraught condition of his men took an emotional toll on the general. *National Archives*

[and] the running gear of our army, but old father Joe will grease it well with bacon & brace it with confidence and soon will be again a flourishing Army."[7]

7 John G. Barrett, *Sherman's March Through the Carolinas* (Chapel Hill, NC, 1956), 112; John J. Huston, letter, Mar. 5, 1865, Huston Family Papers, W. S. Hoole Special Collection, University of Alabama, Tuscaloosa (UASC).

But Johnston's strong bond with his men could do only so much to salve their wounds. He faced the daunting task of pulling and holding the army together after the intense suffering it had endured during the battles around Atlanta and in Tennessee. Settling into their camps around Smithfield, North Carolina, the Rebels greeted the opening of the war's fifth year with grim optimism. Johnston saw obvious signs of the war's toll on them, and their trauma complicated his efforts to make them an effective fighting force again. The stress of the coming days would aggravate his soldiers' pain and overwhelm their hearts and minds.

The anxiety soldiers experience intensified as defeat loomed larger and with each passing day. This stress spawned a wave of fear, despondency, and desertions. Daniel Boyd of the 7th South Carolina told his family about his dim perspective on the regiment's situation, and shared news about those who had left the unit. "It looks like the poor little Confederacy wil[l] soon go up if it has to go. I don't car[e] how soon." Another South Carolinian, Lieutenant Colonel William Stokes, admitted how run down his men were and how badly they had suffered since starting for North Carolina. He lamented his soldiers who had deserted while fighting through South Carolina. "The regiment was in bad condition sure enough; still the others in the Brigade were not a great deal better." For men already deeply suffering from war, the stress of the next few weeks would stir questions about their duty, identities, and morality.[8]

One scarring scene along the march to join Johnston had helped erode Arthur P. Ford's bond with the Confederate cause. An officer of the 1st South Carolina had severely reprimanded a sergeant after the latter had urged his men to desert. The sergeant flew into a rage after the rebuke and fired his revolver at the officer. The column halted instantly, and the sergeant was apprehended. A hastily organized court martial assembled on the roadside instantly condemned him to death, and he was tied to a tree and shot. The execution had a noticeable and deep impact on all the witnesses. It was "an awful sight," Ford recalled, which put a "terrible strain on the integrity" of the exhausted and demoralized troops. Morale would be strained even more within the next few weeks by staggering casualties. His regiment, the 1st South Carolina, lost half their men in the battles at

---

8 J. Keith Jones, ed., *The Boys of Diamond Hill: The Lives and Civil War Letters of the Boyd Family of Abbeville County, South Carolina* (Jefferson, NC, 2011), 137-138; Lloyd Halliburton, ed., *Saddle Soldiers: The Civil War Correspondence of General William Stokes of the 4th South Carolina Cavalry* (Orangeburg, SC, 1993), 192-197.

Averasboro and Bentonville. Ford soon found a way to leave the army and helped spread chaos in the days before the surrender.[9]

In the coming weeks, thousands more would follow Ford's example and steal away from the army. Confederate authorities ordered commanders to take public measures to prevent desertions, including executions to "make an immediate example" of the "ringleaders." Officers knew controlling desertion not only boosted their forces' effectiveness, but also protected citizens from wayward soldiers. Any chance of Confederate success had required maintaining military discipline and keeping the army well fed. Anxiety over starvation was among the most powerful forces breaking down a soldier's military and moral bonds.[10]

Fear of starvation undermined discipline and encouraged theft. Sergeant W. H. Andrews of the 1st Georgia remembered gladly paying the exorbitant sum of a dollar for an ear of corn. He supposed it had been taken from a horse that needed it as badly as he did, but admitted "hunger does not make any man feel very charitably." Charles Colcock Jones of the Chatham Artillery bemoaned the extreme difficulty of getting "either rations for the men, or forage for the battery animals." Another Confederate wrote home that he was "fairing very well in the way of rashings [rations] with what we steal."[11]

Colonel Joseph Waring confirmed the prevalence of theft among some of his cavalrymen from the Jeff Davis Legion of Mississippi cavalry. He confessed his surprises at the degree to which war and hunger corrupted the morals of his men. "They told me of all the deviltries they used to commit. I confess, I was appalled at the utter want of principle displayed in their confessions. . . . I don't believe they know right from wrong." The stress of the final days made the deepest impact on those soldiers who bore the deepest scars of war. Waring's men and others in the Confederate cavalry had experienced one of the longest sustained periods of combat of the war, and became the most violent faction in Johnston's army.[12]

9 Mark L. Bradley, *The Battle of Bentonville: Last Stand in the Carolinas* (Campbell, CA, 1996), 283; Arthur P. Ford and Marion Johnstone Ford, *Life in the Confederate Army: Being Personal Experiences of a Private Soldier in the Confederate Army and Some Experiences and Sketches of Southern Life* (New York & Washington, 1905), 44.

10 OR 47/3:702, 711-712.

11 William Hill Andrews and Richard M. McMurry, eds., *Footprints of a Regiment: A Recollection of the 1st Georgia Regulars, 1861-1865* (Marietta, GA, 1992).

12 OR 47/3:704, 708, 712, 714, 716; Joseph Waring, Diary, May 2, 1865, Southern Historical Collection, University of North Carolina, Chapel Hill (SHC/UNC).

Major General Joseph Wheeler, who graduated 19th in a West Point class of 22 in 1859, commanded Johnston's cavalry. With the outbreak of war, Wheeler resigned his commission and joined the Confederate army. He commanded infantry at the battle of Shiloh and then at the tender age of 25 became the Army of Tennessee's cavalry chief. Wheeler's skill and energy were poured into his authorship of the South's mounted drill manual in 1863. Short, with a heavy black beard, Wheeler was an unimposing commander whose handshake was derisively compared to that of a girl. Wheeler's battlefield competency was unquestioned, but his lack of control over his veterans from Georgia, Alabama, Mississippi, and Texas was known throughout the South, and earned the ire of Confederate civilians. Many of these troopers had volunteered in 1861, but four years of constant campaigning and combat had left them mentally broken, a state of mind reflected in their ragged appearance. A drawing labeled as one of Wheeler's "glorious" horsemen depicted a scruffy figure riding a bucking mule and holding a bottle up to his long-bearded face.[13]

Starting in May 1864, Wheeler's men spent the war's last year engaged with Sherman's army across Georgia and South Carolina. The roughly 4,000 troopers had been engaged 10 of the last 13 months by the time they arrived in North Carolina. As one of the only Confederate forces contesting Sherman, Wheeler's cavalrymen were constantly fighting: swarming around the edges of the Union columns, attacking supply trains, burning bridges, and sometimes brutally killing any Yankees they could find. In February 1865, Confederate leaders sent Johnston more cavalrymen from the Army of Northern Virginia under Lieutenant General Wade Hampton, who had been specially promoted to outrank Wheeler, in order to take control of his lawless men. But shock and rage over Sherman's destruction of homes deeply affected these men too, many of whom were from South Carolina.[14]

The trauma experienced by the Confederate cavalry made them desperate and dangerous to friend and foe alike. Given orders to destroy everything useful to the advancing enemy, they expanded this power and raided civilian farms, private stores, and Confederate depots, such as Columbia, before the city fell. "Some of the men behaved scandalously robbing & pillaging at the depot," George Wise confided to his diary. "Much public & a great deal of private property [was] taken

---

13 St. George Tucker Mason, Diary, 1865, Mason Family Papers, Virginia Museum of History and Culture, Richmond (VMHC).

14 Ezra J. Warner, *Generals in Gray: Lives of the Confederate Commanders* (Baton Rouge, LA, 1959), 398.

Of all the demoralized men in Johnston's army, the troopers of Maj. Gen. Joseph Wheeler's cavalry were the most notorious. By 1865 they had spent almost a year in constant combat, with little oversight. Their behavior and appearance earning themselves an unsavory reputation across the South. A recently arrived officer from the Army of Northern Virginia captured the lawless and wild appearance of these horsemen in a drawing sarcastically titled, "Wheeler's Glorious Men." *St. George Mason Tucker diary, Mason Family Papers, Virginia Museum of History and Culture, Richmond, VA*

by the thieves." Colonel J. W. Black acknowledged the increased number of stragglers from his command who plundered farms and stole horses in South Carolina, noting that "most of the crimes were brazenly committed in broad day light." He managed to arrest only three troopers from Dibrell's division of Wheeler's cavalry. Local citizens beseeched Confederate commanders, begging them to instruct Wheeler's brigands to leave enough food for their survival. The effectiveness of their pleas is doubtful. One Rebel horseman, Munson Buford, before riding out in search of forage, quipped in his diary about "[s]ome picketing & forageing to do just Good exeicize [sic] for a Rebel."[15]

15 Mark Grimsley and Brooks D. Simpson, eds., *The Collapse of the Confederacy* (Lincoln, NE, 2002), 71; *Civil War Diary of Confederate Soldier George D. Wise*, North Jersey History & Genealogy Center Digital Collections, www://jfpl.contentdm.oclc.org/digital/collection/p16100coll2, accessed June 3, 2011; J. W. Black to John M. Otey, March 23, 1865, John M. Otey Papers,

Violence committed by Confederate cavalrymen escalated in the war's closing months. One South Carolina trooper expressed his great hate for the enemy and admitted he took "intense pleasure of chasing, & killing these fiends, taken often in the act of committing crimes upon women too dreadful to mention." Their semi-autonomous operations ensured an unfettered outlet for their thirst for revenge. Union soldiers who fell into their hands could expect little sympathy and no mercy. On the march across Georgia, 64 Union soldiers were found executed. In the Carolinas, this number almost doubled, with at least 109 men found hanged, with throats slit, shot at close range, or even dismembered. A group of carbine-wielding Confederate cavalrymen almost beat a member of the 55th Illinois to death. In mid-February, seven Union cavalrymen, presumably murdered by members of the 8th Texas Cavalry, were found with their throats cut and notices reading "Death to Foragers" pinned to their chests. Another 21 men were executed and left naked in a ravine near Feasterville. The mutilation of captured prisoners revealed a darker streak in the traumatized cavalrymen. After the battle of Bentonville, Union Private David Evans recorded one grisly scene: "Near the creek we found the body of one of our men who had been hanged by the rebels, & chopped with an axe. One leg was broken, one foot cut in two, & his head split in two or three places." Evans found three more mutilated men from the 10th Illinois, with what remained of them hung in trees. A slave who had witnessed the torture and execution led Union soldiers to the shallow grave of another man. The Confederates had cut off his toes, amputated his leg below the knee, hung his body from a tree, and beat him to death. This extreme violence reveals the depths of Confederate trauma. War clouded the minds of these men and skewed their morals to the point that horrific executions became a justifiable tactic. The closest explanation for what they were thinking comes from John Claiborne of the 8th Texas Cavalry, who looked back and tried to explain how they saw warfare. "We did some things that were not credible to our hearts, but they seemed necessary." Claiborne's post-war admission reveals the wartime moral ambiguity he and other cavalrymen experienced.[16]

Perkins Library, Duke University, Durham, NC (DU); OR47/3:721, 772; Munson Monroe Buford Diary, March 31, 1865, Munson Monroe Buford Papers, SHC/UNC.

16 Glatthaar, *March to the Sea*, 128; Daniel E. Huger Smith, Alice R. Huger Smith, and Amy R. Childs, eds., *Mason Smith Family Letters, 1860-1868* (Columbia, SC, 1950), 201; Ulysses R. Brooks, *Butler and His Cavalry in the War of Secession, 1861-1865* (Germantown, TN, 1994), 450; Bradley, *Battle of Bentonville*, 402; OR 47/2:533; John M. Claiborne, "Secret Service for General Hood," *CV* (1901) 9:31.

Alcohol played a prominent role in fueling this violence, as well as the overall demoralization of Johnston's army. Throughout the Civil War drunkenness plagued the armies, but the stress of its closing months fostered an insatiable desire for alcohol among Rebel soldiers. Intoxication dulled many men's issues with trauma and further compromised their judgment. Charles Roberts of the 46th Georgia felt "disgusted" by those around him seemingly consumed by alcohol:

> [D]runkenness is on the increase in the army, for I see men of position get drunk and make fools of themselves in public places without any signs of shame when they become sober. The morals of our people are fast degenerating and it is time for this war to stop if only to save thousands of our men and women from becoming more degraded than brutes.[17]

Besides impacting the rank and file, alcohol severely impacted Confederate leadership during this critical period. The alcoholism of officers like Brigadier General Laurence S. Baker was well known. He had joined the Confederate cause in 1861 and had served in all the major campaigns of the Army of Northern Virginia under Lt. Gen. Wade Hampton and Major General J. E. B. Stuart, both of whom knew about Baker's alcohol abuse but retained him in command. After a serious wounding in November 1864, Baker recuperated in eastern North Carolina, overseeing the safety of the Weldon Railroad. As Sherman's army approached, Baker's drinking problem worsened, and his men's morale plummeted. Lewis H. Webb, one of his officers, left an emotional account of how Baker's drunkenness impacted him and his men, who eventually stole the supplies in their care. According to Webb, "The morals of our troops are very lax indeed & sin abounds among them to a frightful extent." In the coming days, Webb felt great distress over his men, his country, and his pregnant wife. Overwhelmed by stress, he recorded almost daily episodes of sobbing as his war ground to a halt.[18]

To regain control over his men, Gen. Johnston decided a radical reorganization of the army would help him better manage his command and raise its spirits. Many regiments were mere shadows of their former selves, underscoring the sad state of the wilting Confederacy. Johnston consolidated 153 depleted regiments into just 32. Though certainly tightening and trimming the army, the

---

17 Charles Roberts to Maggie Roberts, March 15, 1865, Charles Roberts Collection, Department of Archives and Special Collections, University of Mississippi, Oxford (UM).

18 Sheridan R. Barringer, *Fighting for General Lee: Confederate General Rufus Barringer and the North* (El Dorado Hills, CA, 2016) 80; Warner, *Generals in Gray*, 15; Henry Louis Webb, Diary, March 8, 1865, Henry Louis Webb Papers, SHC/UNC.

shuffle did more harm than good to its morale. Many proud officers suddenly found themselves without a command. And for the men, the loss of respected leaders, as well as their regimental identity, disintegrated cohesion and weakened the remaining bonds with cause and country. Units like the 2nd Tennessee, which had first fought with Johnston along the banks of Bull Run Creek in 1861 and again at Bentonville, were especially devastated. Its merger with nine other Tennessee regiments raised its total to only 441 men. Regimental flags of the deleted regiments, once symbols of pride and honor, were furled, never to fly again. Men now fought under unfamiliar flags alongside unfamiliar faces. The reorganization eroded the soldiers' cohesion with their comrades, and in its place came a powerful desire for self-survival.[19]

Hoping to boost confidence and pride after these changes, Johnston assembled his men on the Everitt P. Stevens farm outside of Smithfield for a grand review. It was the first time the new army saw itself together, and the soldiers realized their sad state. "[T]he review of the skeleton Army of Tennessee," wrote Broomfield Ridley, had been "the saddest spectacle of my life." Only a year ago, he recalled sadly, the army had been "replete with men, and now [it] filed by with tattered garments, worn out shoes, bare-footed and ranks so depleted that each color was supported by only thirty or forty men." On April 6, another review was held for the benefit of a few Raleigh citizens, including Governor Zebulon Vance. After the review, Vance went to fellow Carolinian Major General Robert F. Hoke's headquarters and gave a rousing speech to the boy soldiers of the Junior Reserves regiments. The governor stressed the need for a "proper discharge of duty" in the dire situation and assured them their "cause was by no means hopeless." Perhaps Vance already knew the veteran units would see the hollowness of his words and news heading their way from Virginia would underscore the futility of the Governor's words.[20]

Johnston was unaware that Grant had breached the Confederate defenses around Petersburg, Virginia, in a predawn assault on April 2, forcing the evacuations of that city and Richmond. The sudden attack compromised Rebel plans to link the two armies in North Carolina. It was now a race for Robert E. Lee's army to reach Danville and swing south toward Greensboro and meet

---

19 OR 47/3:696; Robert Underwood Johnson and Clarence Clough Buel, eds., *Battles and Leaders of the Civil War (B&L)*, 4 vols. (New York, 1884-88), 4:699.

20 Broomfield L. Ridley, *Battles and Sketches of the Army of Tennessee* (Mexico, MO, 1906), 456; Johnson Hagood, *Memoirs of the War of Secession: From the Original Memoirs of Johnson Hagood* (Columbia, SC, 1910), 367.

Johnston. But when messages to Lee about the plan went unanswered, Johnston grew nervous. Desperate for news, the general contacted President Davis for information. The replies seemed "favorable," but rumors suggested otherwise. "But there was nothing . . . to suggest the idea that General Lee had been driven from the position held many months with so much skill and resolution" wrote a confused Johnston. On April 4, official dispatches confirmed the terrible news. The fall of Richmond brought more sadness, anxiety, and despair to the hearts and minds of Johnston's army.[21]

These reverses cast a dark shadow over the Confederates camped in Smithfield. "The shades of sorrow are gathering upon us—horrible rumors! . . . Heavens, the gloom and how terrible our feelings!" The emotional reaction to the bombshell consumed the men; one officer wrote that "[t]he wildest excitement seized the troops." Lieutenant Colonel James H. Lewis of the 1st Tennessee Cavalry remembered, "There was little sleep in our camp that night. Brave men shed tears freely. Gloom and despondency settled over the camp." Cavalryman J. W. Evans remembered the news causing unbridled angst. He dropped his regimental flag and "for two days and nights I rolled in the dust, kicked and cussed and vowed, neither ate nor slept much." Another officer, Lieutenant Colonel Joseph Frank Waring, acknowledged the tragedy but remained optimistic: "We have suffered I suppose a good deal [b]ut the end is not yet. We shall succeed to a certainty." Richmond's fall had a devastating impact on the men. Shock, gloom, and uncertainty tore away at the bonds of duty that held men to their cause. But in the coming days, more sensational news would serve to completely break them.[22]

Johnston had further cause to worry about developments in his proposed line of march. Major General George Stoneman and a force of 4,000 troopers crossed the Blue Ridge Mountains from Tennessee and tore into North Carolina on March 23, 1865. Stoneman wreaked havoc in the western and central parts of the state, destroying Confederate supply depots along the railroad from Greensboro to Charlotte. The Yankee cavalry spent days destroying significant supplies at Salisbury, a depot town on the North Carolina Railroad, tore up the railroad, destroyed bridges, and burned mills. Stoneman's horsemen struck again outside Greensboro, and barely missed capturing the fleeing Jefferson Davis and his Confederate administration. But more importantly the raid threatened the lifeline

21 Joseph E. Johnston, *Narrative of Military Operations Directed, in the Late War Between the States* (New York, 1874), 396.

22 Ridley, *Battles and Sketches*, 456; J. W. Evans, "With Hampton's Scouts," *CV* (1924), 31:470.

between Lee's and Johnston's armies. Hastily assembled Rebel infantry, cavalry, and artillery rushed west to confront the raiders in a move that would have dire consequences in the coming weeks. This shift of troops left Confederate depots, packed with supplies and rations for Johnston's retreating army, largely unprotected and vulnerable to pillage.[23]

While some commanders grew despondent, others grew desperate. Brigadier General Thomas L. Clingman hobbled into Johnston's headquarters fuming about the Confederacy's collapse. The once talented orator and gifted politician had fought hard for Southern independence, especially during the Peninsula campaign in 1862. He had been wounded twice in the last year, first at Cold Harbor, on May 31, 1864, and again a few weeks later during the fight for the Weldon Railroad. The trauma of these wounds deeply affected Clingman's mind. For example, he requested a command from Johnston in order to make a gallant, suicidal stand against Sherman's onslaught: "Sir, much has been said about dying in the last ditch. You have left with you here thirty thousand of as brave men as the sun ever shone upon. Let us take our stand here and fight the two armies of Grant and Sherman to the end, and thus show to the world how far we can surpass the Thermopylae of the Greeks." Johnston refused to consider it; he wasn't "in the Thermopylae business," he shot back.[24]

Some soldiers in Johnston's army would have agreed with Clingman, but many more did not. Confederates huddled around their Smithfield campfires wondered if their last campaign was upon them. As the troops tried to steady themselves, their minds grew cloudy while pondering their futures. The foreboding news from Virginia, empty stomachs, and the worsening military situation plagued their restless minds. Haunted by the unforgettable horrors of the battlefield and the ever-present ghosts of the dead, the soldiers of the Army of Tennessee struggled both to survive and to contend with the harmful changes the war had wrought within them.

On April 8, scouts arrived at Johnston's headquarters with news the Union army was preparing to advance. With Lee's fate still unknown, Johnston struggled to craft a plan. The bleak military outlook, the deepening demoralization of his men, and the government in flight all weighed heavily on his troops' minds. Hopes

---

23 Chris J. Hartley, *Stoneman's Raid, 1865* (Winston-Salem, NC, 2010), 262; *OR* 47/3:753-54, 777, 778, 779.

24 Daniel W. Barefoot, *Lee's Modest Warrior* (Winston-Salem, NC, 1996), 305; *Buffalo* [NY] *Commercial*, November 4, 1897.

for a Confederate success grew increasingly dim. Johnston sat in his headquarters on the afternoon of April 9 and issued orders to march west and rendezvous with Lee. But at that same moment, Lee sat in the parlor of the McLean House, surrendering his army to Ulysses G. Grant. The final campaign of the Army of Tennessee was at hand. The Rebels would not undergo the horror of a last battle, but rather a new experience, the long painful collapse of their world that was defeat. It was the final shock for survivors of a painful war.

Chapter 2

Union Soldiers:
"A set of grand thieves as ever stole"

Jacob Allspaugh joked with his men as they trudged along the sandy road toward Goldsboro, North Carolina. Their regiment, the 31st Ohio, barely resembled an army unit in its faded, threadbare uniforms, supplemented by a mad collection of civilian clothes (both men's and women's), Confederate uniforms, and Revolutionary-era tricorn hats taken from homes in Georgia and the Carolinas. As Allspaugh neared the town, he spotted a mounted assembly of Union officers resting beside the road. He recognized the army's commander, Major General William T. Sherman, and cocked an ear as he marched by. Allspaugh heard one officer note the sad state of the men to Sherman, lamenting "those poor fellows with bare legs!" "Splendid legs! Splendid legs!" the general joked. "I would give both of mine for any one of them!" Allspaugh's chest swelled proudly. But then Sherman remarked, "There goes a set of grand thieves as ever stole." The comment stung the troops, but they knew it was accurate. "We didn't relish the compliment much," Allspaugh admitted, "but as there was so much truth about it we had to swallow it." He was one of 60,000 veterans ending a fierce six-month campaign that had shocked the South. Like hundreds of other Union soldiers, he kept a diary and recorded all he witnessed. Allspaugh wanted to remember this epic march, but the ferocity of the war he and his fellow soldiers had unleashed troubled him, so much so that he felt the need to keep his entries secret, recording his thoughts in a complex code only he could read.[1]

1 Henry J. Aten, *History of the Eighty-fifth Regiment Volunteer Infantry* (Hiawatha, KS, 1901), 297; Jacob Allspaugh, Diary, March 31, 1865, Special Collections, University of Iowa, Iowa City.

William T. Sherman, photographed while wearing a mourning ribbon for Abraham Lincoln on his left arm, made national news with his mental breakdown in the autumn of 1861. His recovery left him with a deeper understanding of the power of fear on the mind. He used his insight to lead the Civil War's largest and most successful psychological warfare campaign, which would end in central North Carolina in 1865. *National Archives*

Goldsboro bore ample evidence of the Union army's successful campaign to make Southern civilians feel the harshness of war. Soldiers rode around town using horses, mules, carriages, and buggies taken from families along the march. Men crowded street corners trading and selling watches, rings, jewelry, revolvers, and other booty. Gamblers betting on games of poker and faro wagered with stolen loot and selling lottery tickets packed the alleys. "I doubt whether the history of war shows an organization equal to it in scientific and authorized stealing," an officer observed, and a reporter, noting the troops' rough manner and the corruption of their campaign,said that he doubted "if ever an army enjoyed greater freedom than this . . . it seems to me like a poor school for a young man's morals." Their unscrupulous behavior was the result of four long years of war and the unique campaign devised by their commander.[2]

Like his adversary, Sherman had trained as a professional soldier at West Point, graduating in 1840, 11 years after Joseph Johnston, and saw his first service in the Second Seminole War. Unlike Johnston, Sherman was a man of constant movement and conversation, who exuded an abundance of nervous energy. With the outbreak of war, the 41-year-old Ohioan received a colonel's commission in the 13th U.S. Infantry and led the unit during the Union route at First Manassas. The experience left him deeply troubled. Abraham Lincoln promoted Sherman and sent him to Kentucky, where he eventually took over the Department of the Cumberland. Still rattled by his experience in Virginia, Sherman exhausted himself obsessing over a fear of being overrun by Confederate forces. His belief in impending disaster made him paranoid, depressed, and even suicidal. Sherman's behavior convinced war department officials to relieve him of duty in November 1861—"Sherman's gone in the head, he's luny [sic]," was a common appraisal. Newspapers made his removal headlines and launched a nation-wide discussion of his sanity. After a month at home, Sherman pulled himself together and returned to duty, but he never forgot the impact of war on his spirit. He realized, like armies in the field, that the enemy's mind presented a target for attack.[3]

During the Vicksburg campaign in 1863, Sherman began to conceptualize how to apply this theory in war. He realized civilians' varied roles in supporting not only Southern armies, but the Confederate cause itself. Sherman said, "We are not only fighting hostile armies but a hostile people, and must make old and young, rich and

2   Richard Barksdale Harwell and Philip N. Racine, eds., *The Fiery Trail: A Union Officer's Account of Sherman's Last Campaign* (Knoxville, TN, 1986), 107; *New York Herald*, April 16, 1865.

3   John F. Marszalek, *Sherman: A Soldier's Passion for Order* (New York, 1993), 163-165.

poor feel the hard hand of war, as well as the organized armies." He understood attacking civilian morale undercut the population's affinity and ability to make war. After capturing Atlanta in 1864, Sherman saw an opportunity to attack the Southern mind and spirit. By marching into the Confederacy's interior, he could demonstrate how cruel war really was, while eroding their will to fight, saying, "[e]ven without a battle, the results, operating upon the minds of sensible men, would produce fruits more than compensating for the expense, trouble, and risk." Ultimately, he believed this strategy would prevent greater suffering and would bring the war to a swift end. Ulysses S. Grant and other Union leaders eyed Sherman's audacious plan with skepticism, but they reluctantly agreed.[4]

Their acceptance reflected an evolution of what Union leaders believed was permissible in war. As the conflict grew increasingly harsh, Abraham Lincoln's administration took steps to outline the laws of warfare in 1863 with General Order No. 100, "Instructions for the Government of Armies of the United States in the Field," commonly referred to as the "Lieber Code," after its author, political philosopher Franz Lieber. But the realities of this war conflicted with attempts to wage it in a moral fashion. By 1865, Sherman had pushed interpretation of the code to its extreme. He admitted in his memoirs the necessity to "cut the red tape" in waging war, which was a "dangerous thing for an army to do," but he stressed "war was upon us, and overwhelming necessity overrides all law." Success relied on having soldiers hardened enough to see civilians as the enemy, and callous enough to make the people feel what real war was like.[5]

Nearly 80 percent of Sherman's men who marched across Georgia were veterans. Many had volunteered in 1861 or 1862, and had endured years of brutal combat and hard campaigning. In fact, they were the most experienced army in Federal service, comprised of units which, collectively, had seen action on almost every battlefield of the Civil War. After years of combat, they were bolstered by victories but disillusioned by what it took to survive such a conflict. Their psychological transformation was profound. At the heart of this hardening was a powerful dissociation that men experienced, which changed their concepts of self,

---

4 William T. Sherman, *Personal Memoirs of Gen. W. T. Sherman* (New York, 1890), 2:227; *OR* 39/660.

5 *OR* Series 2, 5/671-682; William J. McNeill, "A Survey of Confederate Soldier Morale During Sherman's Campaign Through Georgia and the Carolinas," *The Georgia Historical Quarterly* (1971), 55:3; William T. Sherman, *Memoirs of General William T. Sherman* (New York, 1984), 404.

numbed their emotions, and altered their morals. They became different men to survive and changed more when ordered to make hard war.[6]

In Atlanta, Sherman took efforts to purge his army of the "sick, feeble, and weak hearted." This "rigorous weeding-out process" ensured that only the most healthy and hardened veterans filled his ranks. Using these men to implement his strategy proved to be a dangerous gamble for Sherman, who intended to use fear as a weapon. The hardening of his men evolved further into a coarsening. Traumatized men grew angrier at civilians, and their will to inflict more punishment increased as the army marched through South Carolina, demonstrating the legacy of their personal trauma and threatened discipline.[7]

Sherman's strategy required his army to live off the land and take what it needed from civilians. Each day on the march from Atlanta to Savannah, regiments organized foraging parties of 15-20 men, which branched away from the marching columns to collect food and supplies. These details fed the army, provided intelligence, and kept enemy cavalry at bay. Soldiers were officially forbidden from entering and plundering private homes, but many officers barely enforced the order, ignored it, or looted themselves. They were joined by soldiers who rode out on their own, unsupervised, to get what they could. Collectively called "bummers," these were the shock troops that brought war to civilians. They often engaged in petty theft, vandalism, or abusive language toward civilians. In some case bummers committed violent felonies such as armed robbery, assault, and, in rare cases, rape and murder. Though he disapproved of the bummers, one Michigan private admitted they were "one of the best weapons of war."[8]

The campaign's success convinced Grant to let Sherman to unleash his men on South Carolina, to punish the state for starting the accursed conflict and for its ill-gotten gains from slavery. Sherman recognized this deep desire for vengeance in the soul of his army. "The whole army was burning with the insatiable desire to wreak vengeance on South Carolina. I almost trembled at her fate, but felt that she deserved all that seemed in store for her." Southern wealth and property were the prime targets of Sherman's men, who admitted they would destroy "everything they could in their route," and take great "satisfaction in knowing that all the

---

6 Glatthaar, *March to the Sea*, 16,39; Michael Fellman, "Inside Wars: The Cultural Crisis of Warfare and the Values of Ordinary People," *Australasian Journal of American Studies* (1991), 10:1-9.

7 Glatthaar, *March to the Sea*, 19-20; Linderman, *Embattled Courage*, 241.

8 Bradley, *Battle of Bentonville*, 51; Glatthaar, *March to the Sea*, 148.

property belonged to the rebels." One Yankee admitted his desire for vengeance: "I have never burnt a house down yet, but if we go to South Carolina, I will burn som[e] down if I can get a chance." An Ohio cavalryman, usually opposed to the plunder of Southern homes, embraced the sentiment common in the army after it entered South Carolina that the Southern "people were entitled to share [the war's] hardships." Sherman's generals echoed that opinion. As Major General Henry Slocum admitted, "It would have been a sin to have had the war brought to a close without bringing upon the original aggressor some of its pains." The intensity of this anger reflected the dramatic psychological changes men were experiencing, and the resulting destruction was proof of its impact on morality.[9]

In February 1865, 60,000 hardened Union veterans stamped into the birthplace of secession with vengeance in their hearts. The destruction unleashed in South Carolina overshadowed that of Georgia. Several towns along the army's path were put to the torch, but its entry into Columbia became the watershed event in the campaign, demonstrating the power of stress to erode discipline. Hardly a conscious decision by commanders, the near destruction of South Carolina's state capital was an important moment; it revealed that the army's psychological state overwhelmed Sherman's control over it. The critical element that made it possible was alcohol.[10]

Colonel George A. Stone's Iowa veterans, the first Yankees to enter Columbia, were greeted by black families clutching pitchers of brandy and bottles of wine. Within an hour, Stone's troops were drunk. Angry Union prisoners released from the city's jails joined the unruly crowd in fueling fires set by retreating Confederates. Some soldiers tried to extinguish the flames, while others cut the hoses off of fire trucks. Another XV Corps brigade entered Columbia to restore order but it, too, got swept up in spreading the destruction. This forced officers to send a third brigade into the city to quell the rioting. "The fire was terrible, the scenes too horrible to describe," one officer remembered. "Large quantities of whisky were found, which the men drank to an alarming extent. My estimate is that forty blocks were burned. So much for giving soldiers liquor." Some soldiers were arrested; those who refused to do so were shot. Another officer speculated that

9 Barbara Bentley Smith and Nina Bentley Baker, eds., "Burning Rails as We Pleased": The Civil War Letters of William Garrigues Bentley, 104th Ohio Volunteer Infantry (Jefferson, NC, 2004), 145, 148; Glatthaar, March to the Sea, 79, 148; Jean V. Berlin and Brooks D. Simpson, eds., Sherman's Civil War: Selected Correspondence of William T. Sherman, 1860-1865 (Chapel Hill, NC, 1999), 775-777.

10 Linderman, Embattled Courage, 196.

about 40 men were killed resisting arrest. Sherman and several commanders blamed alcohol for this behavior. "[F]or awhile all control was lost over the disorganized mass," wrote Major General John A. Logan, because "the citizens had so crazed our men with liquor that it was almost impossible to control them."One soldier summed up the complete collapse of discipline and moral restraint during the march with a chilling admission: "Our army did not feel bound by the ordinary restraints of human warfare."[11]

By the time Sherman's army reached Goldsboro, the cruelty of its method of waging war weighed heavily on those of its members who retained their moral compass. The ones who successfully mitigated their stress and retained the ideals of right and wrong felt conflicted over their comrades' treatment of civilians. Levi Bryant admitted he couldn't bring himself to steal: "I never had face enough on me to go into a house and set up to a young girl and demand her rings or blow out her brains. And I thank God for the heart I have. It is not so hard as some I find." Soldiers wrestled with retribution and the use of force on civilians. John L. Hostetter of the 34th Illinois wrote:

> The Divisions in advance of us were incendiaries. The word is not used in the sense of its common acceptation because there can be no guilt connected with the destruction of property of men who by every means in their power are not only trying to destroy one of the best governments on earth but who also have the blood of the martyrs of freedom slain in this war upon their souls.

Other soldiers, Hostetter included, felt their harsh justice went too far. He admitted "that this system of raiding is rapidly demoralizing our men. There are many who are in quest of gold and silver only and it is feared that many atrocities have been committed in this way, under the plea of authorized foraging, but who were really stragglers."[12]

Lysander Wheeler penned one of the most disheartening descriptions of bumming and its justification in a letter home dated March 29, 1865. "When war is ended and Peace is once more reighning [sic] in triumph the North is ignorant of

---

11 Michael C. Garber, "Reminiscences of the Burning of Columbia, South Carolina," *Indiana Magazine of History* (1915), Vol. 11, No, 4, 285-300; Osborn, *The Fiery Trail*, 129; OR 47/1:227; Glatthaar, *March to the Sea*, 140.

12 Mark H. Dunkleman, *Marching with Sherman Through Georgia and the Carolinas with the 154th New York* (Baton Rouge, LA, 2012), 166; John L. Hostetter, Diary, John L. Hostetter Papers, Special Collections and University Archives, Iowa State University, Des Moines (ISUA).

the effects of war in Comparison with the South here it is dead earnest, the women and Children feel it as well as the men." Wheeler described successive waves of destruction, theft of food, and vandalism in civilian homes, as well as the trauma they caused: "Women and Children Crying and scared to death, expecting the next thing to be killed or something worse." He justified this behavior as a question of survival, adding, "it is a tough matter but if the rebels would rather fight and leave there familys [sic] to starve it is a matter of their own choosing certainly not ours."[13]

Federal officers also struggled with the excesses of their soldiers during the march. Many echoed the sentiments of their men, while others questioned how they lost control. Lieutenant Charles A. Booth justified the necessity of their duties:

> Every effort that could be made was made to check the demoralization of the foragers; but the occupation tended to demoralization, and 'the army must be fed, and the Bummers must feed us.' Thus we reasoned, but deprecated the means used to bring about the result. Some would discriminate, others would not, and thus the few have caused a great deal of unnecessary suffering.[14]

James D. Crozer witnessed soldiers robbing civilians, burning homes, sexually assaulting black women, and torturing civilians to reveal their hidden alcohol. His letters home captured the shock and disillusionment common in soldiers who struggled with the immorality of the campaign. Crozer urged his family not to place any confidence in any soldier, regardless of rank: "The deceit that is practiced in this world wois [sic] enough to make me sick. I have seen more since I've been in the army than I thought mankind could be guilty of."[15]

Captain Russell Tuttle of the 107th New York expressed a similar repulsion, writing, "I am shocked to think there are men in our command who can be so barbarously cruel." Entering South Carolina, a shocked Tuttle witnessed "[d]isgraceful scenes"and felt torn by the "terrible scouraging [sic] at the hands of our troops" that Columbia experienced. It pained him to witness the suffering the Union army inflicted on civilians. "It is heart rendering to contemplate the misery and suffering that must have befallen the poor old men, and women and children in

---

13 Lysander Wheeler to family, March 29, 1865, The Gilder Lehrman Institute of American History Collection, New York City (GLI).

14 Quoted in George S. Bradley, *The Star Corps: or, Notes of an Army Chaplain, During Sherman's Famous March to the Sea* (Milwaukee, 1865), 275-276.

15 James Crozer to family, Mar. 13 and 19, and Apr. 6, 1865, James D. Crozer Collection, North Carolina Department of Archives and History, Raleigh (NCDAH).

the wake of our march." Colonel Thomas Ward Osborn, the Army of the Tennessee's chief of artillery, recorded his moral dilemma but considered the bummers a necessary evil. He believed bumming had a "strong demoralizing tendency" on soldiers; it "cultivates a strong tendency to illegitimate plundering, and requires a firm hand on the part of the commanding officer to keep the spirit under, and even then it is by no means possible to do it." Others took a similar position."It is hard on the women and children," one soldier noted, "but I do not see how that can be helped."[16]

Those who were troubled by the vagaries of the march sought absolution for their sins through the forgiveness of God. "The regimental chaplains are occupying the pulpits of the different churches of Goldsboro and conducting nightly meetings," noted Alexander Downing. "A large number of the boys are attending and a great many are coming forward and professing the name of the Lord. May the work continue until all have made the profession." A religious revival pervaded the camps around Goldsboro, with several baptisms taking place. "It was strange but impressive scene to look down upon a thousand or more stalwart veterans, worshipping," wrote Captain J. B. Brant, the 85th Indiana's acting chaplain. Religion became a balm for souls troubled by sins they and others had committed on the march into South Carolina.[17]

Union soldier J. F. Culver witnessed how the way his army waged war contradicted God's law, and he tried to understand the Almighty's allowance of behavior that otherwise seemed evil. To Sherman's men, it was truly divine retribution, with success serving as validation of both their cause and the retribution they exacted on the South. "God has been very kind to us this far," Culver confided to his diary and admitted, "though there has been so much wickedness He has not cast us off." But the suffering he saw on the march and on the battlefield convinced him of the magnitude of the trauma the nation and its people were suffering. Cavalryman William H. Brown also struggled to resolve faith and service: "You ask me how I enjoy my self spiritually. I must say that I doe not live as faithful as I ought to. . . . You can not Imagine the temptations that beset

16 Osborn, *The Fiery Trail*, 107-110; Robert Cruikshank to wife, April 9, 1865, *Robert Cruikshank Letters (1862-1865)*, www.ehistory.osu.edu/exhibitions/letters/cruikshank/6511, accessed Aug. 29, 2009; George H. Tappan, ed., *The Civil War Journal of Lt. Russell M. Tuttle, New York Volunteer Infantry* (Jefferson, NC, 2006), 195-196.

17 Alexander G. Downing and Olynthus B. Clark, eds., *Downing's Civil War Diary* (Des Moines, IA, 1916), 266; Jefferson E. Brant, *History of the Eighty-fifth Indiana Infantry* (Bloomington, IN, 1902), 119.

a Soldier on every hand. Some times I think if I was not in the army that I could get along better." Soldier Simeon Howe believed Sherman's army was a part of a divine plan, but expressed his doubts as to the depth of their suffering: "Oh God, how long will this continue and how long is it necessary to punish this country for her Sins. Well we are deserving of it all for our sins are very great."[18]

Union commanders were awed by the destructive power of their men, but troubled by their loss of control. Sherman and his lieutenants understood the dire need to restore military discipline, and implemented a variety of methods in order to do so. Court martial sentences were conducted as mass spectacles in Goldsboro. A New York major had his sword broken for allowing his men to plunder houses, while a member of the 70th Ohio was paraded in front of the army "for some of his bad deeds." Moses Allen described this punishment in a letter home: "his head was shaved smooth all over and [he] was marched along in front of 15 regiments with 9 men guarding and the band following after playing the rogues march." Major General Oliver Otis Howard made an example of sixteen-year-old John Bass of the 48th Illinois. Bass's head was shaved and the letters "D R" were scrawled on his body with red ink to identify him as a deserter and rapist. Daniel Kunkleand and four other men of the 38th Ohio were discovered holding down an African American woman while Thomas Kilgore tried, unsuccessfully, to rape her. Testimony by a fellow soldier noted Kilgore grew frustrated and "wanted to see what she had for a thing; [and then] he put his foot on her leg, pulled up her dress and threw a torch between her legs."[19]

Another soldier, Corporal A. C. Warner of the 9th Illinois, was acquitted of attempted rape of an African American woman named Nicy Allen because her husband, sworn in as a witness, was deemed not to have "sufficient intelligence to comprehend the nature of the oath." It was followed by another court martial case concerning allegations of rape against Lieutenant Arthur McCarty of the 78th

18 Vivian C. Hopkins, ed., "Soldier of the 92nd Illinois: Letters of William H. Brown and His Fiancée, Emma Jane Frazey," *Bulletin of the New York Public Library* (February 1969), 73:124; J. F. Culver, Mary Culver, Leslie Whittaker Dunlap, and Edwin C. Bearss, eds., *"Your Affectionate Husband": Letters Written During the Civil War* (Iowa City, IA, 1978), 427; Simeon H. Howe, letter, March 31, 1865, Special Collections, Michigan State University, East Lansing (MSU).

19 Moses Allen to Friend, April 2, 1865, Museum and Collections, Bennett Place State Historic Site, Durham, NC (BP); Glatthaar, *March to the Sea*, 150; Thomas Power Lowry, *The Story the Soldiers Wouldn't Tell: Sex in the Civil War* (Mechanicsburg, PA, 1994), 124-125; Solomon North to wife, April 2, 1865, Nina L. Ness Collection, UM; Brenda Chambers McKeane, *Blood and War at My Doorstep, Volume I: North Carolina Civilians in the War Between the States* (Bloomington, IN, 2011), 277.

Ohio. The McCarty family made up the backbone of the company when it was formed, but all were gone due to death, wounds, or capture, leaving only Arthur by 1865. He had been commissioned a second lieutenant in 1864 to fill their shoes. But war broke him. McCarty was caught and found guilty of raping Martha Clowell in her home near Bennettsville, South Carolina. His punishment included having his head shaved, and he was dishonorably discharged with a two-year sentence in a state prison. But McCarty's connections reached into the White House, and he received a pardon from President Andrew Johnson. Another member of McCarty's regiment, Henry Quinn, was charged with assault with intent to kill. In an ominous letter home, Bliss Morse commented on the number of men arrested for sexual assaults: "a man is going to be shot the P.M. for committing a foul deed, then killing the victim, while on our trip through the Carolina's. Many more for the same crime deserved like treatment."[20]

The most dramatic execution witnessed by Sherman's men was that of recruit James Preble of the 12th New York Cavalry. The entire XX Corps, some 13,000 men, was formed into a massive square around a single coffin to watch his death by firing squad. Preble raped Letitia Craft and attempted to rape two more women, Rebecca Drake and her 17-year-old cousin, Louise Jane Bedard. Guards marched Preble into the square to the sounds of the regimental band playing the "dead march." The grim parade halted next to a coffin and a freshly dug grave. Soldiers shot Preble dead from twelve paces away, and his body was placed atop the coffin. Afterwards soldiers were marched by the corpse to make sure they got the message—some crimes would not be tolerated.[21]

To help recalibrate the army, officers reinstated drills, a novelty since the fighting in Georgia, and units were soon seen awkwardly marching in formations. "Had battalion drill today for the first time in a year with colors and music," wrote one soldier, who admitted the event was "done very poorly." Camps were laid out in neat company streets, a practice unheard of during the campaign. Details were organized to draw rations and perform guard duty. Men were issued new uniforms and cleaned up those they had in preparation for formal reviews. Members of the 2nd Iowa wanted to impress their commander during their dress parade. "A number of the boys were sent down town to buy all the white gloves and white

---

20 Thomas P. Lowry, *Sexual Misbehavior in the Civil War* (Bloomington, IN, 2006), 133, 138; Loren J. Morse, ed., *Civil War Diaries of Bliss Morse* (Pittsburg, KS, 1963), 197.

21 "A Military Execution Near Goldsboro," *The Maysville* [OH] *Tribune*, May 17, 1865; "Goldsboro during the Civil War," *Goldsboro* [NC] *News-Argus*, April 4, 1976.

collars they could find, besides shoe blacking and shoe brushes, and then we spent all the time till the parade in fixing ourselves up," wrote one soldier. To further unit cohesion, special corps badges were approved for enlisted men's uniforms. Stars, arrows, and acorns appeared, as did one for the XV Corps that featured a miniature cartridge box with the inscription "40 Rounds."[22]

As the army pulled itself back together, Sherman left Goldsboro for a council of war in Virginia. On March 27, 1865 he reached City Point and met with Lincoln, Grant, and Admiral David Porter. There they devised a plan for Sherman to march to Virginia and link up with Grant's forces in order to break the ten-month siege of Petersburg and destroy Lee's army. Both generals considered Lee's army a more important target than Joseph Johnston's force in North Carolina. Sherman speculated that either Johnston would try to slip into Virginia and join Lee, or that Lee would come to North Carolina. Sherman boasted that he could certainly handle his old adversary in a fight, no matter which strategy Johnston chose. "I feel certain from the character of the fighting that we have got Johnston's army afraid of us. He himself acts with timidity and caution. His cavalry alone manifests the spirit but limits its operations to our stragglers and foraging parties." In addition to the military plans for the war's end, the men discussed the aftermath of Confederate defeat. Lincoln expressed his desire to reunite the country and heal a nation that had suffered so much. It was a sentiment Sherman agreed with and took to heart. But implementing the president's unofficial wishes would become impossible after the dramatic events of the next three weeks. Sherman returned to Goldsboro and prepared for what he hoped would be the final campaign.[23]

By early April, Sherman's army had added two more corps, the X and XXIII, increasing its strength to 88,948 men supported by 91 pieces of artillery. He considered his army unstoppable, but knew it's size would make the pursuit of a fleeing enemy, especially the skillful Joe Johnston, a difficult endeavor. The additional hungry mouths also forced an enlargement of his quartermaster system and complicated the logistical support the growing army required. The railroads branching out from Goldsboro afforded Sherman an opportunity to resupply, allowing him to prohibit foraging. His men may have not been happy about returning to a diet of hard tack and salt pork, but they were assured that food would

22 Allen Morgan Geer and Mary Ann Andersen, eds., *The Civil War Diary of Allen Morgan Geer, Twentieth Regiment, Illinois Volunteers* (Bloomington, IL, 1977), 212; OR 47/1:42; Downing and Clark, eds., *Downing's Civil War Diary*, 267.

23 OR 47/3:368; Oscar Osburn Winther, ed., *With Sherman to the Sea: The Civil War Letters, Diaries & Reminiscences of Theodore F. Upson* (Baton Rouge, LA, 1958), 161.

be available. Unlike the march through Georgia and South Carolina, food was less of a motivator for the army, but if self-preservation came into question, the practice of foraging could easily be reinstated, with dreadful consequences.

Sherman began hauling an estimated 1,500 tons of freight per week up the Neuse River to the recently captured town of Kinston, where it was unloaded onto wagons and escorted 23 miles to Goldsboro. Rapid repair of the railroad was critical, and Sherman ordered that no expense should be spared in fixing the rail lines that ran to Wilmington, New Bern, and Morehead City. Once the rails were made serviceable, Sherman ordered that they be made fit to carry at least 300 tons of freight per day, with the highest priority given to ammunition. Hundreds of formerly enslaved men found work repairing the damaged lines and unloading incoming supplies for the army. With their help, the lines were put back in working order in just two days.[24]

Preparations for a movement to Virginia were suddenly halted by dramatic news. Just as afternoon drill ended on April 6, the men of the XX Corps heard heavy cheering in the direction of Goldsboro. The roar traveled like a wave, washing over each regiment, with each in turn erupting into celebration as the thrilling news shot down the line. Richmond had fallen. "The army was wild with joy," wrote a member of the 102nd Illinois. Men erupted into "outbursts of feeling. With enthusiasm that knew no bounds." Another Ohio private recalled, "such cheering as seldom vibrates on mortal ears. The men are in a state of excitement bordering on insanity." They danced, yelled, prayed, and rolled around on the ground, and some considered it worthy of a July 4th-type celebration. "One of the favorite devices," wrote William Wirt Calkins of the 104th Illinois, "was to put powder in a canteen, then bury it and light it with a fuse." The great news sent many men and officers on a joyous bender. Henry Pippitt recorded that his officers were "on a small drunk" after the news hit and that the celebration lasted into the next day: "All drunk at Hd Qr."[25]

The news made Sherman and his men supremely confident. "I don't think an Army ever started on a campaign with brighter prospects before them" wrote

24 OR 47/3:7.

25 OR 47/3:109; F. M. McAdams, *Every-day Soldier Life, or A History of the One Hundred and Thirteenth Ohio Volunteer Infantry* (Columbus, OH, 1884), 149; Robert Hale Strong, author, and Ashley Halsey, ed., *A Yankee Private's Civil War* (Chicago, 1961), 165; William Wirt Calkins, *The History of the One Hundred and Fourth Regiment of Illinois Volunteer Infantry, War of the Great Rebellion, 1862-1865* (Chicago, 1895), 310; Henry Pippitt, Diary, Betsey B. Creekmore Special Collections and University Archives, University of Tennessee, Knoxville (UTK); Joshua Pettit, Diary, Rare Books and Special Collections, St. Bonaventure University Archives, New York (BUA).

William Bentley of the 104th Ohio. Young Powell of the 2nd Iowa said "[t]he Soldiers, are all cheerful and in high spirits at their success on the last two campaigns, and think that there never was such a man as Sherman or as they all call him (Crazy Bill) and he has got his men to believe that they cant be whipped." An amateur songwriter, George Lawson of the 45th Illinois, tempered these high spirits: "The enemy cannot withstand us. They are whipped and they know it, but I suppose their hearts are hardened like Pharoahs."[26] Hospital Steward Joseph M. Stetson was cheered to hear the news because it meant the army would move. He lamented the "Enuie" of camp life and preferred campaigning, believing that the next one would bring victory and a return home: "I think and hope Shermans Army will move onward until the last rebel shall return to the United States & peace Shall have spread her white wings on our land then Mother I Could return & Enjoy the comforts of home."

For Sherman and his men, the goal was clear: Destroy Joe Johnston's army and end the awful war once and for all. The prospect of peace sent troubled spirits soaring. For Sherman and many of his men, victory meant and end to the cruelties of the horrible war. But for some, the war would never end. Peace was at hand but the perceived joys it would bring would be disappointing for men who would forever wrestle with the war they made.[27]

26 Bentley, Smith, and Baker, "Burning Rails as We Pleased," 147; Young J. Powell, Diary, Ellen Aumack Papers, Special Collections, DU. George Lawson, Diary, March 26, 1865, Library and Archives Room, Atlanta Historical Society (AHSL).

27 Joseph M. Stetson to Mother, April 2, 1865, Joseph M. Stetson Papers, DU.

CHAPTER 3

Southern Civilians:
"No lark could pipe to skies so dull and gray"

North Carolinians who picked up Raleigh's *Weekly Standard* on April 5, 1865, saw their glum outlook set to word on the front page in a melancholy verse, "A Farewell," by British poet Charles Kingsley. "My fairest child, I have no song to give you; No lark could pipe to skies so dull and grey . . . And so make life, death, and that vast for-ever; One grand, sweet song." The poem captured the citizenry's collective foreboding of the disaster seemingly destined to befall the Confederacy and themselves. Other pages of the paper carried equally disturbing news from across the state: military reverses, deserters, violence on the home front, and a long list of the wounded who recently inundated Raleigh's homes and hospitals. The *Standard* also introduced otherwise unacquainted readers to a dangerous, particularly unnerving kind of Yankee, the now infamous "bummer." The article asked readers to contemplate the worst when encountering these thieves, as they would in the coming weeks. "Think how you would admire him if you were a lone woman, with a family of small children, far from help, when he blandly inquired where you kept your valuables. Think how you would smile when he pryed [sic] open your chests with his bayonet or knocked to pieces your tables, piano and chairs; tore your bed clothing in three inch strips, and scattered the strips about the yard." As an illustration of the venomous threat, the article included an account of a woman who offered a Union soldier a jug of sorghum to fill his canteen. Before giving it back, he took the wad of tobacco from his mouth and stuffed it in the jug. The surprised woman asked why he had spoiled the rest.

"Oh, some feller'll come along and taste that sorghum, [and] think you've poisoned him," he explained, "then he'll burn your damned old house."[1]

Other local newspapers, along with eyewitness accounts and rumors, fueled the powerful anxiety gripping Raleigh and central North Carolina in early 1865. Four years of war had taken its toll on citizens, and the dawn of the fifth promised even worse. People felt a new unease as they followed Sherman's march across Georgia and prayed they would be spared a similar fate. Their anxiety worsened as the Union army swung into South Carolina and headed north. Raleigh resident Mary Bayard Clarke wrote to her son and speculated about the arrival of Federal soldiers. "I believe the enemy will march right up here, but you must not be uneasy if they do and you don't hear from me for I shant try to run away they wont stay here long and I shall stick it out I have seen too much misery and suffering among refugees for me to be willing to run off from home." Locals were keenly aware of how fleeing the enemy could be just as disastrous as enduring its arrival. But over the next two months, the anxiety of Raleigh's citizens began eroding that belief as distraught refugees related stories of the cruelty suffered at the hands of Sherman's men in South Carolina. The destruction of that state's capital, Columbia, struck a deep fear, and they wrung their hands in worry, wondering if they would be the next Confederate state capital to suffer that fate. Charles Dewey, a Raleigh banker, informed his son about the frantic activities of his neighbors and his feelings of great despair, writing, "we are on the edge of the crater, and it is crumbling beneath our feet every moment."[2]

Raleigh, the capital of North Carolina since 1792, was largely unscathed by the war. In 1861, it boasted a population of 4,780 residents, and was served by two railroads: the Raleigh and Gaston, completed in 1840, and the North Carolina Railroad, finished in 1856. The latter line connected the state's major cities in a great arc, from the major port of Wilmington to Charlotte. With secession, the capital became the headquarters of the state's war machine, with training camps, arms manufacturing facilities, and supply depots transforming the city into a busy industrial complex. Raleigh's location also made it an ideal refuge for terrified

---

1 [Raleigh] *Weekly Standard*, April 6, 1865.

2 Mary Bayard Clarke, Terrell Armistead Crow, and Mary Moulton Barde, eds., *Live Your Own Life: The Family Papers of Mary Bayard Clarke, 1854-1886* (Columbia, SC, 2003), 175; Charles Dewey to Thomas Dewey, April 10, 1865, Drury Lacy Papers, SHC/UNC; [Raleigh] *Daily State Journal*, February 18, 1865.

people fleeing war zones across the South. Since the earliest days of the conflict, traumatized refugees had inundated the city seeking safety and comfort.[3]

The flood of displaced persons swelled as armies raged across Virginia and eastern North Carolina. The panic within the state started in August 1861, with the Union army's invasion of the coastal islands. Affluent plantation owners packed up what valuables they could carry and left friends, families, and fortunes—an experience that left them distraught and shaken. Towns and cities of the central and western parts of the state were quickly overrun with frightened refugees. When lodging could be found, it was expensive. The increased pressure on resources sent food prices skyrocketing to crisis levels by the summer of 1863. The threat of financial ruin and fear of harm took a heavy psychological toll on thousands of North Carolinians. This stampede split up and scattered families, and tore apart people's kinship and familiar networks. Without this support system, the experience of flight became more traumatic due to the lack of a support system to help refugees deal with the stress. Those who fled the fighting in New Bern arrived in Raleigh shocked and frightened, and obsessed with worry over the capital being the Federal armies' next target. The war forced one of the state's richest planters, Josiah Collins, III, to flee his plantation, "Somerset Place," in August 1862. He moved his family inland to Hillsborough but died within a year under the burden of severe stress.The most notable refugees flowing in from Virginia were President Jefferson Davis's wife and family, who arrived in the city in May 1862. Varina Davis described herself as "greatly depressed and heavy with anxiety" after her flight from the fighting that raged outside Richmond. Each new arrival served as a dark omen of what was to come.[4]

The influx of refugees and soldiers created a crisis for their hosts. Many brought disease with them that spread in overcrowded cities and towns. A yellow fever outbreak in the fall of 1862 sent people scrambling away from Wilmington, sparking fears of a statewide contagion. The epidemic reportedly killed 1,200 of the 3,000 residents who remained in the city. A simultaneous outbreak of smallpox spread among the rest of the state's major cities: Fayetteville, Charlotte, Salisbury,

---

3 Elizabeth Reid Murray, *History of Wake County*, 2 vols. (Raleigh, NC, 1983), 1: Appendix A.

4 Margaret Supplee Smith and Emily Herring Wilson. *North Carolina Women: Making History* (Chapel Hill, NC, 1999), 70; David Silkenet, *Driven from Home: North Carolina's Civil War Refugee Crisis* (Athens, GA, 2016), 151; Murray, *Wake County*, 489-490.

and Raleigh. The movement of civilians and soldiers ensured the spread of infectious disease across the state throughout the war.[5]

Refugees also inflamed the long-held fear of slave rebellion. Many wealthy families brought their enslaved property with them on their flights. The greater number of slaves fraternizing during a time of inadequate oversight made people nervous. One Raleigh planter, William Boylan, recalled his property, in faraway Yazoo City, Mississippi, back home. Large numbers of the enslaved gathering fostered a great fear of uprisings and other nefarious behavior, and this belief grew with each passing year of war. The Carolinians' worries were not unfounded: newspaper advertisements for runaway slaves dramatically increased, as did accounts of slaves attempting to kill masters, some of which succeeded. A panic ensued in early 1863 when slaves in Orange County killed two of their owners. Citizens stepped up patrols with what manpower remained. The enslaved took advantage of the chaotic situation by running away, feigning illness, and undermining the weakened control of masters. And as Union armies stormed into the state's interior, fear of slave rebellion surged.[6]

Civilians also staggered under the weight of helping to care for the wounded soldiers who had overwhelmed the Confederate hospital system. Throughout the war, a constant stream of wounded arrived from Virginia, bringing home the shocking reality of the conflict for civilians. The sight of bleeding and disease-ridden men bore witness to the transformative power of war. Besides the drain on already stretched resources, the steady influx of mangled men complicated the daily lives of civilians and took a toll on their own mental health. From 1861–64, Raleigh's various hospitals serviced roughly 7,000 patients. The crisis peaked after the battles of Averasboro, Bentonville, Fort Fisher, and Kinston in the first three months of 1865. The wounded packed the cities, filling hospitals, churches, homes, and every available space a man could lie. Raleigh resident Margaret Devereux voiced the exhaustion many felt while trying to deal with the

---

5 Surgeon General's Office, *Report on Epidemic Cholera and Yellow Fever in the Army of the United States During the Year 1867* (Washington, DC, 1868), XXIV-XXXV; [Charlotte] *Evening Bulletin*, December 13, 1862; *Fayetteville Weekly Observer*, February 2, 1863; [Salisbury] *Carolina Watchman*, February 9, 1863; *Daily* [Raleigh] *Standard*, December 21, 1868; *The* [Raleigh] *Confederate*, March 15, 1865.

6 B. H. Nelson, "Some Aspects of Negro Life in North Carolina During the Civil War," *North Carolina Historical Review* (April 1948), 25:146, 156; Silkenet, *Driven from Home*, 143-145.

waves of wounded men, who became "the greatest taxes upon our resources, and the event that brought the war very closely home to us."[7]

The wounded also overwhelmed the citizens of Greensboro. With a population of 1,000 as of 1860, Greensboro was a popular stop along the North Carolina Railroad. It became critical to Confederate strategy in 1864 with the completion of the Piedmont Railroad, which linked it to Danville, Virginia, thus connecting the front lines of the war's Eastern Theater with the Deep South. A Raleigh newspaper noted the city's new role: "Greensboro has become a very important point in the Confederacy and with exception of a few places in Virginia, more soldiers, and especially sick and wounded ones pass through this place than any other." This role brought unprecedented stress to the city's residents.[8]

The wave of wounded that washed over Greensboro crested in late March and April of 1865. In addition to casualties from battles in North Carolina, cars of injured soldiers rolled in from the fighting in Virginia. Shocked residents suddenly found their city inundated with wounded men. Mary Smith, wife of Presbyterian minister Jacob Smith, noted, "On that memorable night, without warning or preparation, the wounded were brought to Greensboro, in such numbers as to fill the churches, the court house, and every available space in the town." For Smith and other townspeople, the sheer number of the wounded weighed heavily on their spirits. "That night in the old Presbyterian church and lecture room I saw the first wounded and dying men and witnessed the grief of their comrades." This was a shocking and repulsive sight. Her experience with mass casualties deeply scarred Mary Smith. Although bemoaning the lack of supplies, she also stressed the most pitiful scarcity: anesthesia. Doubtless she had heard screaming men suffering on operating tables. One soldier who convalesced in Greensboro later wrote that there were so many deaths that the bodies were "laid out until they turned black."[9]

Increasingly, North Carolina families saw their lives turned upside down, and blamed their government for its inability to provide for its people. Greensboro's newspapers reinforced the growing crisis with the publication of the Confederate

---

7 *North Carolina* [Raleigh] *Standard*, March 24,1865; H. H. Cunningham, "Edmund Burke Haywood and Raleigh's Confederate Hospitals," *North Carolina Historical Review* (April 1958), 35:157; Margaret Devereux, *Plantation Sketches* (Cambridge, MA, 1906), 151; *The* [Raleigh] *Confederate*, March 15,1865.

8 *Greensboro* [NC] *Patriot*, September 29, 1864.

9 Adrian L. Whicker and Bradley R. Foley, eds., *The Civil War Ends: Greensboro, April 1865* (Greensboro, NC 2008), 8-11; United Daughters of the Confederacy, *Recollections and Reminiscences 1861-1865 through World War I* (Columbia, SC, 1990), 5:231-232.

government's summons of all militia officers to service, calls for more food and bandages to aid the city's hospitals, and the demands of Guilford County farmers to pay their taxes in food stuffs as soon as possible. The conscription of men, supplies, and livestock helped replace passion for the Confederate cause with a focus on survival. One notable Greensboro citizen, John A. Gilmer, observed the gloom of the situation when he wrote, "The discouraging spirit of despondency is to be dreaded more than the enemy." Fearing ruin at the hands of their own countrymen, nervous Greensboro citizens published an appeal to Johnston and his army to be more "thoughtful" and respect the rights of citizens. Their plea would fall on deaf ears in the coming weeks.[10]

State treasurer Jonathan Worth saw the increasing despair of his neighbors from his window in downtown Raleigh. "All sensible men know the days of miracles are past—and that nothing but a miracle can save us. The continuance of the contest, without a miracle, is but to add to the hecatombs of slain and further destruction of property." The heart of former North Carolina Governor Charles Manley sank as he anticipated the crisis to come. "The horrible deeds perpetrated by the Yankees in Fayetteville & the not less lawless & atrocious acts of our people in Johnston & Wake exceed the enormities of Barbarians. Between the two fires of desolation, plunder & actual starvation awaits us. God help the country." Bartholomew Figures Moore, a Raleigh attorney, put it pithily: "God save us from retreating friend and advancing foe."[11]

Soldiers described civilians in the western portion of the state as "badly whipped and r[e]ady to submit." Rumors spread by refugees entering Charlotte threw the town into chaos, with "the wildest panic and confusion on every hand." The refugees and soldiers in Raleigh resulted in "disgusting" scenes of drunkenness. The *Daily Progress* newspaper applauded the closure of liquor stores during the "extraordinary public peril" the city faced. The paper blamed the military reverses they now faced on the abuse of alcohol, and bemoaned its effect

10 *Greensboro Patriot*, March 23, 1865; Richard E. Yates, "Governor Vance and the End of the War in North Carolina," North Carolina Historical Review (October 1941), 18:315-38.

11 Richard E. Yates, "Governor Vance and the End of the War in North Carolina," *North Carolina Historical Review* (October 1941), 18: 315-338; McGee, "On the Edge," 254; Jonathan Worth and Joseph Grégorie de Roulhac Hamilton, eds., *The Correspondence of Jonathan Worth*, 2 vols. (Raleigh, NC, 1909), 1:362-363, 367.

on the people as a whole. "There can be no doubt but the excessive use of liquor has done much to cause existing demoralization and to wreck our cause."[12]

Despite the sagging support for the war, Governor Zebulon Vance issued an appeal in March 1865 for North Carolina families to provide more foodstuffs for the besieged Rebel army around Petersburg, Virginia. University professor William Battle scoffed at the notion: "What do you think," he asked a friend, "of Gov. Vance's appeal to a half starving people to send provisions to a half starving army? Won't it give aid and comfort to the enemy to see how we are reduced?" Other citizens replied to Vance with their own desperate letters. One woman begged him to "stop the cruel war" for the sake of "poor women and children." She said she was "without one mouthful to eat for myself and five children and God knows when I will get something," and urged him to make peace on any terms, "let the rest of the poor men come home and try to make something to eat."[13]

Home front morale suffered further from deprivations committed by desperate Rebels. After a visit from Confederate cavalry, one victim asked, "are citizens to be thus treated, and without remedy?" The writer acknowledged the damage these visits caused: "Bread is as essential to war as powder, and if the power to produce it is taken from the farmers, we are a gone people." Catherine Devereux Edmondston's plantation became a temporary corral for impressed horses. She did not think this arrangement would last over a month because the Confederacy could not feed them. "In a few weeks their bones will whiten the red clay hills of Warren & Granville [counties] through which Johnston returns." She resented this forced patriotism, which agitated feelings of distrust and betrayal amongst many North Carolinians for the Confederate government. "The feeling against it is intense throughout the country" Edmonston said. "[E]re long hearts will be alienated away from the Government & system that thus tramples on our rights, our feelings, & our sacred honor." The seeming inability of the Confederate authorities to protect citizens from their own soldiers also stirred resentment. Swarms of men absent from Johnston's command skulked around Raleigh, causing some citizens to worry about mob violence from their own troops. General Braxton Bragg, writing to Johnston about the troubling situation, noted that "[t]he country is perfectly

12 [Raleigh] *Daily Progress*, February 23 and 25, 1865.

13 W. H. Battle to Kemp Battle, March 6, 1865, Battle Family Papers, SHC/UNC; Unknown to Zebulon Vance, undated, Governors Papers, NCDAH; McKean, *Blood and War*, 1:294.

infested, and the most atrocious outrages are being committed." Without an active cavalry, Bragg warned the situation could not be brought under control.[14]

The threat to survival civilians experienced made them desperate, and drove them to extremes. In February 1863, women calling themselves "regulators" broke into a grain warehouse in Bladensboro. A month later a mob of 50 angry women attacked stores in Salisbury, where owners had taken advantage of shortages and increased prices. Armed with axes, the women assaulted price-gouging merchants and forced them to hand over barrels of flour, salt, and molasses, as well as cash. For the next two years, women across North Carolina's Piedmont targeted speculators and Confederate agents, and they rioted in Wilmington, High Point, and Boon Hill in late 1864. All strata of society were moved to action in the face of starvation. Twenty "respectable" Raleigh citizens forced a sale of flour, wheat, and corn. As the end closed in, desperate citizens eyed the Confederate storehouses as their only chance for survival.[15]

Despite the hardships North Carolinians faced, the magnitude of death and loss they experienced made the deepest wounds. Brothers, fathers, and sons left for war, never to be seen again except in coffins. A deep, debilitating sadness filled the hearts of many families and redefined how they thought about death. Research suggests that around 125,000 North Carolinians entered Confederate service; around 32,000, roughly one out of every four military aged males, died during to the war. Many of those who had returned were mangled and sometimes unrecognizable. In the wake of the battle of Gettysburg, the *North Carolina Standard* took three separate issues to list the names of all the dead and wounded. Raleigh's Mary Bryan wondered when "this human butchery" would end. Emotionally exhausted by news of the dead arriving weekly, Bryan and other women found themselves plunged into a constant state of mourning.[16]

14 *Raleigh Weekly Standard*, April 5, 1865; Marc W. Kruman, "Dissent in the Confederacy: The North Carolina Experience," *Civil War History* (December 1981), 27:293-313; *North Carolina Standard*, March 24, 1865; Wilson Angley, Jerry L. Cross, and Michael Hill, *Sherman's March through North Carolina: A Chronology* (Raleigh, NC, 1995), 56; OR 47/3:694.

15 *Greensboro Patriot*, April 16, 1863; Victoria Bynum, *Unruly Women:The Politics of Social and Sexual Control in the Old South* (Chapel Hill, NC), 128, 134; Andrew F. Smith, *Starving the South: How the North Won the Civil War* (New York, 2011), 51-52, 64; [Raleigh] *Daily Confederate*, December 13, 1864.

16 Mark A. Moore. *The Old North State at War:The North Carolina Civil War Atlas*, Jessica A. Bandel and Michael Hill eds. (Raleigh, NC, 2015), 178; Bynum, *Unruly Women*, 120; David H. McGee, "'On the edge of the crater': The Transformation of Raleigh, North Carolina during the Civil War," Ph.D. dissertation, University of Georgia (UGA), 1999, 208.

Intense grief from the war's death toll traumatized an already struggling Southern populace. Some turned to opiates for solace and developed addictions. In Chapel Hill, the deaths of her sons drove Lucy Battle to a dependence on "medicine," most likely laudanum, and she became frantic when Sherman's army threatened her supply. *Southern Historical Collection, UNC*

The deaths of loved ones psychologically broke some grieving families and left them forever scarred. Sarah Smedes, wife of a girl's school rector in Raleigh, suffered crippling grief after losing two sons during the war. The news of their deaths left her inconsolable, and she "retreated into [a] shadowy world of grief from which [she] never fully emerged." Sudden news of her son's death shattered another Raleigh woman; neighbors noticed the dramatic effect the loss had on her: "She does nothing but walk up & down & repeat his last letter." News of a fallen son elicited a deep despondency in one Cumberland County family. A neighbor observed, "it seems they have nothing to live for now. I never saw people in such trouble before." In Chapel Hill, grief overwhelmed another woman and drove her to addiction. After the death of her two sons in the Confederate army, Lucy Battle turned to laudanum for the solace she needed to deal with her depression. With Sherman approaching Raleigh, she believed her supply would be cut off and panicked, leading her husband ask their son for help, "Your mother thinks she is afraid she will soone be unable to procure the medicine that she is in habit of taking and that the consequence will be that she will be unable to sleep and get back into the measurable condition in which she was some years ago. If she does I fear it will almost kill your mother."[17]

Battle was not alone in her addiction. Others gravitated to opium and other narcotics to deal with problems the war brought into their lives. Families sought help for the worst of these cases at the North Carolina Insane Asylum in Raleigh.

---

17 McKean, *Blood and War*, 2:636-637, 640; R. H. Battle to Kemp Battle, April 4, 1865, Battle Family Papers, SHC/UNC.

Opened in 1856, the hospital swelled with soldiers and civilians who developed chronic issues spawned by the conflict. Doctors examined patients and tied their issues to causes like fright, bereavement, loss of husbands and fathers, exhaustion, loss of property, and ill health. But a majority ended up in the care of asylum doctors for reasons they were unable to discern; these causes were listed as "unknown." In some cases, the doctors simply attributed patients' manias to "the war," and these cases increased as the war drew closer.[18]

Civilians held their breath as the opposing armies prepared to march. Many hoped Sherman would join Union forces in Virginia and spare central North Carolina, but once news of Richmond's fall arrived, Sherman's direction became terrifyingly clear. The Federal army would no longer bypass North Carolina's interior. The approach of Sherman's men aggravated the civilians' continuing mental problems. The emotional and psychological strain took a physical toll on the bodies of civilians. One of the largest plantation owners in central North Carolina, Paul Cameron, complained about the ill effects of stress in mid-March 1865: "These nights loss of sleep—and the unpleasant excitement that I have suffered for some days past render me unfit for anything—I really feel very badly." Laura Elizabeth Lee remembered the physical effects of stress on her mother, who worried for their safety. "Such horrible stories my mother had heard of what might happen to her daughters gave her so much real pain."[19]

By April 1865, North Carolinians had felt the war as deeply as anyone else in the Confederacy. They suffered years of stress and were increasingly tormented in their daily lives, but the arrival of war on their doorsteps led them to believe they now faced Armageddon. Their greatest fears and terrors lurked just over the horizon: great armies poised and ready to unleash chaos on helpless men and women. The violent convulsions of the Civil War's final weeks amplified the pain suffered by a traumatized people. North Carolinians struggled to deal with a deep, crippling sadness, making their lives miserable. The power of this experience left a wound on the minds of survivors that would take years to heal. Some, who felt the war the most, would never be free from the dark shadow it cast on their lives.

18 Admission logs, Dorothea Dix State Hospital Collection, NCDAH.

19 Alex K. Hall to father, April 9, 1865, Alexander K. Hall Papers, ADAH; John G. de Roulhac Hamilton, ed., *Papers of Thomas Ruffin* (Raleigh, 1920), 3:448; Ethel Stephens Arnett, *Confederate Guns Were Stacked, Greensboro, North Carolina* (Greensboro, NC, 1965), 15; Laura Elizabeth Lee, *Forget-Me-Nots of The Civil War: A Romance, Containing Reminiscences and Original Letters of Two Confederate Soldiers* (St. Louis, MO, 1998), 161.

CHAPTER 4

April 10-12:
"My mind is doing finely but pains me a great deal"

April 10, 1865

On this day, Charles W. Hutson confided to his diary, "I am often busy now, trying to talk good cheer into the hearts of some of the despondent: for I am sorry to say, there are some badly whipped men around me." Hutson wrote to reassure himself of the Confederacy's ultimate triumph, and he planned how it could still win the war. His delusional strategy reflected the dire state of affairs for the South. Hutson envisioned a great campaign in which the Army of Tennessee would link up with other Confederate units across the Mississippi River and surge into the North, eventually capturing Washington. Previously unthinkable, Hutson now believed Southern victory would be assured "if we carry negro troops with us." He confidently believed victory easy to see through the lens of history and believed success required faith in a just God. "[O]thers cannot appreciate the merits of a great cause and lack faith to feel the full assurance, which our wisest thinkers hold themselves justified in feeling," he wrote, "that the God of justice will watch over our destinies and ensure our triumph." Hutson's fantasy mirrored those of the most stalwart Confederates, especially officers, who still professed victory possible in the spring of 1865. Unable or unwilling to consider defeat, these believers were a shrinking minority in Joseph Johnston's army.[1]

---

1 Charles W. Hutson, Diary, April 10, 1865, Charles W. Hutson Papers, SHC/UNC.

Surrounding Hutson were many men whose hopes of success, and even survival, were extinguished by years of horrific war. Captain John L. Swain of the 17th North Carolina described his despondency in letters to his brother. Avoid the army and stay home with their mother, he advised, as any further sacrifices for the Confederacy would be futile. "The laws of the land now give no room for the display of patriotism . . . it is not rewarded." Sights of the battlefield tempered Swains optimism into melancholy. "There is a dark cloud hanging over our country and every passing breeze comes laden with the din of war, devastation and death." Like many men in Johnston's army, Swain wrestled with the war's meaning and cost. "The sun in his course at midday is frequently Shut out by a dense column of Smoke from consuming wealth but it is useless to describe it is perfectly horrible." Gathering rumors of Robert E. Lee's surrender in Virginia further darkened spirits in the army. The Texans of Granbury's Brigade were among the first to hear them, and their hearts sank further. Captain Samuel T. Foster remembered, "We hear that General Lee has surrendered which has a very demoralizing effect on this army. I do hope and I believe that we will whip this fight yet." General Johnston also heard the stories, and worried as he sat on the veranda at his headquarters, deep in thought. His head spasmodically jerked side to side, the effects of a mild palsy, as he pondered his next move. Even without a plan, Johnston knew he must continue moving his fractured army and keep it together until a solution presented itself.[2]

Johnston decided to march his roughly 30,500 soldiers via two parallel roads west toward Greensboro and wait for Lee's army. Hardee's corps would march along the North Carolina Railroad while the two corps under Maj. Gens. Alexander P. Stewart and Stephen D. Lee would trudge together on the Louisburg Road. If the junction of the armies succeeded, the joint force would move west via the railroad and rely on the supply depots Johnston was currently stocking. But several obstacles on this route posed series problems for Johnston. Reports revealed Stoneman's Union cavalry had severed the railroad in several places between Greensboro and Charlotte. The general also faced the difficult crossing of the Haw and Yadkin rivers, whose bridges which had been washed away. Johnston ordered all available pontoons hauled on wagons from Augusta to Charlotte with all possible speed in hopes of rendezvousing with him as he reached these waterways.

---

2 Joseph B. Cummings, "How I Knew the War was Over," *CV*, 1901, 9:18; John L. Swain to "Julius," April 10, 1865, John L. Swain Collection, SHC/UNC; Samuel T. Foster and Norman Brown, eds., *One of Cleburne's Command: The Civil War Reminiscences and Diary of Capt. Samuel T. Foster, Granbury's Texas Brigade, CSA* (Austin, TX, 1980), 163; Nicholas W. Schenck Reminiscences, SHC/UNC, 35-36.

If the Confederate army delayed on the march or failed to cross the rivers, they faced destruction at the hands of the pursuing Union forces.[3]

To stall the pursuit, Johnston deployed his cavalry in a 30-mile arc at the rear of his army. He posted Joseph Wheeler's troopers on his left flank to observe the Wilmington and Weldon Railroad as well as roads heading north in order to determine if Sherman was heading to Virginia. Anchoring the right flank, Wade Hampton positioned his forces to block the Neuse River Road and the direct routes to Raleigh from Goldsboro. The cavalrymen built barricades, felled trees, and positioned cannons to slow the enemy's advance. Johnston knew he could not stop Sherman's army, but he needed to stall the Union advance to give him time to link up with the Army of Northern Virginia.

With the rearguard of the army formed, Johnston started their march toward Raleigh. The general hoped he'd instilled enough discipline in his weary men to keep them together. The result of Johnston's reorganization was obvious as the new army started to move. New regiments and unfamiliar officers took all day to begin marching amid the downpour. The weather also sowed confusion among commanders, who spent the day trying to keep troops moving on the right roads. Major General Benjamin Franklin Cheatham's command waited until 6:00 p.m. to start its march, and stopped after making only six miles. The dearth of reports from adjutants and commanders reveals the disorganization that plagued the day's movements. The confusion enabled those men who had had enough of war a chance to slip away from the army. Those who remained marched on into unknown future that was growing ever darker.[4]

Thirty miles southeast in Goldsboro, another army woke and prepared to make war. Bugles pierced the dull patter of rain falling on the Federal camps. Sherman's men ate their breakfasts and packed their camps amid the foul weather, which dampened prospects for an easy start to the march. At 5:30 a.m., bands serenaded Maj. Gen. Charles R. Woods's division as it marched north along the Weldon Railroad toward Virginia. The rest of the XV Corps, which Sherman had first led during the Vicksburg campaign, came next. These Yankees were no strangers to hard marching but found this slog through the Carolina countryside one of its worst. The torrential rain made their routes impassable; regiments were forced to halt and wrench heavily loaded wagons out of the mud and drag them

---

3 Bradley, *This Astounding Close*, 79, 88; Joseph E. Johnston, *Narrative of Military Operations During the Civil War* (New York, 1874), 396.

4 OR 47/1:1083.

along slick, wet roads. At particularly deep troughs, soldiers cut trees and stole fence rails to corduroy the road. Skirmishers soon discovered Wheeler's cavalrymen blocking their path and exchanged shots, igniting the day's fighting. Woods's soldiers steadily pushed the Rebel horsemen, who reported their advance along the Weldon Railroad. To Johnston, it appeared that Sherman was heading toward Virginia. But when the blue columns reached Nahunta Station, they abandoned their feint and turned west toward their true objective, Raleigh.

The rains delayed the corps throughout the day and into the night. Woods's worn-out division halted in an abandoned Confederate camp, while the rest of the corps camped several miles to the south in what Cornelius Platter recalled as a "little pine grove without tents or blankets or anything to eat." Platter, however, managed to find alcohol, which served "to refresh the 'inner man.'" Orderlies from headquarters were dispatched to hurry the remaining wagons into camp while others lit fires along the road to guide their way. But the night was not without its dangers, as Confederate horsemen prowled the shadows waiting to grab any stray Yankee they could. One orderly, Sam Marot, had the unfortunate luck to be "killed by a Guerrilla."[5]

At 7:00 a.m., Maj. Gen. Frank P. Blair's XVII Corps marched out of its camps around Goldsboro and headed north. It, too, slowed upon hitting soggy roads that had been transformed into Carolina swamps. The conditions frustrated some of the troops. The unforgiving mud and thorns tore at Allen Greer's heavy load until he could take no more and tossed away the new equipment he had been issued just days earlier. Though disgusted and exhausted, Greer declared in his diary that the "rebellion reels it must be closely followed till it falls helpless at our feet." Blair's men swung west from the railroad and headed toward Whitley's Mill on the Little River.[6]

Sherman sent Maj. Gen. Henry Slocum's Army of Georgia directly toward Raleigh. The morning's rain made roads completely impassable for XIV Corps soldiers, who splashed their way west on the direct Stage Road. Men and horses slipped and fell, and wagons sank. Then came the sudden shock of the Rebels' terror weapon: a hidden naval mine buried in the road that exploded when an unfortunate member of the 104th Illinois tripped it. This weapon enraged

5 Cornelius Platter, Diary, University of Georgia, Athens (UGA), 166; William H. Chamberlin, *History of the Eighty-first Regiment Ohio Infantry Volunteers, during the War of the Rebellion* (Cincinnati, 1865), 166-167.

6 Geer, *The Civil War Diary of Allen Morgan Greer*, 212.

Sherman, who had encountered an officer with his foot blown off by a similar device on the march through Georgia in 1864. "This was not war, but murder," a furious Sherman declared. He retaliated by forcing Confederate prisoners to probe the route of march with shovels and picks in order to discover any other hidden mines. Union soldiers had discovered more of these booby traps, planted by Southern cavalry along the roads in South Carolina. Apparently enemy tactics would not change here.[7]

A few miles further on, skirmishers began exchanging shots with Confederate cavalrymen, who slowly gave ground until the fighting reached a wide, swampy waterway called Moccasin Creek. Here, Wade Hampton had positioned two regiments in earthworks, supported by a battery of horse artillery on a slight rise 200 yards to the rear. As Union pickets surged forward, Capt. Frantz Fleischman of the 108th Ohio fell dead, struck by canister balls ripping through the canopy of pine trees. The rest of the brigade deployed behind the Ohioans and pressed forward. Cannon fire greeted the men of the 34th Illinois as they topped a ridge. "There was a tremendous cracking over our heads and a shower of bark and splinters" one soldier wrote. He also noticed the serious and silent expressions on the faces of his companions as they moved into position. All of them wore tightened faces and "compressed lips," consumed with fear of being killed just as the war seemed to be ending. Union artillery quickly deployed and dueled with the Confederates on the opposite bank of the creek. They also covered another Federal brigade, which had crossed upstream and outflanked the Rebel earthworks at a cost of seven or eight casualties. After the battle, soldiers found a cabin heavily damaged by shot and shell between the lines, and discovered a woman and three children consumed "in mortal terror" inside.[8]

On a parallel route further to the south, the XX Corps marched up the Brogden Road, which hugged the meandering Neuse River. A unique corps in Sherman's army, most of its regiments hailed from eastern states, and the cultural differences between it and the westerners in its sister corps, the XIV, put them at odds, even to the point of outright disdain. This rivalry would prove fatal before the war's end. For the present, the slick, muddy roads made it a hard slog forward for all of Sherman's men. Besides being wary of Rebels lurking in the woods, the troops of the Third Division fretted about their commander, Brig. Gen. William T.

---

7 Calkins, *The History of the One Hundred and Fourth*, 311; Sherman, *Memoirs*, 194.

8 Lyman S. Widney and Robert I. Girardi, eds., *Campaigning with Uncle Billy: The Civil War Memoirs of Sgt. Lyman S. Widney, 34th Illinois Volunteer Infantry* (Bloomington, IN, 2008), 351-354.

Ward. As they marched by, the men cocked an eye to gauge his level of sobriety. Weeks earlier, the 33rd Indiana had encountered a drunken Ward along the road, a condition "quite common to him." After some of the soldiers complained about being hungry, Ward flew into a rage and placed the entire regiment under arrest.[9]

Ward's weakness for alcohol may be partly explained by his experiences on the battlefield, and the impact of war on his men was easy to see. The 33rd Indiana fought in the first Union victory in Kentucky, at the battle of Camp Wildcat, in 1861. But they were soundly beaten at Thompson's Station, Tennessee, in 1863, suffering the most casualties of all Northern units involved. Major General Nathan Bedford Forrest's Rebel horsemen killed, wounded, and captured 505 out of 606 soldiers engaged. The regiment rested for a year, but had not fully recovered before joining Sherman's campaign for Atlanta in May 1864. The regiment's colonel, John P. Baird, resigned due to the mental strain, and died in an asylum in 1875.[10]

John R. McBride of the 33rd Indiana recorded some of the physical problems that plagued his regiment after the hard campaigning. He described some "moon-eyed" men, who could not see at night, or experienced double vision. McBride knew of one fellow soldier, Simon Lasley, who suffered so severe a case of this affliction that it eventually killed him. Some men lost their voices. Before the battle of New Hope Church, Capt. J. L. Banks inexplicably lost his voice and was rendered useless. He was so determined to redeem his reputation after murmurings of cowardliness that he led his men forward in the regiment's next charge and suffered a fatal wound. The 33rd's lieutenant colonel also fell victim to this mysterious affliction of speech. The strain of campaigning affected other soldiers in the regiment in different ways. John Clifford had a hard time understanding military life and fitting into the army. Fellow soldiers described him as a man whose "mental endowment was not rich," and remembered several times when Clifford had been knocked senseless during fatigue duty or had collapsed while carrying his oversized knapsack. During the battles around Atlanta, Clifford was wounded, but he returned to service and now marched with the regiment toward Raleigh. Within five years, he would die in an asylum in Washington, D.C.[11]

9 John Randolph McBride, *History of the Thirty-third Indiana Veteran Volunteer Infantry During Four Years of Civil War* (Indianapolis, 1900), 237.

10 OR 23/1:75; J. E. Brant, *History of the Eighty-fifth Indiana Volunteer Infantry* (Bloomington, IN, 1902), 63.

11 McBride, *Thirty-third Indiana*, 222, 238.

Bright's Disease, called nephritis today, refers to various inflammations of the kidneys. Cases surged during the war and ravaged veterans in the post-war years including generals like Judson Kilpatrick and Stephen D. Lee. The disease tormented many soldiers who struggled to deal with the pain caused by the disease. Brigadier General James L. Selfridge battled the pain until he ended his life by suicide on May 19, 1887. *Library of Congress*

The XX Corps continued its march until around 9:30 a.m., when scouts encountered Confederate cavalry blocking the road. Brigade commander James L. Selfridge deployed skirmishers and pushed forward. Two companies of the 123rd New York moved up and exchanged fire with Rebels posted on the opposite side of an extensive plantation. The New Yorkers dashed across the fields and pushed back the cavalry. The discovery of the main Confederate line along the opposite bank of Aiken's Creek temporarily halted the skirmishing, but the Yankees reformed and charged into the waist-deep water. For two hours they struggled to cross the creek, finally chasing the Rebels off at a cost of two killed and five wounded.[12]

Selfridge complimented his men for the action, but his ability to lead them suffered greatly from the cumulative physical toll of the war. He had enlisted in 1861 and earned a commendation for his leadership during the fighting at Peach Tree Creek. After the war, Selfridge embarked on a successful life in business, dabbled in politics, and became a staunch supporter of the North's largest veterans' organization, the Grand Army of the Republic (GAR). But by 1887, Selfridge was consumed with Bright's disease, an umbrella term for several kidney ailments that became prominent in post-war veterans. The pain of this disease, rooted in his wartime service, led Selfridge to take his own life with a bullet to the head.[13]

12 OR 47/3:614, 673, 698-700; Rice C. Bull, *Soldiering: Civil War Diary of Rice C. Bull, 123rd New York Volunteer Infantry* (San Rafael, CA, 1977), 238.

13 "An Old Soldier's Suicide," *The* [Philadelphia] *Times Newspaper*, May 20, 1887.

The XXIII Corps followed the XX Corps out of Goldsboro. The corps was part of the Army of Ohio, which fought with Sherman in the campaign for Atlanta; but missed the March to the Sea, instead opposing the Confederate invasion of Tennessee in late 1864. After a circuitous route, the corps sailed to North Carolina and fought its way inland to rejoin Sherman in Goldsboro. The transformation of their old comrades caught them unprepared, and they were shocked at the destruction the XX Corps left in its wake. "The stragglers in the army have become much worse than they were in the Atlanta Campaign," wrote XXIII Corps commander Maj. Gen. Jacob D. Cox, who was angered by each burned house he passed. He suspected that one home where he stopped had been set ablaze by stragglers from other corps: "Two of the best residences along our road were burned today. One, the house of a Mr. Atkinson where I stopped at noon to take lunch, was in flames half an hour after we left it; the soldiers suspect him of being a conscription agent for the rebel government, and this may account for his house being burned." That evening, Cox issued an order noting the unprecedented arson and directing the "summary trial and drum-head court-martial and execution of [any Federal soldier] guilty of such outrages."[14]

The last of the Union army to step off this morning were expected to deliver the death blow in Sherman's plan for the campaign. The general believed the Confederates would make a final stand along the Neuse River, 15 miles east of Raleigh. To attack the expected location of the Rebel right flank, or even appear behind their lines, Sherman would use the river as a screen, sending the X Corps and Kilpatrick's cavalry along the south bank toward the capital. Kilpatrick's force numbered around 5,600 men, while Maj. Gen. Alfred Terry's command counted just over 12,000. New to Sherman's army, Terry's X Corps was unique. One of its three divisions was made up of United States Colored Troops (USCT), the first African Americans Sherman had commanded.[15]

In all, the Federals fielded 88,948—an army that matched all the Southern forces in Florida, Georgia, and the Carolinas. Unquestionably, Sherman's overwhelming numbers would win any battle, but could they catch the retreating Confederates before they escaped? Sherman worried that a failure to bag

14 Cox, *Reminiscences*, 458

15 Bradley, *This Astounding Close*, 284-285, 287.

Johnston's army would result in its dispersal, and could transform the conflict into an ugly guerilla war.[16]

Sherman's columns struggled throughout the night to keep up with the rest of the army. Some soldiers were lucky enough to get a few hours of sleep which allowed them to take stock of the day. The Northerners were confident but worried about a final, bloody battle in the coming days. The desperate fighting their enemies had unleashed at Bentonville underscored the danger they still posed, and they could not rest believing that a major battle for Raleigh loomed. The chaos of the Confederates' own march, however, revealed how disjointed their own army was, despite Johnston's attempts to make it whole. Men talked amongst themselves, and tried to understand if and how victory could still be achieved. It was an uncomfortable night, but it was decidedly overshadowed by the devastating news morning brought.

An hour after midnight, the telegraph at Joseph Johnston's headquarters delivered a coded dispatch from President Davis confirming the surrender of the Army of Northern Virginia. Reeling at the news, Johnston struggled to comprehend his new position. He felt compelled to keep his army moving until he figured out what to do. The impact of this news upon the nerves and spirit of his frayed men would be devastating and herald the death knell for the Army of Tennessee and the Confederacy.

April 11

Before the sun rose, Johnston's men rolled out from under their blankets and crowded around low fires to ward off the morning chill. The warmth of the Carolina morning swelled as the tired veterans formed for yet another hard day's march. They attributed their aches and pains to old wounds and their respite in Smithfield, but they also knew the long campaigns were taking their toll on their bodies. Thin rations made the muddy march unbearable and hastened the shrinkage of their already depleted ranks. One Rebel officer described this movement as "the most severe march we have had." Soldiers dropped out of the ranks and began to beg for food as the army crossed into eastern Wake County. Major General James Patton Anderson's division started the morning with a total of 1,499 men, but only 214 answered the evening roll call; some caught up to the army while others would never return.[17]

The spirits of Johnston's troops momentarily rose when they reached Raleigh, where cheering citizens lined the city's main thoroughfares. This reception, a kind gesture in a dark moment, moved the tired soldiers. The thin companies closed up their ranks and tried to put on a bold face, but once civilians realized the dilapidated state of the army and saw the downtrodden expression its men bore, the cheers faded. Charles Johnston appreciated the civilians' support but could not stop himself from begging for food. One eyewitness noted the soldiers' spirit, but "their careworn faces told the sad tale." Another citizen reckoned the stark contrast between the bright, strong volunteers who had marched through the streets 1861 with these men: "ragged, dirty, pale, and sickly in appearance to a large degree, and most of them barefoot." Young girls from St. Mary's School watched the army march past on Hillsborough Road. The sorrowful sight left a lasting impression on Kate McKimmon, who remembered the "footsore, ragged, hungry" soldiers, who were "emaciated from lack of food and clothing." McKimmon and other students gathered around the school's front gate and handed out food to the men. The Confederate retreat ominously signaled the impending occupation by the Union army, and this deeply troubling prospect left Raleigh women inconsolable. One soldier remembered them "all in tears and almost in despair at the news from Va, the retreat of our Army, the prospect of the Citys being pillaged by our Cavalry during the night and the certain advent of the Yankees in the morning."[18]

Johnston's rearguard cavalry continued fighting to keep Sherman's army at bay, unleashing their anger and frustration on any Union soldier they could grab. They captured and executed several men from 12th Indiana, including one unfortunate Yankee hanged by Col. John Logan Black's cavalry. South Carolina troopers of Brig. Gen. Mathew C. Butler's command extracted their own revenge on four captured Union soldiers of Giles A. Smith's division. Butler's men probably knew that these Yankees had been among the first to pillage Columbia, but it hardly mattered. Robbed and then arranged in a row facing away from the Rebels, William C. Crockett of the 11th Illinois Cavalry inquired as to what command his captors belonged. "None of your [damn] business," came the reply;

17 Hagood, *Memoirs*, 368; Bradley, *This Astounding Close*, 91.

18 Jane Constance Hinton, "The Reminiscences of the Key Basket," Laurens Hinton Collection, SHC/UNC, 7; *OR* 47/1:1083-1084; W. W. Gordon, Diary, Mily Gordon Collection, SHC/UNC.

the next instant, the quartet of Yankees received a bullet fired into the backs of their heads. Crockett's bullet glanced off his skull and he fell wounded. A check of each victim's pulse revealed that Crockett was still alive, and he received another shot, into his back, and was left for dead. Amazingly, he crawled to the nearest home for help and lived to recount his story.[19]

Stories like these fanned terror among civilians who were as fearful of the approach of lawless Confederates as of the Yankees—especially Rebel cavalrymen with reputations as common thieves and outlaws. As the horsemen drew nearer, Raleigh citizens worried if they would get the same treatment as those in South Carolina's state capital. Weeping families huddled over bibles praying for salvation and deliverance filled parlors and bedrooms throughout the city. Men and women wrestled with the agonizing decision of whether they should remain in the city or pack what they could and flee. The refugee experience was particularly torturous to those who had the most to lose. Prosperous white families piled up what few possessions they could carry, abandoned their homes, status, identities, and joined a mob of others from Goldsboro, Wilmington, and Columbia traveling west with the army seeking safety.

Those who remained in Raleigh braced for the worst. Desperate to save family treasures, women spent hours hiding what they could in every conceivable place. They sewed gold, watches, and silverware into hoop skirts, stockings, collars, pocket-handkerchiefs, and dresses in hopes of preventing their loss. Charlotte Grimes hid "$200.00 in gold quilted in a belt under my corsets, a stout bag filled with forks and spoons around my waist, and the front of my corsets filled with jewelry." She already fretted about her husband, Maj. Gen. Bryan Grimes, who served under Lee in Virginia and whose fate was unknown. Civilians nervously awaited their fates, hoping that both they and the capital would survive the immediate future. Obsessive anxiety weighed heavily upon them and the stress ate away at their worn nerves.[20]

But heading toward Raleigh were two men were who had conquered their fear to save their suffering state. Former governors David L. Swain and William A. Graham had spent their lives modernizing North Carolina. At the turn of the century, it had earned derogatory nickname of the "Rip Van Winkle" state for its

---

19 Upson, *With Sherman to the Sea*, 160; Lewis C. Paxson, *Diary of Lewis C. Paxson, 1862-1865* (Bismarck, ND, 1908), 60; Bradley, *This Astounding Close*, 105; *Philadelphia Inquirer*, April 28, 1865.

20 Murray, *Wake County*, 503.

The burning of Columbia in February 1865 marked the destructive climax of Sherman's South Carolina campaign. Union commanders were shocked by the destructive power of their men, and blamed alcohol for unleashing their inner demons. The soldiers' anger flared again when they attempted to burn North Carolina's capital two months later. *Library of Congress*

dearth of progressive spirit and development. But in the three decades before the war, Swain and Graham took the lead in helping North Carolina catch up with the rest of the nation. The approach of Sherman's vengeful army threatened the hard-won triumphs of a poor state that had struggled to improve itself. The former governors decided it was time to act in order to save what they fought so hard to build.

They knew the desperate situation demanded decisive action. Since the war seemed close to its end, they decided to propose a plan to save the capital, the state university in Chapel Hill, and all North Carolinians from unnecessary hardships. They hoped to persuade the current governor, Zebulon Vance, to seek a separate peace and, if need be, secede from the Confederacy. Swain went to Raleigh to propose the idea to Vance and convince him to invite Graham to join him on a peace mission. Vance agreed and Graham began his journey toward the capital. As he neared Raleigh, the former governor passed through Johnston's retreating army; the men's sad condition affirmed both his mission and its urgency.[21]

21 Bradley, *This Astounding Close*, 93.

Entering the city early that morning, Joe Johnston continued striving to save his army, but the task was taking an emotional toll on him. He spent a hectic day trying to communicate with his commanders and a government in full flight while simultaneously trying to feed his army. Shepherding his troops forward through these catastrophic circumstances required significant effort of a commander who still struggled to devise a plan in the wake of Lee's surrender. In addition to the stress of command amid the chaos, Johnston suffered from cruel aspersions on his generalship. John Bell Hood's report on his disastrous Tennessee campaign of the previous autumn and winter, blamed Johnston for ruining the army's fighting spirit by his constant retreats before Atlanta. Johnston angrily wired Hood of his intention to press charges in a court-martial for slander. The general's growing realization that he was going to face the onerous task of surrendering also weighed on his mind. The prospect of becoming the scapegoat for the Confederacy's failure had angered Johnston when he was first recalled to duty on February 22, 1865 and now it seemed his fears were justified. His stress erupted as the general dined that evening at the home of Rufus Tucker.[22]

Reverend Anthony T. Porter and Maj. Gen. William Hardee joined Johnston as they supped and enjoyed polite conversation. At one point Porter expressed his regret at Johnston's removal as commander of the Army of Tennessee in 1864. He told Johnston that he, and the rest of South Carolina, had been extremely saddened by that event. "[A] black pall fell over the State when you were relieved; we all felt that General Sherman would never have reached Columbia if Johnston had not been removed from Atlanta." Johnston rose from the table and, pacing briskly back and forth, proclaimed: "Since you have said so much, I will tell you. I was in command of as splendid an army as [a] general ever had." He continued with increasing emotion: "It was stronger and larger the day I reached Atlanta than it was the day I began to retreat. It took me seventy-three days to fall back seventy-four miles. I never lost a wagon or a caisson. I put almost as many of the enemy hors de combat as I had in my army." Stunned, Porter and Hardee slowly rose as Johnston's emotional outburst intensified. "Men who were at home flocked to me. I had put fifteen thousand of Governor Brown's militia on the fortifications, and Atlanta was impregnable. I had 'tolled' General Sherman just to the place where I wanted him." At this point, as tears began flowing down his cheek, the excited Johnston turned and walked out on the piazza. In the uncomfortable

---

22 OR 38: 3/628-629; Symonds. *Johnston,* 343, 353.

silence that followed, Hardee turned to Porter with tears in his own eyes and offered a defense of the general.[23]

Unlike his opponent, Sherman began his day confident but concerned. As his army took to the roads and approached the Neuse River, it braced for a day of battle. If Johnston planned to defend Raleigh, it would be today, Sherman reasoned. Anticipation of another battle made skirmishers jumpy and generals nervous. But the Confederates were not to be found, and Sherman pushed his troops forward to overtake the retreating enemy. The warm Carolina spring made for another day of laborious travel for the men, and some soon fell victim to the heat. "Two of our Brigade died & several took sick," wrote an Illinois soldier after marching 20 miles; "I had but six men of my Company with me, all the rest had fallen out."[24]

"We were loaded down," one soldier remembered, and "the men played out fast the day being extremely hot." Cornelius Platter complained to his diary: "The last three days have been very hard indeed more severe on the men than any we have experienced for some time." Platter and others had only gotten 4-5 hours of sleep per night, and the constant marching exhausted men in the ranks. One of them, John A. Cundiff of the 99th Indiana, was also suffering from the unrelenting brutalization of the war, and hard marching only stirred these troubled thoughts. His role in the death of a Confederate prisoner weeks earlier still rankled. In mid-February, the hatred between the opposing cavalries had degraded into tit-for-tat executions of prisoners and a running debate on the laws of warfare. Cundiff found himself in a firing squad for one of these revenge killings; shooting a bullet into another man haunted him forever. After the war, he claimed that his neighbors were Rebel spies and dead Confederates were coming to get him. He would take his gun and blanket and sleep in the woods for days to avoid these imaginary enemies, or hide weapons under his bed. Another member of the 99th suffered his own mental injury that hampered his service. James D. Campbell, suffered lingering mental impairment after a Confederate cannonball exploded over his head at Missionary Ridge in 1863. His comrades considered him to be

---

23 Anthony Toomer Porter, *Led On! Step by Step, Scenes from Clerical, Military, Educational, and Plantation Life in the South, 1828-1898* (New York, 1898), 182.

24 Culver, *Your Affectionate Husband*, 432.

John A. Cundiff of the 99th Indiana Infantry enlisted in August 1862. His unit had participated in the siege of Vicksburg, but Cundiff's baptism of fire came in Sherman's campaigns for Atlanta and the Carolinas. Cundiff's breaking point came after he served on a firing squad that executed a Confederate soldier in February 1865. He was haunted by the man's death in the post-war years and believed dead Confederates were coming to get him. To avoid them he would take his gun and blanket and sleep in the woods for days, or hide weapons under his bed. *Deborah Branigan, descendant*

nervous and unsound afterward. So serious was his brain injury that Campbell was taken off the line and detailed as a teamster for the rest of the war.[25]

The colonial-era town of Smithfield, with its bridge over the Neuse River, was the chief target of the Union advance. The 75th Indiana, spearheading the XIV Corps, dashed through the town to try and capture the crossing intact, but Rebel cavalry successfully kept them at bay while it burned. While waiting for the bridge to be rebuilt, Union soldiers explored Smithfield. Presently they discovered three barrels of applejack brandy and rolled them into the regiment's camp. After a few drinks, both officers and men were feeling "glorious," according to soldier Lew Ginger, who confessed, "I believe [only] one man in the regiment was sober and he was on guard at the Quartermaster's a half-mile away." The Hoosiers' division commander, Maj. Gen. Absalom Baird, appeared among the drunken men. He complimented them on the day's fighting and gave them permission to "have all the fun they wanted" so long as they refrained from destroying property. With their commander's apparent approval, the men wasted little time vandalizing the town. They burned the stocks on the courthouse lawn, graffitied court records, and ransacked churches. One soldier inscribed an admonishment to the congregation in the Methodist church's record book: "Remember the hard lessons of taking up arms against the

25 George P. Metz Papers, DU; Brown, *History of the Fourth Regiment*, 399; Platter Diary, UGA,168-169; Dean, *Shook Over Hell*, 61-62, 127.

government," he chided. Another unknown soldier expressed sympathy: "I am Sore [sorry] to see this church and Books Missused so, but you must look over it, you must bare and [bear in] mind that there is some Rootless [ruthless] men in the army that don't cear [care] any thing for them Selves nor any body Else."[26]

Several drunken men discovered the Odd Fellows and Sons of Malta lodges, with their colorful masks and ritual regalia, donned the costumes, and dashed about the streets frightening the nervous African Americans watching the scene. A young enslaved man named Frank Freeman was initially uncertain who the men "dressed in blue" were, but when they "began breaking up things and taking what they wanted," he realized they were Union soldiers. The marauding Northerners were shocked to find in one box a skeleton whose bones had been wired together. One (doubtless inebriated) soldier grabbed the skeleton and threw it out the window. Glass and bones landed on the men below, causing great shock and amusement. Federals disinterred some of Johnston's freshly buried soldiers from a church cemetery, hunting for hidden valuables. Jacob Allspaugh only hinted at the full scope of the behavior of his fellow Yankees by confiding in his coded diary, "Some depredations were committed in town."[27]

For a second day the XXIII Corps, unaccustomed to the new practices of war, marched through the destruction left by the XX Corps. Having witnessed the profitable and gratifying practice of bumming, they decided to seize their share. The diary of the 8th Minnesota's Lewis C. Paxson revealed some of the resulting pillage: "Fine big white house burned, and others less fine also burned." (This reportedly was retaliation against civilians by Union soldiers angered over the Rebel cavalry's execution of a Federal.) Paxson pointedly noted their fury: "An Indiana boy hung by Major Black; the man living in this white house accessory to some. The girl made to play piano until nearly scorched." The 8th Minnesota had already made its own kind of hard war against indigenous tribes in the Dakota territories. The so-called "Indian Regiment," formed in 1862, spent its first two years killing Native Americans. These soldiers had burned Sioux villages without orders and dug up the bodies of the Indian men and women. Paxson himself pocketed teeth and sent some of the skulls home to his family as trophies. Now these men were making hard war on Carolina civilians.[28]

26 Bradley, *This Astounding Close*, 98-99; John Smith, WPA, 11/2:278.

27 Frank Freedman, WPA, 11/2:321; Allspaugh Diary, UI.

28 Lewis C. Paxson, *Diary of Lewis C. Paxson* (Bismarck, ND, 1908), 38, 60; "The Board of Commissioners," *Minnesota in the Civil and Indian Wars 1861-1865* (St. Paul, MN, 1890), 1:395.

The destruction and the lack of discipline incensed corps commander Maj. Gen. Jacob Cox, as he rode past the smoking ruins. He believed this rampage was worse than the Atlanta campaign. His men had vented their anger on Thomas Atkinson, who was mistaken for his twin brother, William, a rumored Confederate conscription agent. The scotched rumor saved his life, but his home was burned to the ground anyway. Cox poured his anger into a circular to his men the following day admonishing their behavior, especially with the war's end in sight. He hoped his threats might curb their brutal behavior:

> Since we left Goldsborough there has been a constant succession of house burning in the rear of this command. This has never before been the case since the corps was organized, and the prospect of speedy peace makes this more than ever reprehensible. Division commanders will take the most vigorous measures to put a stop to these outrages, whether committed by men of this command or by stragglers from other corps. Any one found firing a dwelling-house or any building in close proximity to one, should be summarily shot.[29]

Blazing trees along the road marked Sherman's line of march through the dark spring night, and the roaring flames cast an eerie glow visible for miles. The sight struck John McBride of the 33rd Indiana: "Mile after mile of pitch pine trees would be in a blaze a height perhaps forty or fifty feet, making at times a beautiful sight, but the smoke was unbearable." The thick, black smoke from the Carolina pines "was blinding and, minus soap, the smoke became imbedded in the skin, so that some of the men were almost beyond recognition." To any onlooker it appeared as if an army of black devils was emerging through flaming corridors from the underworld. It was an image that added to the legend of Sherman's men as hellish fiends who came to destroy the South.[30]

April 12

A ship docking at the port of Wilmington bore two Federal officers with important news for Sherman. Riding through the night by the light of a full moon, they found the general at his headquarters in Smithfield, where they delivered an official dispatch from General Grant announcing the surrender of Lee's army at

---

29 Bradley, *This Astounding Close*, 101; OR 47 3/188-189.

30 McBride, *Thirty-third Indiana*, 179.

Appomattox Court House on April 9. An overjoyed Sherman quickly composed a reply: "I have this moment received your telegram announcing the surrender of Lee's army. I hardly know how to express my feelings, but you can imagine them." Sherman then dictated his own official announcement, Special Field Order No. 54, and ordered it distributed to the army. It elicited a powerful emotional response in his men, and sent their spirits soaring.[31]

The news shot through the army with lighting speed. Soldiers would never forget where they were or how they felt when they heard the news. Robert Strong of the 105th Illinois observed the reactions of men as the news rolled down the line:

> [We] saw, way ahead of us, hats being thrown in the air. Cheers and shouts went up. Pretty soon we were halted and then we could see a courier coming down the road. As he passed along, the boys seemed to go wild. When he reached the head of our regiment, our boys went wild too. We at the rear could not hear what he said. As he reached us, he yelled: "Lee has surrendered!"[32]

Henry J. Aten was sitting alongside the road during a halt when Sherman's order was proclaimed. The news "electrified" the men, Aten remembered. "Glory to God and our country, and all honor to our comrades in arms, toward whom we are marching!" Sherman punctuated the order with a nudge: "A little more labor, a little more toil on our part, the great race is won, and our Government stands, regenerated, after four long years of war." Nelson Stauffer and his comrades had just finished corduroying a road with fence rails when their commander, Brig. Gen. John E. Smith, galloped down the line. The men leapt to their feet to get out of his way. Waving his hat, Smith yelled, "Boys I have good news for you. General Lee has surrendered his entire force to General Grant. . . .Then it seemed that the dark cloud of war rolled back and vanished away. Our hearts were full, and it seemed that the scape valves were too small and something would surely burst." An air of celebration swiftly consumed the ranks. "The soldiers acted like a lot of escaped lunatics," wrote one Federal. "After four years of the bloodiest war the world ever

---

31 Henry Hitchcock, *Marching With Sherman: Passages from the Letters and Campaign Diaries of Henry Hitchcock, Major and Assistant Adjutant General of Volunteers, November 1864-May 1865*, M. A. DeWolfe Howe, ed. (New Haven, 1927), 295.

32 Strong, *Yankee Private*, 196.

saw, in which half a million men had lost their lives, it was ended, and not a star had been erased from the glittering folds of Old Glory."[33]

Sherman's aide, Maj. George Ward Nichols, remembered the emotional outbursts of the entire army:

> Our army went wild with excitement when this glorious result was announced. . . .Our troops gave cheer after cheer to express their joy, and then, when cheers became too feeble an expression, uttered yell upon yell until they waked the echoes for miles around. Then the bands burst forth in swelling strains of patriotic melody, which the soldiers caught up and re-echoed with their voices. Every body was proud and glad.[34]

According to Rice C. Bull of the 123rd New York, "The men went wild, ranks were broken, and shouting and crying, the men in their joy hugged and kissed each other. Never have I witnessed such happiness." Another wrote, "Immediately we forgot all about our fatigue, our rags, our dilapidated shoes, our sore feet and danced about like school boys just let loose from school." Members of the XV Corps celebrated the news with music from the "D[ivision] band. Songs by the 7th Iowa. Speeches cheering & c. &c.—in fact a grand jubilee." Alexander Downing cheered, "We forgot all about our hard marching, and the whole brigade commenced singing songs—'John Brown's body lies a-mouldering in the grave, As we go marching on!'" One ecstatic 21st Wisconsin soldier smashed his rifle against a nearby tree. The regiment's commander, Lt. Col. Michael H. Fitch, laughingly admonished the soldier saying, "That will cost you $14.00 my boy, and besides we have not settled with General Johnston; you may have use for a gun [y]et." The young man replied, "Colonel, I have carried that rifle for nigh three years. I don't know how many Johnnies it has hit, or knocked over. It has done its part. I will gladly pay Uncle Sam for the rifle, for the good news is worth that to me. As for Genl. Johnston and his men, Why, they will be glad if we will let them go home." But the celebration got out of control when a nearby warehouse containing turpentine, pitch, and rosin caught furiously afire, sending flames 100 feet into the

33 Aten, *History of the Eighty-fifth*, 302-303; *OR* 47/3:180; Nelson Stauffer, *Civil War Diary*, Norman Tanis, ed. (Northridge, CA, 1976); William Royal Oake, *On the Skirmish Line Behind a Friendly Tree: The Civil War Memoirs of William Royal Oake, 26th Iowa Volunteers*, Stacy Dale Allen, ed. (Helena, MT, 2006), 317.

34 Nichols, *The Story of the Great March*, 293.

air. Burning tar flowed into an adjacent waterway and carried downstream, spreading the fire to nearby forests as well.[35]

The news reached Kilpatrick's cavalry just as it launched Sherman's flank attack. Johnston did not make a stand along the Neuse River, but Hampton's cavalry still guarded the crossings and the army's rear. The Union horsemen charged across Swift Creek at the troopers of the Jeff Davis Legion and Cobb's Legion. Over the gunfire a courier arrived and spread the news of Lee's surrender. Jubilant soldiers with spirits soaring, began to shout, scream, and sing. The blue troopers vigorously renewed the charge and overran the confused Rebels. The surprise and ferocity of the attack pushed the Southerners back toward Raleigh. Sherman's strategy and his cavalry's tenacity had succeeded in surprising Wade Hampton and his men. The rapid Union advance drove a wedge between the Confederate rearguard and Johnston's army in Raleigh.

In the capital, the situation's gravity was unmistakable: no crowds turned out to welcome Johnston's remaining units as the marched through the streets. Soldiers recognized the panic among citizens who looking to their own survival rather than hospitality. Ex-governors Swain and Graham spent the morning attempting to convince Governor Vance to make peace at any price to save North Carolina. Columbia's pillage and fiery fate loomed large in these discussions, and Vance realized the suffering of his people and the magnitude of the threat they faced. Finally, he authorized Swain and Graham to negotiate an armistice with "authorities of the United States, touching the final termination of the existing war." Vance wanted their mission to be a secret, which gave it the best chance of success from still-dedicated Confederates. Vance did ask General Hardee to authorize sending a flag of truce into the Union lines, but he hid the true purpose of the request. Vance risked removal, imprisonment, and dishonor, all in hopes of sparing citizens further suffering, while Swain and Graham were about to risk their lives for peace. With Vance's note in hand, the men prepared for their clandestine journey to meet with Sherman.[36]

The former governors discreetly assembled a party of sympathetic military officers to escort them, but news of their mission leaked. Diehard Confederate supporters wired Johnston in Greensboro about Vance's intentions, and orders

35 Bull, *Soldiering*, 241; Widney and Girardi, eds., *Campaigning with Uncle Billy*, 353-354; Downing, *Downing's Civil War Diary*, 267-268; John Henry Otto, *Memoirs of a Dutch Mudsill: The "War Memories" of John Henry Otto*, David Gould and James B. Kennedy, eds., (Kent, OH, 2004), 359; Paxson, *Diary*, 60.

36 *OR* 47 3:178.

quickly arrived in Raleigh prohibiting Swain and Graham from meeting with Sherman. But the peace mission had already entrained and set off toward the faint sounds of battle in the distance. After a few miles, Hampton's troopers intercepted the train. Hampton reviewed Hardee's order, but he was skeptical of the mission and ignorant of Johnston's order to halt the committee, so he reluctantly let them pass. Minutes later, though, he received orders to arrest them, and he instantly dispatched a rider to bring them back.

Just as the peace commissioners began to relax, they spotted one of Hampton's breathless cavalrymen dashing toward them, and he delivered the general's order recalling the train. Swain and Graham realized they had failed. There was no hope now of protecting the capital and the university. Dallas Ward, the young conductor, threw the engine into reverse and, in a few minutes, reached the angry Hampton, who revealed his orders from Johnston and sent the commission's train back to Raleigh. The train chugged slowly on until reaching its intersection with the Smithfield Road, six miles from the capital. Suddenly, the passengers saw Kilpatrick's blue coated troopers dashing toward them. The riders riddled the engine with gunfire, forcing everyone in it to take cover. Once the train rolled to a stop, Yankee cavalry "piled down on us like wild Indians," according to Ward.[37]

As the passengers were forced off and ushered to the rear, Ward heard the increasing volume of gunfire behind them as the Union troopers attacked Hampton's forces. He never forgot the fever of the fighting and its aftermath, with bleeding, wounded men and horses lining the railroad embankment. They soon encountered a "greatly excited" General Kilpatrick sitting on his horse and peppering the men with questions: "Do you think Johnston will make a stand to fight us in Raleigh? How many men do you suppose he has?" As the skirmishing intensified Kilpatrick grew angry and cursed while ordering the train and its passengers on to Sherman's headquarters. The peace commissioners reboarded the train escorted by 40 Federal troopers, with another 40 riding on top. Swain and Graham would finally meet Sherman and they hoped to convince him to spare the state before it was too late.[38]

After arriving at Gully's Station, the commissioners made their way to Sherman's headquarters. Swain instantly greeted the general as if they were old friends and noted the fact that both had been college presidents. In practically the

---

37 Dallas T. Ward, *The Last Flag of Truce* (Franklinton, NC, 1915), 12; William Collin Stevens Papers, BL-UMI; *The Charlotte Democrat*, March 6, 1885.

38 Ward, *The Last Flag of Truce*, 13.

same breath, he "seized upon two or three members of [Sherman's] staff whose parents and pedigrees he knew and was soon at home among them." The commanding general greeted the delegation cordially and listened as Graham explained their mission and read Vance's offer.[39]

Sherman agreed to honor their flag of truce and spare the university and capital. The general recognized the peace commissioners as an opportunity to work with Vance and take North Carolina out of the war, thereby removing a keystone from the crumbling Confederacy. After quick consideration, Sherman issued orders for Vance's protection and for all members of the state government to return to Raleigh. Swain and Graham were quietly elated, for the great weight of bearing the responsibility to save their state had been lifted. Both were eager to return and announce the agreement, but Sherman warned them about the dangers of doing so; he urged them to stay as his guests, to which the commissioners reluctantly agreed.

The conversation around the campfire that night between enemies was pleasant. The commissioners' demeanors had made a favorable impression on Sherman and his staff, as did their desire to end the war. These impressions would be critical in the coming days as the army's emotional balance got severely tested. But Sherman's agreement to the former governors' proposals did not reach Vance in Raleigh, and after hours pacing the capitol, Vance finally decided to flee the city leaving Raleigh residents to deal with the arrival of the Yankees by themselves.

Dusk brought an end to the fighting. Kilpatrick's attack isolated Hampton's force and compelled them to spend the evening riding around Union positions to reach Raleigh. Despite success and the impending occupation of another Rebel capital, the Union camps grieved the men lost in the day's battle. Cavalryman Cornelius Baker recorded the death of his brother, Samuel, who was mortally wounded in the attack and left on the field; he had been "wounded in the Left Lung While assisting to inspire Courage into the men who were almost worn out with Constant Engagements With The Enemy and rapid marches By day and night." Baker and his saddened friends returned to his brother's grave to say goodbye a week after the skirmish that claimed his life.[40]

Cavalryman John Green survived the clash but suffered horrific physical and mental wounds that would plague him for the rest of his life. A Confederate pistol

39 Zebulon B. Vance, *Life and Character of David L. Swain* (Durham, NC, 1878), 16.

40 John W. Rowell, *Yankee Cavalryman: Through the Civil War with the Ninth Pennsylvania Cavalry* (Knoxville, TN, 1971), 247-248.

ball shattered the right side of Green's face, blowing out some of his teeth and damaging his skull. Green lived but was forever tormented by his wound, which left him in constant pain and deaf in his right ear. In the years after the war, his posture worsened and his ability to stand hot weather decreased dramatically. The ghastly wound completely transformed the mind and body of the boy of 17 who had gone to war in 1863. By the time of Green's death in 1883, friends and family remembered that his wound had reduced him to the state of a "raving Maniac."[41]

Most Union soldiers celebrated that night. Sergeant Theodore Upson was just placing his guard at the headquarters of XV Corps when Brig. Gen. Charles Woods came out of his quarters. "Dismiss the guard, Sergeant, and come into my tent." Upson asked why. "Don't you know Lee has surrendered? No man shall stand guard at my Quarters to night. Bring all the guard here." As Upson returned with the guards, officers were hurrying from every direction to Wood's tent, where a large bowl of alcoholic punch beckoned. Upson, the guards, the officers, the general himself, and several regimental bands all got exceedingly drunk. Rousing choruses of patriotic songs and music accompanied speeches celebrating the news. But as the bands drank more, the songs grew worse. When they could play no more, Woods picked up the bass drum, other officers grabbed horns, and together they led a great parade through the camp. The joyful display provided a significant release of stress for the men. "I dont realy think the singing was a grand success from an artistic stand point at least," Upson admitted. "But it answered the purpose and let out a lot of pent up exuberant feeling that had to have an outlet." The overwhelming desire for exaltation coursed through Sherman's massive army. A cacophony of patriotic songs filled the night air for miles. "The bands throughout the army played National airs during the evening," Robert Cruikshank wrote. "There was rejoicing everywhere. The men indulged in very little sleep. We all sat up late and talked over the prospect of the War coming to a close."[42]

With the enemy close on his heels, Johnston pushed his army to stay ahead of Sherman's pursuit. He ordered Wheeler to detail 200 men as a rearguard in Raleigh. Given Wheeler's struggles, it was an unfortunate choice, but Johnston had few options. Hampton also had concerns over the order, and he sternly warned Wheeler that he would be "held strictly accountable for any misdemeanors which may be committed in the city." Hampton detailed some of his own men from

---

41 Pension application, John Green/Melissa J. Green, NARA.

42 Upson, *With Sherman to the Sea*, 166; *Robert Cruikshank Letters (1862-1865)*, ehistory.osu.edu/sources/letters/cruikshank/index.cfm, accessed August 29, 2009.

Butler's division to keep Wheeler's unruly men in check, but they proved unequal to the task.[43]

That night's chaos consumed Raleigh. Citizens and Confederate authorities desperately tried to save what they could. Wheeler's troopers spread more panic: they spent the night drinking, stealing clothes, and thrashing about the city streets. The unruly cavalry so terrified twelve-year-old Patsy—the youngest of nine enslaved people working for Alexander M. Gorman's temperance paper, *Spirit of the Age*—that she "squatted like a rat" when the troopers rode by. She described how the soldiers stole drying clothes off the line, especially women's pantaloons, tied the legs together, and then filled them with meats, hams, and other loot. Another witness, a free woman of color named Adora Rienshaw, considered the Rebel cavalry the "meanest troops what wuz." Civilians flinched at the sounds of their own cavalrymen shouting as they tore up the town. The worry over the looting taking place and the capital's impending fall caused them extreme duress in many civilians. Men and women remained sleepless in their beds, fully clothed, expecting at any moment to have to flee from burning homes. One Raleigh citizen remembered it as a night of "extreme anxiety." [44]

Panicked civilians and government employees packed wagons, buggies, and carts, preparing to follow the army west. All serviceable train cars rolled out of Raleigh's station filled with military supplies, the state's historic archives, and what remained of its treasury. Conductors hauled the heavily laden cars west throughout the night to smaller stations along the North Carolina Railroad in hopes of keeping the vital supplies ahead of the advancing foe. Wounded Confederate soldiers collected from across the city were packed into wagons or packed in rail cars for evacuation. James A. Hall, a wounded officer who struggled through the evacuation with his wound and the mental stress it caused, "My mind is doing finely but pains me a great deal." Brigadier General Dan Reynolds bade farewell to the Haywood family as his staff loaded him onto a train car for the move west. Reynolds had received a horrific wound at the battle of Bentonville when a cannon ball passed through his horse and took off his leg when it exited the other side. He and the rest of the wounded spent a fretful night rattling through the cool spring air

43 OR 47/3:795.

44 Adora Reinshaw, WPA,11/2:213-15; Moses N. Amis, *Historical Raleigh from Its Foundation in 1792; Descriptive, Biographical, Educational, Industrial, Religious; Reminiscences Reviewed and Carefully Compiled* (Raleigh, 1902), 184.

to the small depot town of Morrisville, whose citizens offered the injured prayers, but little else.[45]

For Margaret Devereux and her family, the pressure of caring for the endless procession of wounded over the past weeks weighed heavily on their minds; their exertions caused "the greatest taxes upon our resources, and [it was] the event that brought the war very closely home to us." She tried to nurse several wounded Rebels, the Butler brothers, at her family's home in Raleigh: Capt. James, Brig. Gen. Mathew C., and the most seriously wounded, Nat, who had suffered from a shot through the right arm during the Confederate cavalry's March 10 attack on Kilpatrick's headquarters at Monroe's Crossroads. Doctors urged amputation of the limb but he refused. Margaret remembered the traumatic experience of Nat's bleeding, festering wound. "[T]he poor old captain [was] frantic with terror and [I was] quite unable to do anything for the patient . . . senseless and bleeding upon the bed," she wrote years later. "I can never forget his ghastly appearance." She recalled rushing to his bedside and compressing the wound until the doctor arrived, and being shocked to find herself covered in his blood.[46]

Besides comforting the wounded soldiers and her two young daughters, Mrs. Devereux had the added stress of caring for an upset family of refugees that filled her home. Together they faced enemy occupation and fretted over the unthinkable terrors it would bring. "[E]xcitement and turmoil" dominated the days before the expected occupation. Her desperate neighbors "were leaving town in a panic, and going they knew not whither," Devereux remembered. They pleaded with Margaret to hold their boxes, barrels, heirlooms, and other family treasures that they could not carry with them. Amid all the turmoil, a small group of cavalrymen and civilians with glowing lanterns gathered in the city cemetery beside a shallow grave.[47]

Lieutenant Wiley Howard of Cobb's Legion had caught the full fury of Kilpatrick's attack over Swift Creek earlier that day: "one of the hottest encounters in the range of my experience," he called it. Howard and his men tried to resist the assault, but the murderous volleys from the Yankees' Spencer repeating rifles rained the bullets "like hail." Two of Lieutenant Howard's fellow officers,

---

45 James A. Hall to Father, April 12, 1865, ADAH; Gordon Collection, SHC/UNC; Daniel H. Reynolds Papers, Special Collections, University of Arkansas, Fayetteville (UA). Reynolds prospered in postwar life but a son, Daniel Reynolds Jr., suffered a mental breakdown and was institutionalized.

46 Devereux, *Plantation Sketches*, 151-155.

47 Ibid.

including his best friend, Tom Dunnahoo, were wounded. Noticing his friend had fallen from the saddle, Howard raced back in the face of the attacking enemy to help. Howard reached him and "raised his head on my lap, his horse and mine standing there, and he gasped his last breath. [T]he blood from his bosom had bespattered the picture of his little motherless daughter which he carried." Howard and others threw Dunnahoo's lifeless body over his horse's saddle and dashed away. The other lieutenant killed in the attack, Charles Metcalfe of the Jeff Davis Legion, was an "irreparable" loss to his men. Now wrapped in an army blanket, their two lifeless bodies were lowered into the grave, followed by a few prayers. The known location of their final resting place offered loved ones offered a modicum of comfort. For other families the lack of information about fallen soldiers would be a constant source of sadness.[48]

Soldier Dick Eustis, took a bullet in the spine during the fighting and was left on the field. When the war ended, Eustis did not come home, and his disappearance caused great anxiety for his family, which doggedly sought any information about his fate. A mid-July issue of Raleigh's *Weekly Standard* contained a notice searching for news of Eustis. All the family had were rumors of his possible capture, and at least some hope he might still be alive. The notice appealed to anyone who knew anything to supply details to his "exceedingly anxious" friends. Eustis, however, shared the fate of several men killed in the war's final days. Confusion, destruction, and loss of records, not to mention the sweeping events themselves, obscured the fates of loved ones for years, if the information ever became available at all. It was yet another crushing burden of the war for thousands of missing men on both sides.[49]

48 Bradley, *This Astounding Close,* 106; Wiley C. Cobb, "Sketch of Cobb Legion Cavalry and Some Incidents and Scenes Remembered," August 19, 1901, SHC/UNC, 18-19.

49 Joseph Frank Waring Papers, SHC/UNC; Orrin L. Ellis Diary, USMHI, 31; *The* [Raleigh] *Daily Standard,* July 17, 1865.

CHAPTER 5

April 13–16:
"The greatest of human crimes for us to
attempt to continue the war"

April 13

Explosions

shook Raleigh during the stormy morning of April 13, as munitions set alight by retreating Confederates exploded and sent showers of metal skyward to fall with the rain. Burning piles of food, uniforms, and supplies sent heavy black clouds into the gray dawn. The last of Johnston's army rattled through the streets in the pre-dawn hours, heading west. Retreating Rebel artillerymen paused long enough to unlimber and bombard the train station in a final effort to deny its use to the Yankees. With their departure, the city was empty of all but straggling horsemen, some of whom were thoroughly drunk by dawn.

With these wild men roaming the streets, the fiery farewell by Confederate forces, and the approach of the Federals deepened fears that Raleigh would become another Columbia. No news from the Graham-Swain peace mission and the governor's flight left its leading citizens anxious and deeply worried about their fate. Thus, before sunrise another committee gathered to try surrendering the city. The mayor had been pulled from his sickbed to join former U.S. senator Kenneth Rayner and others to ask the invaders for mercy. The buggy filled with the dignitaries rattled down the abandoned streets and waited under a white flag on the city's southern outskirts in hopes they could still save the city.[1]

Meanwhile, Graham and Swain eagerly anticipated their return to Raleigh with their peace pact to ensure its enforcement. The two men bade Sherman farewell and boarded their train, hoping to beat his soldiers into town. Dubious of the surrender and skeptical of all Southerners, Judson Kilpatrick met the statesmen at their rail car and issued a chilling warning: He would honor Sherman's agreement but promised "relentless fury" on all armed traitors if he met any resistance while entering the city.[2]

As the train lurched forward and rolled out of sight, Kilpatrick ordered his columns forward. Unsure about their reception, nervous Union scouts expected an attack. They soon spied what at first appeared to be a Confederate advance, but a closer look by calmer heads revealed it to be only a buggy sporting a white flag. The cavalrymen cautiously approached and discovered Rayner's committee wishing to surrender the city. An hour passed before Kilpatrick arrived to accept these second terms. Rayner's and his companions' nerves had grown edgy waiting in the cold rain for the general to arrive. As Rayner rose and began to beg for the safety of the capital, he faltered almost immediately, overwhelmed by his emotions. Choking on his words, he broke down in sobs. Kilpatrick listened but was unmoved by the plea and pressed on to claim his prize.[3]

The commissioners' train slowed to a halt before reaching the burning station. Hurriedly disembarking, the men split up. Swain darted down the deserted streets to the capitol to await Kilpatrick's approach. He quickly spied a group of Confederate horsemen, whom he recognized as Wheeler's brigands, ransacking a jewelry store across from the capitol grounds, the same behavior they had engaged in during the evacuation of Columbia.[4]

These actions threatened the deal Swain had just struck for the safety of the city. He confronted the men and informed them of the agreement with the Federals for Raleigh's surrender. A heated exchange erupted, with one soldier

1 *Groesbeck* [TX] *Journal,* January 13, 1910; A. Wood, "The Last Shots by Gen. Johnston's Army," in *Confederate Veteran Magazine (CV),* 40 vols. (Nashville, TN, 1893-1932), 16:585.

2 Moses N. Amis, *The City of Raleigh: Historical Sketches from its Founding* (Raleigh, NC, 1887), 59.

3 Bradley, *This Astounding Close,* 122; Noah A. Trudeau, *Out of the Storm: The End of the Civil War, April-June 1865* (Baton Rouge, 1995), 210.

4 Spencer, *The Last Ninety Days,* 157-160; George Knox Miller to Celestine McCann, February 23, 1865, George Knox Miller papers, SHC/UNC.

barking, "D[am]n Sherman and the town too"; they cared for neither. The argument ended when Swain pointed to a Federal column marching up the southern end of the street.

One of Kilpatrick's officers saw "about half a dozen [Confederate] stragglers ... looting a store just opposite the Capitol." One Rebel horseman emptied his revolver at the Federals and galloped out of town, but his horse fell at the corner of Morgan Street, throwing him to the ground. He did not get far before Kilpatrick's staff captured him.[5]

An enslaved woman named Milly Henry watched as Union soldiers dragged the captured Confederate to the lawn of the capitol, where he confronted an enraged General Kilpatrick. Milly remembered the soldier stating his name as Robert Walsh of the 11th Texas Cavalry. When Kilpatrick asked why he fired on the Union column Walsh replied, "[Bec]ause I hate de Yankees and I wush dat dey wus daid in a pile." Kilpatrick, who had found his men executed by the Confederate cavalry, ordered his troopers to take the captive to a place where none of the ladies could see and hang him. What struck Milly most about the scene was the trooper's reaction to his death sentence. He began laughing and kept repeating "Kin[d] of you sir" as he waved goodbye to the crowd. "He died brave to" Milly added, "an he kep laughin' till his neck broke."[6]

Fearing his surrender had been endangered, a shocked David Swain watched Federal cavalry dismount and approached the capitol. The nervous Swain quickly proclaimed, "I am just from your commanding General and have his promise that this edifice shall not be injured." The officer replied, "I know you, sir, and have orders to attend to your wishes." Swain again breathed a heavy sigh of relief, but it would not be the last time Raleigh faced mortal danger from Sherman's army.[7]

Kilpatrick's cavalrymen saluted him with three cheers as they rode through the city. The general paused for only 30 minutes to gloat over the newly captured capital before he put his men into action. Sherman had ordered Kilpatrick to pursue the retreating Confederates as aggressively and relentlessly as possible. The electric effect of Lee's surrender, the capture of Raleigh, and Sherman's orders for a

5   Trudeau, *Out of the Storm*, 219; Murray, *Wake County*, 507-509; Gibson, *163 Days*, 248; John D. Taylor Reminiscences, in John D. Taylor Papers, NCDAH; Joseph Kittinger, Diary, United States Military History Institute (USHMI), 204; George W. Pepper, *Personal Recollections of Sherman's Campaigns in Georgia and the Carolinas* (Lexington, KY, 1968), 421.

6   Milly Henry, WPA, 11/2:400-404.

7   Spencer, *The Last Ninety Days*, 162.

determined pursuit invigorated the Union troopers. Kilpatrick left a single regiment to guard the city and dispatched the rest of his command in pursuit of the Rebels, thereby igniting the hardest day's fighting of the campaign.

Wheeler's men had camped just outside of Raleigh's western outskirts. As they cooked breakfast, they heard a low rumble and felt the ground shake. O. P. Hargis of the 1st Georgia Cavalry heard the bugle call "to mount quick and we sprang for our horses, and by the time we got into our saddles the Federal cavalry was right on to us and every man had to take care of himself. It was the worse stampede I ever saw." Kilpatrick's cavalrymen were amongst the Rebels, firing pistols and hacking with sabers. The Confederates dashed off in every direction, fighting pell-mell through the pine thickets. The surprise attack shook the nerves of Hargis and his brother, who hatched a plan to escape the army in the coming days under the guise of impressing horses from a local cousin's farm.[8]

Fighting hand-to-hand, the Georgians pushed back the Federals. An intoxicated Texan named Tom Burney remembered Federal cavalry so thick that the men were pushing each other into the gullies and through fences trying to get away. As the fighting crossed over a small creek, Burney witnessed one man robbing a dead soldier lying in the muddy water. Wheeler's and Kilpatrick's forces continued skirmishing throughout the day, covering over a dozen miles. At one point, Confederate cavalryman Wiley C. Howard, who had suffered in yesterday's skirmish over Swift Creek, received a grisly injury when a thorny blackjack tree punctured his eye. Blinded, Howard was led to the rear as Union artillery began shelling the Southern position. The fear that came with his loss of sight during the battle rattled the veteran: "I cannot picture the demoralizing effect of the situation, stone blind and suffering while I was retreating, subjected to this horrible cannonading from the rear," the distressed soldier lamented. "It remains to-day amid all my experiences a living, vivid memory beyond my descriptive powers. It was my last experience under fire and was received with all the force and dread which my introduction to shell and shot produced at Cold Harbor."[9]

The Federal advance culminated in an attack on a stranded train filled with supplies and wounded soldiers that had left Raleigh the previous day. Union cannons shelled the Morrisville town depot as the cavalry moved into position for an attack. The blue troopers' headlong charge came within 100 yards of capturing

8 O. P. Hargis, Reminiscences, SHC/UNC.

9 *Groesbeck* [TX] *Journal,* December 9, 1909; Wiley C. Howard, *Sketch of Cobb Legion Cavalry and Some Incidents and Scenes Remembered* (Atlanta, GA, 1901), 19.

the train before withering Rebel fire stopped it. But to save the train, Wheeler ordered the cars of desperately needed supplies uncoupled, while those with the wounded remained attached and escaped. At 3:00 p.m., Kilpatrick informed Sherman about the day's fighting, noting that his men had "taken barricade after barricade of the strongest character" and had "fought over nearly every foot of ground from Raleigh." The general also reported the capture of 21 cars filled with mostly corn and other supplies and an intercepted telegraph message noting heavy fighting down the tracks in Salisbury by Maj. Gen. George Stoneman. The news was welcomed in Sherman's headquarters. Stoneman's raid would hamper Johnston's retreat giving his army a better chance to catch the fleeing Rebels.[10]

Sherman established his headquarters in the "Governor's Palace." As the rest of the army moved into Raleigh officers took over residences for their own command centers. Major General John Schofield and his staff made their headquarters in William Grimes's home. They took over two front rooms and the dining room; tents appeared on the lawn. For the Grimes family, the occupation started well, until an incident occurred that underscored how alcohol influenced the judgement of men who morality hung in the balance.

An intoxicated staff officer, Maj. Samuel M. Letcher of the 12th Kentucky, stumbled into the Grimes house. Letcher entered the war as a nineteen-year-old private in October 1861, but due to his gallant conduct at the January 1862 battle of Mill Springs (Logan's Crossroads), Kentucky, he was personally recommended by Maj. Gen. George Thomas for an officer's commission. Drunk, belligerent, and stressed out by three and a half years of hard war, Letcher took his anger out on the Grimes family. Grabbing William Grimes in his hallway, he began interrogating him: "Well sir, what part are you taking in this war?" Grimes rebuked the officer and denied his authority to question him in such a manner. An angry Letcher then pulled out his pistol and pointed it at Grimes's head. Mrs. Grimes leaped between the two men. "Don't you dare shoot that pistol!" she ordered. The fortuitous arrival of Letcher's commander ended the confrontation.[11]

The conflict shocked Letcher back to his senses and made a deep impression on him. In July 1866, Letcher wrote to Grimes and apologized for the incident, blaming alcohol for his behavior. The major admitted that if he had killed Grimes that day he would now be "an outcast without ambition or friends." It was the

---

10 *OR* 47/3:198.

11 William Grimes, Recollection, Grimes Family Papers, SHC/UNC.

confrontation with Grimes that made Letcher realize how far war had pushed him, and he admitted that since that day he had decided to turn his life around.

One of Grimes's neighbors, former governor Charles Manly, "hosted" some of Sherman's staff, who had pitched their tents in his front yard and taken over his office. Manly was shocked when the soldiers tore down his fences for fuel, destroyed his gardens, stole horses, and "tore off doors, flooring, and weatherboarding of my out-houses and barns for tents." But his plantation, "Ingleside," three miles from Raleigh, fared much worse. The homes of 70 enslaved people were "plundered of their clothing and provisions" and the farm was sacked. "My dwelling-house was broken open, weatherboarding, flooring, and ceiling carried off, every window-sash and glass broken out, and every article of furniture for house or kitchen either carried off or wantonly destroyed." Manly bemoaned the crisis after the soldiers carried off all the livestock and provisions, "leaving the whole place entirely bare, so that my negroes had to come in town for rations."[12]

Terrified townspeople flocked to Sherman's headquarters, desperately seeking protection from soldiers who were starting to enter private homes. Kemp P. Battle, a prominent lawyer and railroad president, sought a guard for his sister, the wife of Confederate Brig. Gen. William R. Cox. One of her slaves brought Battle the alarming news that Union soldiers were looting their home. Battle rushed to the Governor's Palace, introduced himself to Sherman, and requested a guard. "Certainly," Sherman replied, "Go see General Joseph Mower yonder." Mower promptly denied the request. "I cannot do it. I cannot trust Wheeler's men. They will steal up at night and shoot the guard." Eventually, Battle managed to find a Federal to guard the Cox house and escorted him to his post. As they arrived, another soldier was leaving with a jar of preserves and a sack of flour. But when Battle insisted that the guard force the return of these goods, all he got was the cool reply: "I wasn't sent to make anybody put back what they have got but to keep them from getting things after I have arrived." The looting finally ceased, but only after a brigadier general camped in Cox's yard.[13]

Charles Brown of the 21st Michigan enjoyed terrifying locals who came to request guards. Brown wrote home relating Southerners' interest in the bummers and the joy he derived by inflaming the stories about their dark work. "[I]t was fun

12 John G. Barrett, *Sherman's March Through North Carolina* (Chapel Hill, NC, 1956), 72; Betty Forman Cheshire, WPA, 7:30.

13 Kemp Plummer Battle, *Memories of an Old-Time Tarheel* (Chapel Hill, NC, 1945), 193-194.

to hear their questions & some I did scare almost to death the very name of 'Sherman's Bummers' would cause all to turn pale." Brown seemed to relish describing their activities, and related some of these scenes to his family:

> Boys pounding Piano keys with their hatchets to see who could make the most noise or pile up a pile of plates & "order arms" on them to see who could break the most or try to & see who could dress themselves in the best suit of womens clothes & them make the lady of the house play for them to have a cotillion & if the music did not suit slash their hatchet through the top of the piano to improve the time.

But Brown related much more insidious stories that went beyond those of malicious vandalism. One account told of a soldier who made a woman "kneel to them & beg for Gods sake to leave enough for her children in her house. [And then t]urn from them with oaths & take the last morsel of food on old woman," all at the end of a cocked revolver. Brown recoiled in disgust and began to sympathize with Southerners:

> I have been thankful ever since I have been in the Army that this war is south. You never can imagine a pillaged house, never—unless an army passes through your town & if this thing had been in the North I would Bushwhack until every man was either dead or I was. If such scenes be enacted through Mich[igan] I would never live as long as one of the invading army did I do not blame the south & shall not if they do go to Guerrilla warfare.[14]

Bummers proliferated as the army approached Raleigh. Foragers from the XV Corps crossed the Neuse River, discovered whiskey, and commenced to "have a big drunk." Several diarists encountered intoxicated soldiers. "The bummers found whiskey to-day," Charles Wills noted; "I saw a number dead drunk by the roadside." Wills was one of Sherman's soldiers who still tried to fight the war while preserving some morality, but also knew alcohol's power to subvert their beliefs. When his fellow soldiers had entered Columbia, he noted that whiskey and wine had "flowed like water and made the whole division drunk." He saw the necessity of Columbia's destruction, but disagreed with the way it was carried out. "This gobbling up of things so, disgusts me much. I think the city should be burned but would like to see it done decently."[15]

---

14 Charles S. Brown to Mother and Etta, April 18, 1865, Charles S. Brown Collection, D3U.

15 Charles Wright Wills, *Army Life of an Illinois Soldier* (Washington DC, 1906), 369-370; Diary of Robert Armstrong, Allen County Public Library; James F. Overholser Diary, April 13, 1865, Wright State University (WS).

At the "Broomfield" plantation just below Raleigh, Jane Constance Hinton prepared for the worst and panicked trying to save what she could. She hid her family's food in the walls of her kitchen and sent the animals away. She remained at the home with her four small children, determined not to suffer the agony of refugeeing. The first Federals who arrived were polite and raised their hats to Hinton, asking if any other Federal soldiers had passed by; they warned her, "you had better take care of your things—look out for bummers." But as the bulk of the army started passing by, the madness began. Waves of soldiers swarmed the house and grounds, breaking locks on doors and cabinets, taking every edible they could find. One particularly prized saddle was stolen but Mrs. Hinton appealed to a nearby general, who ordered it returned; nevertheless, another soldier took it shortly afterward. Hinton's hidden food was looted after her slaves revealed where its location. The sight of a helpless mother and her children moved one soldier to return his share of the loot. Hinton remembered him walking across the porch. "Madam, will you have this? For I have never seen anyone treated as you have been treated today."

All day long, soldiers barged in, searched the house, and took whatever they desired, but Jane Hinton refused to leave Broomfield. When she learned around five o'clock that black troops would be passing that night, however, fear moved her to make the agonizing decision to leave. She and her children walked through the circle of Yankee soldiers sitting in rocking chairs on her front porch and headed toward Raleigh and safety. Charles Wills camped near the vandalized plantation that night, which was the fourth anniversary of the firing on Fort Sumter. Ruining the Hinton family's ostentatious home and their livelihood built on slavery gave the soldiers great satisfaction, and the irony was not lost on Wills. "How are you, chivalry?" he asked his diary that night.[16]

General William B. Woods also worried about a repeat of the Columbia debacle as his command approached Raleigh. From his headquarters at Wilder's Plantation, Woods issued Special Order No. 66, strictly curtailing foraging and imposing punishments for violations. It also stripped mounted foragers of their horses and mandated that only officers could supervise foraging parties. Determined to keep his men under control, Woods ordered the apprehension of any other miscreant foragers the officers discovered. "The division detail will arrest

16 Hinton, "Key Basket," 8-13, SHC/UNC; Wills, *Army Life of an Illinois Soldier*, 369; OR 47/1:284-285.

any and all other foragers that may be discovered through the country belonging to his division, sending them to these headquarters under guard."[17]

Besides curtailing their own men Union soldiers remained vigilant against a active enemy. In the rear of the army, the XXIII Corps lumbered toward Raleigh. One column encountered a panicked Federal lieutenant galloping down the road shouting, "Take the left hand road and drive like h[el]l; Wheeler's cavalry is just up that right-hand road and will capture the last one of you! Drive for your lives I tell you!" About 60 wagons turned and dashed down the road. But the blue-coated horseman was actually a Southerner dressed in the uniform of an officer captured earlier that day. Confederate horsemen bolted from their concealed positions and attacked the guards of the 104th Ohio, shooting horses and burning wagons they were unable to haul away. They killed mules that could not be carried off and cut up their harnesses. Alerted by the sound of gunfire, a detachment of men from the 100th Ohio pounded down the road and scattered the Rebels, but their pursuit managed to recapture only a few mules and several of the Union prisoners; they also bagged two Confederates.

Angry at the betrayal, the troopers of the 104th Ohio returned to the crossroads where the trap had been sprung. Suspiciously eyeing the nearby home of Henry and Elizabeth Finch, the soldiers convinced themselves that the occupants were in on the ambush and decided to make them pay. They rushed the house, barred the doors, and set it on fire. Flames soon engulfed the home with the family still inside. Mrs. Finch frantically forced herself through a window despite soldier's threats from below to shoot her. She screamed that she would "rather be shot than burned," and fell from the inferno.[18]

Accompanying the 104th was its notable mascot, Harvey, Lt. Daniel M. Stearns's pit bull, beloved by his master and the regiment. His special collar proclaimed: "I am Lieutenant D.M. Stearns' Dog. Whose Dog Are You?" Harvey followed Stearns throughout the war and was wounded twice. The dog managed to recover from his wounds, something his owner did not do. Stearns originally went to war in 1861 with the 8th Pennsylvania. After his enlistment expired, he reenlisted in the 104th Ohio and rose to become Company F's first sergeant. He earned another promotion to second lieutenant in December 1862. But war soon took its toll on his mind.

17 *OR* 47/3:193.

18 Whitaker, *Reminisces*, 254-255.

Lieutenant Daniel Stearns' dog, Harvey, was both a regimental mascot and an emotional support pet for his master. Stearns's mental state continued to deteriorate after the war. He could not work or concentrate, and suffered from hallucinations. He blamed his erratic behavior on sunstroke suffered during the Atlanta campaign in 1864. Stearns's family eventually committed the veteran to the Northern Ohio Insane Asylum, where he died in 1890. *Susan Scullion, descendant*

Stearns himself believed that sunstroke he suffered during the Atlanta campaign caused the mental problems that plagued him for the rest of his life. One particularly bad episode happened after Stearns was in the saddle for the better part of two days, leading his men in an assault on a heavily entrenched Confederate position in late July 1864. For the next four days, Stearns suffered high fever but returned to his regiment, then in the thick of combat at Utoy Creek, on August 5. Four months later at the battle of Franklin, Stearns and his regiment caught the fury of Maj. Gen. Patrick Cleburne's frontal attack that sheered the Ohio regiment in half near the infamous Carter cotton gin. By the time Stearns arrived in North Carolina he was a wrecked man, with only his dog for support and friendship. Indeed, friends thought Stearns "seemed to think more of [Harvey] than anything else." Harvey's death before 1886 could have been the last straw for the unreasoning, distraught Stearns. His inability to function and wild mood swings forced his family to commit the veteran to the Northern Ohio Insane Asylum, where he died in 1890.[19]

19 Testimony of W. B. Slawson, William H. Batchelor, Charles W. Stearns, Julia Stearns, Daniel M. Stearns Pension file, NA. Stearns returned home from war an irritable, nervous, lethargic, and unbalanced man, obsessed with his army service and with Harvey. Family and friends found him incapable of concentrating, and he failed miserably in numerous jobs they lined up for him. Grasping his head, he constantly complained of raging pain as though an iron band were constricting it. His wife testified it resembled a headache, and when he walked "the pavement seemed to be rising in front of him." Harvey comforted and stayed with his master over the years as his condition worsened; Stearns eventually was committed to the asylum in 1888 after showing signs of insanity. The doctor's assessment noted that he was both suicidal and homicidal, and attributed his insanity to heredity and intemperance. He died of Bright's disease in 1890.

The ambush on Stearns's column highlighted the growing frustration of the Confederate cavalry. But other incidents showed how stress morally bankrupted these men, causing them to become more violent as the prospects for their cause grew darker. After the XXIII Corps passed, several Union soldiers were lured into a home by women and captured by waiting Rebel scouts. They were found with their arms tied behind their backs, and their tongues had been cut "from their mouths, and nailed them to a tree beside their owners." Confederate horsemen lurking outside Goldsboro executed a Union officer, Capt. John McGuire, and a small group of soldiers from the 175th New York who had ventured outside the lines collecting boards to build shanties. They killed most of McGuire's party, except for two who escaped. It took twelve days to recover the captain's body, which "was badly mangled"; he had been shot seven times and his throat was slit from ear to ear. For men whose minds and judgment were clouded by war, these actions were warranted. The horsemen continued to lash out at friend and foe throughout the closing days of the conflict. Though some would carry this anger for the rest of their lives, events were in motion that would end the war and break the spell it had on them.[20]

On this day, Joe Johnston received orders to meet with President Davis and his cabinet in Greensboro. Johnston and Davis had thoroughly disliked one another from the war's earliest days, and their animosity deepened as the war dragged on. Now as Confederate fortunes dimmed, both men bristled at the meeting, but an immediate war council was necessary to determine the fate of the cause, the country, and the army.

Once his cabinet members assembled, Davis queried them and Johnston about how best to continue the war. The room was silent. Only after Davis prompted the general did he express his thoughts—in a "tone & manner almost spiteful," Postmaster General John H. Reagan remembered. "Our people are tired of war, feel themselves whipped and will not fight," Johnston began. "Our country is overrun, its military resources greatly diminished, while the enemy's military power and resources were never greater and may be increased to the extent desired." In an exasperated tone, Johnston declared that his "small force is melting away like snow before the sun, and I am helpless of recruiting it." Silence once again gripped the room. Johnston continued and stressed the urgency to mercifully end the war, "for

---

20 Nelson A. Pinney, *History of the 104th Regiment Ohio Volunteer Infantry from 1862 to 1865* (Windham, OH, 1886), 81; Joseph Crowther Diary, April 13, 1865, Virginia Military Institute (VMI).

under such circumstances it would be the greatest of human crimes for us to attempt to continue" it. Several of the cabinet members agreed with Johnston's assessment, as did the rueful president, who authorized Johnston to contact Sherman and inquire what terms they could expect for surrender. The dishonor of surrender was Johnston's greatest fear, but he took solace in the relief it could provide to both his tortured people and his lacerated army. Davis dictated the message to Sherman—which was sent to Hillsborough for delivery to Union lines—but Johnston signed his name to it.[21]

April 14

The second day of Raleigh's occupation occasioned a daunting display of force. Major General John A. Logan's XV Corps approached the city with orders to prepare for a review by Sherman. Around 11:00 a.m. his troops marched through Raleigh under the commanding general's watchful eyes as he sat on the grounds of the capitol. The review was aimed at straightening up his men as they passed through the city, and it emphasized military authority. It would also serve as a vivid sign of Northern power to Raleigh's citizens. According to George Metz, "[a]t every corner you could see Women and Children standing with open mouths and eyes watching us as we passed through." Captain James Crozer noticed one upset woman watching the parade. "She hardly knew what she was about [she] kept crying snarling & snapping at the Yanks all the time they were passing just because her nigger went off with the Yanks."[22]

Major General Carl Schurz remembered that "[a]s far as the eye can reach is a sea of bayonets." He also took note of woeful locals watching the parade, especially one young woman who raised a handkerchief to her eyes and declared, "It is all over with us; I see now, it is all over. A few days ago I saw General Johnston's army, ragged and starved; now when I look at these strong, healthy men and see them coming and coming—it is all over with us!" Other citizens took off their hats as a sign of respect as the soldiers passed, a silent admission of their subjugation.[23]

---

21 Jefferson Davis, *Rise and Fall of the Confederate Government*, 2 vols. (New York, 1961) 2:519-520; Johnston, Narrative, 396-398; Symonds, *Joseph E. Johnston*, 355; Stephen R. Mallory, "Last Days of the Confederate Government, *McClure's Magazine* (December 1900), 16: 240-241.

22 Carl Schurz, *Intimate Letters of Carl Schurz, 1841-1869* (Madison, WI, 1928), 333.

23 *OR* 47/3:209; George P. Metz Diary, April 14, 1865, Metz Papers, DU; Letter to family, April 14, 1865, James D. Crozer Papers, NCDAH.

The XV Corps pressed on through the city to the northwest and nervous citizens braced for the worst. Margaret Devereaux and her family watched as the corps lumbered toward her home. She compared the arrival of the rain-soaked columns, clad in their dripping, rubberized ponchos, to that of a slithering snake. "It was towards noon upon that fatal day we espied a long blue line crawling serpent-like around a distant hill. Silently we watched, as it uncoiled itself, ever drawing nearer and still nearer, until the one great reptile developed into many reptiles and took the form of men." Their arrival brought chaos to the Devereux farm: "men in blue tramping everywhere, horsemen careening about us with no apparent object, wagons crashing through fences as though they had been made of paper. The Negroes stood like dumb things, in stupid dismay . . . then the only feeling was of awe."[24]

As his army entered the city Sherman began the next phase of his pursuit of Johnston. He issued Special Field Order No. 55, which outlined the new route of the march. Sherman would maintain the feint of pursuit along the railroad, but the bulk of his army would race Johnston's on a parallel course and catch him around Charlotte. This route would force the Union army to abandon its supply lines and return to living off the land.[25]

Johnston continued to push his men forward as fast as possible while he waited for his armistice offer to reach Sherman. He foresaw Sherman's plan to intercept him and decided to split his force in order to move faster. The commands of A. P. Stewart and S. D. Lee moved to Hillsborough on roads that shadowed the railroad tracks. The men of Hardee's corps would go cross-county on backroads. They prepared for the march under the worst of conditions. Exhausted from the previous day's 22-mile march, morale sank even lower with rumors of Lee's surrender. News of Stoneman's raid in their front stirred more uneasiness as they prepared to move west. But the weather now became a new enemy. The spring rains flooded the numerous creeks and rivers, and the worries Johnston envisioned for traveling across the state became reality. The difficulty in crossing these roaring waterways brought panic to his nervous men.

Hardee's column left Chapel Hill and marched over the rolling hills toward the first of their dangerous crossings, the raging Haw River. The corps crossed with only the loss of a few young men of the Junior Reserves, who were swept away by the rapid current. But the rain continued to fall, further angering the flooded

---

24 Jones, *When Sherman Came*, 303.

25 *OR* 47/3:208, 215.

creeks. By the time the men reached the Great Alamance Creek, rain had turned it into an impassible torrent that washed away the bridges. Anxious men now realized the danger they faced. If in close pursuit, the Yankees could pin them against the river and easily destroy them. Men cautiously waded into the water holding the hand of the next, but the powerful water current was too much and swept them away.

Major General Frank Cheatham rode to the head of the column to discover the problem with the crossing and grew agitated with the slow efforts. Riding to the riverbank, he ordered the lead teamsters into the water, but "[w]ith a crack of the whip, and a shout to his mules he is in and under, rises, struggles, and is swept away." Another two wagons tried to cross with the same result. Cheatham ordered more men to cross, but with "some pretty lively swearing" they refused to obey. The general's anger boiled over. He grabbed the closest man and tried to force him into the water, but the soldier resisted, and a scuffle ensued. Soldier William Clark watched Cheatham and the soldier wrestling on the ground and rolling into the water. With rain pouring, and the river rising, Hardee could see no other options. He had to get his men across or risk being killed or captured, so he rashly ordered destruction of all the wagons and supplies. Major General Robert F. Hoke intervened, suggesting that a more viable crossing might be located and asking permission to look. Fortunately, Hoke's scouts found such a crossing over a railroad bridge just four miles upstream. [26]

Wheeler's cavalry served as Hardee's rear guard and fought to keep the Union pursuit at bay. The troopers rode into Chapel Hill and set up their defences. The troubling accounts of the men's recent rowdy behavior, especially in Raleigh, made people nervous. Residents regarded the troopers warily and met the men to see if the stories about their character were true. Cornelia Spencer found them "utterly demoralized, lawless, and defiant" with "more than a few" interested only in plunder." Further, the townspeople had the unfortunate task of informing the men of Lee's surrender, news that shocked the troopers. Some "denounced it as a Yankee lie" while one Georgian trooper proclaimed, "they won't get me." Another assured Mrs. Spencer that "he would join the army of France and take his allegiance and his revolver over the water." Many were simply stunned and "had absolutely no where on earth to go and knew not what to do." She described Lt. James Coffin, a former university student, as a completely ruined man. He "had not seen his

---

26 Walter Clark, *Histories of the Several Regiments and Battalions from North Carolina in the Great War 1861-65*, 4 vols. (Goldsboro, NC, 1901), 4:60; Dunkerly, *Confederate Surrender*, 43.

[Tennessee] home within a year and had recently learned that his wife and children were homeless because the enemy had burned it to the ground." News of Lee's surrender finally broke his spirit, and he "covered his face with his hands to hide a brave man's tears," Spencer noted. Many of the heart-stricken men spoke frankly about the sad state of affairs, and the news soon spread to the rest of the army, with catastrophic effects.[27]

The arrival of parolees from the Army of Northern Virginia inflamed an already dire situation. The hungry parolees fought for whatever resources they could find, to the consternation of Johnston's shaky troops. But the fact of Lee's surrender signaled a much greater disaster. It foreshadowed their own capitulation, the end of the Confederacy, and the ruin of Southern society. The monumental changes defeat portended elicited powerful emotional and physical reactions among the troubled men in Johnston's army. Sidney Wilkinson of the Junior Reserves said he had "never . . . witnessed such a scene when the news hit camp. "[S]ome were sad, some joyful, some crying, some shouting at the top of their voices and here and there you could find a squad dancing, and every little distance an officer would have a stand making a speech, trying to quiet the uproar." J. W. Evans reacted viscerally to Lee's surrender: "[F]or two days and nights I rolled in the dust, kicked and cussed and vowed, neither ate nor slept much." Captain Thomas Pickney heard the news as he lay wounded in a railcar in Hillsborough; he dragged himself to the open doorway and "launched such a philippic at the crowd soon collecting as I had never indulged in before, telling them it was a disgrace to the uniform they wore for the soldiers of the Confederate States to be circulating reports which they knew to be untrue and which were becoming only to weak-kneed old men and women at the rear, who knew nothing of the spirit of the army." After seeing a parole from one of Lee's men, Pickney recoiled, admitting "it required time to take in this stunning blow." The parolees helped deplete the rapidly dwindling supplies of food. Charles Jones of the Chatham Artillery recalled 10 horses and mules died for lack of forage, and the near impossibility of getting "even a limited amount of corn, fodder, and peas . . . for twenty-five miles round for forage."[28]

27 Spencer, *The Last Ninety Days*, 167-168; Journal, Cornelia Phillips Spencer Papers, SHC/UNC.

28 Dunkerly, *Confederate Surrender*, 28; J. W. Evans, "With Hampton's Scouts," in *CV*, 32:470; "Capt. Thomas Pinckney," in *CV*, 24:343; Charles Colcock Jones, *Historical Sketch of the Chatham Artillery During the Confederate Struggle for Independence* (Albany, GA, 1867), 216.

The impact of Lee's paroled men was felt in towns and cities all along the North Carolina Railroad, from Hillsborough to Charlotte. Greensboro's post commander, Brig. Gen. Alfred Iverson, quickly grasped the effect parolees were having on the broken spirits of his men. "I am pained to say that the disposition of the command is not good," he confessed, "there being much demoralization." Iverson had a precarious hold on the town, with the majority of his forces being unreliable "men collected together for the emergency." He noted that most of the Virginia troops had already deserted and that trying to round up stragglers was futile. Iverson suggested that moving the men to a less congested area might help. Outside the city, Brig. Gen. Collett Leventhorpe witnessed the rise of discontent among his men to the west of Greensboro when he noted swiftly plummeting morale and a "growing number of desertions." During the previous night, "200 men of one battalion" deserted and the remainder "state openly their intention to return to their homes." Massive demoralization, he said, was "indisputable." The same was true for commanders around the city and across central North Carolina.[29]

The appearance of both Lee's men and Stoneman's Union raiders spread demoralization around the town of Lexington. The town's desperate commander, Col. A. M. Booe, wired Governor Vance about the crumbling morale of his soldiers, who were "very impatient under the present excitement . . . their property in different counties have been plundered by raiders and tories. The army of Generals Lee and Johnston falling back, with discouraging accounts, renders it almost impossible for me to hold them together."[30]

R. P. Leinbach recorded the confusion and anxiety coursing through his neighborhood in Salem. "The country was in a pitiful condition; bands of soldiers straggling thro' the country, . . . some stealing, others borrowing, some taking openly; the people uneasy and anxious, some few at work, others hiding their horses, and none able to appreciate the solemn [Easter] season." Fear impelled citizens in the small Moravian community to form a vigilance committee to protect the town day and night from the hundreds of hungry parolees passing through.[31]

Lee's surrender sent shockwaves to posts in the east that had been isolated by Sherman's march inland. Matters worsened, for example, for the far-flung command of Brig. Gen. Laurence S. Baker in Warrenton. Baker's alcoholism had

29 OR 47/3:799-800; Bradley, *This Astounding Close*, 153.

30 OR 47/3:800.

31 Daniel C. Crews and Lisa D. Bailey, *Records of the Moravians in North Carolina*, 13 vols. (Raleigh, NC, 1865), 7:603-604; McKean, *Blood and War*, 1:1,067.

long affected his leadership and his relationships with officers and men. The breakdown in discipline made men "disorderly, every one helping themselves." Only tearful pleas by junior officers kept the men together. "[F]or a while Tears choked my utterance & I was compelled to desist—The men some of them wept with me & all promised implicit obedience," wrote Capt. Lewis Webb. Baker's generalship and Webb's emotional state would both wane in the coming days.[32]

Confederate deserters drifting into Union lines broadcast demoralization as well. "The Rebs are coming in by droves and give themselfes up…[their] army is discouraged and will not fight any more," noted one Union soldier. Desertion into Federal lines often seemed preferable to some Southerners than starvation, death, or a return to their ranks. Federals described the Confederates coming into their lines as "in a sad plight. Weary and way worn, unpaid, and almost without exception, entirely dependent on the people for subsistence. Very few … regretted the failure of the Confederacy, for the very good reason that as a class, they could have gained nothing from its success." One Yankee said that the common Confederate soldier had been "taught" that every reverse of their army was a "blessing in disguise," and they were in "the mood to accept this … greatest reverse … as the greatest blessing." Johnston's officers were divided over the war. Some opposed their men's opinion; others "admitted . . . they had been thoroughly beaten, and . . . their cause . . . irretrievably lost, [but] still urged that if they [had succeeded], the south would have been better off." Some thoughtful officers confided that "they would have succeeded better, contending for the same thing, under the old flag."[33]

Unlike those cities and towns under Confederate control, those occupied by Union forces remained calm and orderly. In Raleigh, John Woods noticed the reserve of his fellow soldiers, believing the prospect of peace helped ease the anger many felt toward civilians. "[T]he respect showed by all officers & men to the union feeling of this place," he wrote home, "is most manifest when contrasted with the recent habit of this very army who have been lighting their way by burning houses . . . cribs sheds & cotton gins." Realizing friends back home might not understand, he quickly explained:

---

32 Lewis H. Webb, Diary, Lewis Henry Webb Papers, SHC/UNC.

33 OR 47/3:209-10; Metz Diary, April 14, 1865, DU; Wills, *Army Life of an Illinois Soldier*, 369-370; Robert Cruikshank Letters (1862-1865), www.ehistory.osu.edu/osu/sources/ letters/cruikshank/index.cfm, accessed August 29, 2009; James A. Mowris, *History of the One Hundred and Seventeenth Regiment, N.Y. Volunteers* (Hartford, CT, 1866), 214-215.

This may seem barbarous to you but I assure you it makes the Rebels feel that there is war in the land that they have sowed the wind & are reaping the whirlwind. It times the ardor of a man who is fighting to enable some other men simply to keep a 'nigger' when he sees the rafters of his own house burned black & charred through a sheet of flame.

Sherman's army helped vanquish slavery, saved the Union, and made the South pay for its treason. Now, the prospect of peace overjoyed Sherman's men, but with it came with a realization that the bonds they forged with one another, intimate relationships grounded on the deepest levels, would soon be broken. The realization of this loss grew as the end neared, prompting them to commemorate and preserve this special brotherhood before returning to civilian life. Major Generals John Logan and Frank P. Blair gathered their corps officers at the capitol building in Raleigh and proposed creating an entity to memorialize their service together. Thus was formed the Society of the Army of the Tennessee, a formal organization of officers who had "served with honor" to preserve "that kindly and cordial feeling" that had characterized their army. Logan continued to be active in the expanding organization's future, and was also instrumental in creating the Union army's largest veterans' organization, the Grand Army of the Republic. He served as its first commander and promoted a national day of mourning that eventually became Memorial Day. Groups like these played an important role in supporting the old soldiers, and also gave them a place to talk about their war in the Carolinas, especially their emotional reactions to the news that was heading their way.[34]

On the night of Good Friday, April 14, an assassin shot President Lincoln in Washington's Ford Theater at 10:15 p.m. Lincoln died early the next morning, shaking the nation and its armies. The assassination profoundly affected events in North Carolina and in the hearts of Federal soldiers. As the news of the tragedy made its way to Raleigh, other news arrived to balance the blow.

A Confederate officer and private rode through a cold, relentless rain to deliver Johnston's request for an armistice. Around midnight Union pickets halted the pair and then escorted them to Kilpatrick's headquarters in Morrisville. Johnston's armistice offer shocked Kilpatrick, and he instantly sent it on to Sherman in Raleigh. The message literally heralded peace for a broken country but making good on the offer would be difficult to achieve.

34 *Report on the Proceedings of the Society of the Army of Tennessee*, 45 vols. (Cincinnati, OH, 1865-1922), 1:6; James P. Jones, *John A. Logan: Stalwart Republican from Illinois* (Carbondale, IL, 1982), 19.

April 15

The offer of armistice made its way through the rainy night to Sherman's headquarters. The general was elated to read Johnston's request and at once sent a reply accepting his offer and agreeing to meet with Johnston and halt the advance of his army. He also intimated that Johnston could expect to receive the same generous terms that Lee had received from Grant at Appomattox Court House. Sherman ended his note by echoing Johnston's thoughts: "I really desire to save the people of North Carolina the damage they would sustain by the march of this army through the central or western parts of the State."[35]

The prospect of returning home elicited great, but not unsullied, joy. Some soldiers predicted the difficulty of returning to civilian life. Those struggling with moral burdens worried about how to describe the war they fought to families and friends. Men who waged hard war feared their wives, children, and neighbors could not understand the truth about war and how it changed men. On this, his fourth anniversary in the army, veteran Charles Wills pondered his military experience and wondered what his return to civilian life would be like. He felt as if army service had stalled his life and dreaded his discharge, believing the transition back "would sorely [be] against the grain for a while." It would take time, he thought, to readjust to home. "Citizens are not like soldiers and I like the soldier ways just the best." Unfortunately, transformation would have to wait. The war was not yet over. Sherman's men were still campaigning, and more hard war awaited them.[36]

The XIV Corps continued its march from Raleigh toward the Cape Fear River and the crossing at Avent's Ferry. Foraging by the army was reinstated, causing some to lament the return to stripping civilian farms. Commissary officer Dexter Horton felt "sad to see the system of Bummy commenced again" and bemoaned the devastating effects it had on civilians. The return to foraging also put Union soldiers back in harm's way. Those who fell into the hands of the traumatized Rebel cavalry could expect no mercy.[37]

A detachment of the 88th Indiana escorting pontoon wagons discovered the aftermath of one Confederate attack. Chaplain John J. Hight described seeing dead horses still harnessed to wagons packed full of supplies. Scattered around the

---

35 *OR* 47/3:207.

36 Wills, *Army Life of an Illinois Soldier*, 70.

37 Clement Eaton, "Diary of an Officer in Sherman's Army Marching Through the Carolinas," *Journal of Southern History*, 9:252.

carnage were corpses of eight executed Union soldiers. Hight knew the trauma the violent ambushes could inflict. A month earlier, he had tended to John Medsker, a soldier in his regiment, who had survived an attack outside Goldsboro with only a shot in the side. Greatly painful, the wound limited his mobility. Years after the war, the old wound still caused Medsker to spit up blood, eventually causing a mental injury. The old soldier convinced himself that his wound was bleeding perpetually. The unhealed injury he envisioned eventually became too much for him to handle. Medsker sought help in the Indiana Hospital of the Insane in 1901. There he complained of being restless and unable to sleep, and he attempted suicide.[38]

Minister Hight had witnessed what war did to men. But the true scourge on the army was alcohol, which he condemned as causing many problems. "Whiskey is a great curse in the army, as it is everywhere else." Hight noted the varied attitudes officers expressed toward it, believing only "vulgh [vulgar] soldiers abuse it, but 'refined' staff need it for its electrifying effects." Ubiquitous alcohol use prevailed in the ranks of both sides as suffering soldiers sought benumbing relief from the war. As the sun set, Confederates in Govan's Brigade spent the evening swilling brandy from a 40-gallon barrel discovered while setting up camp. "We can say with confidence," a soldier recounted, "that few barrels of brandy have ever made more a jolly crowd than ours was on that occasion." Of himself, Robert Collins admitted that the "effect of the fluid extract of apples on the mental and physical outfit of the writer was such that he cannot keep in the middle of the road in an effort at describing what the boys said and done during the remainder of the day and night." Even the regimental chaplain "got drunk as an 'English lord.'" Captain Samuel T. Foster remembered, "Every one helped themselves, and of course some get funny, some get tight some get gentlemanly drunk and some get dog drunk, of this latter class all the officers from our Maj[or] up. Kept up a noise nearly all night, but no one gets mad—all in good humor." One junior officer joked, "General S. succeeds in having a barrell of peach brandy…Yum! yum! ha! ha! We are taking it along for medical purposes."[39]

Alcohol might have soothed the troubled minds of soldiers but it likewise revealed problems that would lead to long-term addiction in those traumatized by

38 John J. Hight, *History of the Fifty-eighth Indiana Volunteer Infantry* (Princeton, 1895), 518; Dean, *Shook Over Hell*, 112.

39 Collins, *Unwritten History*, 294-298; Foster and Brown, eds., *One of Cleburne's Command*, 165; Ridley, *Battles and Sketches*, 458.

war. Some veterans could put up the bottle while others, like Capt. William J. Dixon, could not escape it. Dixon had enlisted as an enthusiastic private in the 1st Georgia in 1861 and became an officer with the 63rd Georgia when it was organized in 1862. But the war wore down his mental state. He fought in the 1863 defense of Fort Wagner in South Carolina, under Johnston in north Georgia, and under Hood at the crushing defeats at Franklin and Nashville. His zeal had long since given way to melancholy, and with surrender he became "deeply chagrined and depressed." To deal with the ills of war, Dixon began drinking, and he developed a lifelong dependency on alcohol. He was admitted to an asylum just four years after the war ended but he never overcame its painful legacy.[40]

Perhaps the most powerful effect of alcohol was its power to impair judgment. Drunkenness complicated the ability of Johnston's confused men and helped spread chaos that accelerated the Confederacy's disintegration. Drunken men mingled with desperate citizens forming mobs that filled the streets. The situation grew volatile with arrival of starving parolees from Lee's army. The city's warehouses were packed with food, cloth, and other material meant for Johnston's army made lucrative targets. Some sympathetic guard who believed the war was over began handing out the goods they guard which further excited the growing crowds. The city's military commander, Brig. Gen. Alfred Iverson, claimed only 500 men were available to guard the city and wanted the first organized unit to reach it to arrest any soldier without a command to maintain order. The "indiscriminate issue of clothing &c. [was] having a bad effect" on the city's soldiers, and without a reliable guard Iverson could not stop the process. "Men are now waiting here for the opportunity to plunder," he warned.[41]

Quartermasters recognized the danger that stockpiles of alcohol presented. To assure public safety, orders were issued to destroy the copious stores of liquor that remained in the city. Artilleryman Robert Herriot remembered the destruction of an entire trainload of liquor belonging to the medical department; barrel heads were smashed and the whiskey was poured into the streets, where it made a pool a foot deep. Herriott recounted how soldiers were scooping up so much of it that the officer in charge ordered the conductor to keep running the train back and forth over the pond to keep it out of the soldiers' reach. Nonetheless he managed to get a

---

40 Diane Miller Sommerville, "'Will They Ever Be Able to Forget?': Confederate Soldiers and Mental Illness in the Defeated South," in Stephen Berry, ed., *Weirding the War: Stories from the Civil War's Ragged Edges* (Athens, GA, 2011), 327.

41 OR 47/3:799-800; Alfred Iverson to George W. Brent, April 16, 1865, George W. Brent Papers, DU.

kettle full, and the young teenager took his first drink, joining a host of others. Vast amounts of alcohol remained in the city, and soldiers easily found it. Brigadier General George Gibbs Dibrell's command arrived and took advantage of the flowing liquor.[42]

Dibrell's troopers had been sent to protect the fleeing Jefferson Davis and his cabinet, but stocked warehouses of food and goods immediately distracted the drunken troopers. Colonel William C. Breckinridge's Kentuckians led an attack on the city's Confederate commissary, charging down the streets with pistols blazing. As the warehouse guards scrambled for cover, the troopers along with the accompanying mob surged inside. Parolees from Virginia arrived amid the chaos and joined the riots. James W. Albright found Greensboro in a "perfect uproar—Yankees expected every minute, Goods of the army are going in every direction—went in for my share and got a good deal." Stephen Mallory, the Confederate secretary of the navy, witnessed the looting: "Hundreds of armed men, swarming like locusts into well filled warehouses, struggling, cursing, yelling, every one for himself, in utter disregard of all authority … many a bronzed, weather beaten veteran was seen to emerge from such a crowd, strangely burdened with more plunder than he could take care of." More troops were quickly dispatched to quell the riot.

Robert A. Jenkins rushed through streets with a detachment from the 12th North Carolina toward the besieged warehouses, remembering that "[a]s we rushed up and ordered the mob to disperse, some of them wheeled[,] drew their pistols and fired upon us, but without hurting anybody. We immediately returned the fire with a better effect than they had. We killed two men and one horse and wounded one man. They took flight running at the quickest speed in every direction."[43]

The upheaval rattled Maj. Gen. P. G. T. Beauregard, and he worried about the safety of President Davis and his cabinet. As disorder threatened to destroy the city, Beauregard pulled any unit he could find into the city and authorized them to use artillery with double canister to keep the peace. Sentries were posted and

42 Robert Herriot, "At Greensboro, N.C., In April, 1865," *CV*, 30:102.

43 Ridley, *Battles and Sketches*, 455, 458; Robert Alexander Jenkins, "From Harper's Ferry to the Surrender," in Gertrude Jenkins Papers, DU; James W. Albright, *Greensboro 1808-1904* (Greensboro, NC, 1904), 298; James S. Harris, *Historical Sketches of the 7th North Carolina Troops, 1861-1865* (Mooresville, NC, 1893), 61; *The* [Raleigh] *Morning Post*, August 17, 1905; Dunkerly, *Surrender at Greensboro*, 66.

bonfires set on street corners. But the drunken mob did not disband and, led by Wheeler's men, attacked another warehouse late in the afternoon.[44]

A detachment of veterans from the 7th North Carolina under Capt. Thomas P. Mulloy met the horsemen's assault. Far from home guards, these troops were veterans of the Army of North Virginia. After a short and furious skirmish, the horsemen fled, leaving one dead and three wounded. Trooper James Brown of the 8th Tennessee Cavalry was one of those who fell with a mortal wound. Fellow soldiers considered Brown "an extra good soldier," and his "cold blooded murder" infuriated them.[45]

Confederate Admiral Raphael Semmes darted around the city's riotous streets and recorded the scenes of anarchy: "all the public stores ha[d] been plundered," and the "vultures [were] scouting their prey for ten miles around." Semmes bemoaned the state of the Confederacy and the disintegration of his unit, which had lost 250 men in the last 10 days. "Commissioned officers slunk away from me one by one, and became deserters! I was ashamed of my countrymen. Johnston, by reason of his great personal popularity, was enabled to gather around him the fragments of several armies. . . . But the moment the news of Lee's surrender reached him, there was a stampede from his army."[46]

Chaos spread to other towns along the railroad. A mob raided and cleaned out Company Shop's warehouses. Further down the tracks in Graham, soldiers and citizens attacked Confederate storehouses. News of the looting reached Governor Vance, who fired off a dispatch to Johnston and accused his men of the robbery. The exasperated governor abhorred the lawlessness prevailing in his state: "stores of leather blankets &c. at Graham were pillaged and I confess I am getting tired of it." Johnston dispatched Brig. Gen. Richard C. Gatlin to investigate Vance's claims. Gatlin arrived at the depot and found storehouses sacked, as well as officers who feared parolees from Lee's army would storm them again. To try to save the remaining supplies, Gatlin agreed to transport them back to Greensboro, but he found the city much more dangerous upon his return. "[A] mob of citizens and soldiers crowd[ing] the streets laden with shoes[,] cloth & clothing," greeted

---

44 Dunkerly, *Surrender at Greensboro*, 68.

45 Lindsley, *Military Annals of Tennessee*, 676.

46 Raphael Semmes, *Memoirs of Service Afloat, During the War Between the States* (Baltimore, 1869), 819-820; Dunkerly, *Surrender at Greensboro*, 43.

Gatlin's arrival. Civilians, parolees, and soldiers fought for any items that could be eaten, traded, sold, or worn.[47]

With no official word from Johnston about the Army of Northern Virginia many soldiers were still unaware of its destruction but whispers of disaster grew louder. Rumor after nerve-wracking rumor swirled around campfires, deepening the men's dismay. "Very bad rumors afloat about Lee's Army. Hope none of it is correct," wrote Thomas Sullivan. He also noted the dire military situation they faced and acknowledged their last remaining hope for victory. "It is also rumored that the enemy are advancing on us from 4 different points. We will put our faith and trust in God for our success in the future." But when Lee's paroled men stumbled into the camps it provided proof of Lee's surrender and extinguished what hope remained. Shocked soldiers struggled to understand what the surrender meant. Major General Johnson Hagood confessed, "Tonite, Colonel Olmstead, of the First Georgia regiment tells me positively that General Lee has surrendered. Great God! can it be true? I have never for a moment doubted the ultimate success of our cause. I cannot believe it." The news sent shock waves through Johnston's army and signaled that their moment of reckoning was at hand.[48]

That night, Rebel soldiers heard another, more devastating rumor. The confirmation of Johnston's meeting with Sherman to discuss surrender elicited a powerful reaction. Their minds reeled with thoughts of what the news meant and what they should do. Men wrestled with their urge for self-preservation and their loyalty to the Southern cause. Wheeler's cavalrymen huddled around campfires that night trying to understand how they felt and what surrender meant. Several members of the 51st Alabama Cavalry held a council and unanimously decided, "No surrender, disband and in small squads strike for home, and later we probably can reassemble west of the Mississippi river, with Gen. E. Kirby Smith." These men felt the need to fight on. Duty still held some of them to the cause; for others surrender meant possible imprisonment or execution for the war they had waged. Some nurtured a desire to continue killing. In their clouded minds, escape and continuing the war were their only options.[49]

47 Wilson Angley, Jerry L. Cross, and Michael Hill, *Sherman's March Through North Carolina* (Raleigh, NC, 1995), 81-82.

48 Thomas L. Sullivan Account Book, April 15, 1865, Tennessee State Library and Archives (TSLA); Hagood, *Memoirs of the War of Secession*, 368.

49 Edward Kennedy, "The Last Work of Wheeler's Special Confederate Scouts," in *CV* (1924), 32:60.

April 16

The rising sun witnessed the Alabama cavalrymen make good on their decision to leave the army. Mounting their horses, they bade their Texas comrades good-bye and rode past groggy infantrymen, who looked up from cooking their meager rations with disbelief. The sight of the cavalrymen leaving ignited a fear among the soldiers. Men worried the army was surrounded or worse, and that surrender was imminent. If they left now, some surmised they could avoid the risk of the unknown. If they were lucky, they could grab a horse or mule and make it home in enough time to plant a spring crop. "Every one supposes this army is to be surrendered shortly and of course there is great excitement about it," wrote Capt. Samuel T. Foster. He confirmed the demoralization but still expressed hope; "The whole army (or at least as far as I know) are badly demoralized and there are various suggestions which, if Johnston could act upon would of course save the army."[50]

Those of Wheeler's command that remained fortified their defensive positions outside Chapel Hill. Anxiety of civilians as they watched soldiers prepare to defend the town. With the war's end at hand, further death and destruction seemed ludicrous to many. Terrified residents assembled a delegation to appeal to Wheeler to leave the town in order to save the university. The general listened silently as the citizens expressed their fears pleaded for peace. Eventually he agreed and wrote a brief order withdrawing his forces and leaving the town to the Federals.[51]

With one threat averted townspeople prepared for the next. People dashed about, frantically seeking places to hide their silver, gold, and other valuables. Boxes and bags of family heirlooms were packed into hollow logs or buried in holes. Wells, stumps, rock walls, and even the university's telescope became hiding places. With preparations completed, Chapel Hillian then spent several anxious hours waiting for the arrival of the enemy, unsure of what occupation would bring. Expecting the Yankees as they looked down the streets, the residents saw only the walking skeletons from Lee's army coming into town. They were on the verge of starvation, surviving only on parched corn for the past five days. One officer reported that his men were so weak with hunger that in the last charge, they could scarcely stay in their saddles. The citizens rushed to their aid. "They look wasted,"

---

50 Ed Kennedy letter, July 1927, 51st Alabama Cavalry file, ADAH; Foster and Brown, eds., *One of Cleburne's Command*, 164.

51 Charles P. Mallett, Diary, April 16, 1865, C. B. Mallett collection, SHC/UNC.

remarked Cornelia Spencer. Paroled Rebels arriving in the afternoon brought the electric news that they had seen Federal cavalry approaching the town.[52]

Around dusk, 40-50 Union troopers dashed into Chapel Hill and inquired for Wheeler's men. "Some separated from the others and behaved badly, took away some watches &c.," wrote one resident. After scouting the town, the soldiers informed residents that their entire force would return tomorrow. Citizens thus endured a long, sleepless night of worry. The appearance of the enemy represented the reality of defeat that shocked Spencer. "[O]ur hearts died within us," Cornelia Spencer told her diary.[53]

The Union cavalry that occupied Chapel Hill was the left flank of Sherman's advance. The right flank was anchored in Durham Station, some 19 miles to the northeast. But Yankee patrols scouted the countryside where they skirmished with retreating Rebels across some of North Carolina's largest plantations. Dr. James and Polly Cain's farm, "Hardscrabble," enslaved 41 people. One of these, Sarah, had been taken from her mother at an early age to be a servant for Polly. As the sounds of battle grew closer, Sarah remembered her sobbing mistress's distraught reaction: "Listen Sarah, hear those cannons? They're killing our men!" The young girl relayed Cain's emotional state to the family's enslaved cook, Aunt Charity, who believed all the emotion stemmed from fear that the slaves were going to be set free. Retreating Confederate cavalry arrived on the farm soon afterward and took out their anger on the enslaved. Stealing what they could from the farm's storehouses, they asked the slaves if they wanted to be freed. If they said yes, then the troopers shot them, but if they say no, the terrified men would be left alone. Sarah remembered. "Dey took three of my uncles out in de wood's an' shot dey faces off."[54]

Union horsemen soon followed, but they were almost as terrifying as the Confederates, ransacking the house, kitchen, pantries, and smokehouse looking for loot. One soldier scared Sarah by shouting questions at her about where the family's valuables were hidden. The terrified girl told the soldier she did not know because they had been spirited away while she slept. The soldier pushed Sarah off the step, pulled out his pistols, and threatened to shoot her toes off if she did not dance for him. When the horsemen left, they took all the meat, flour, pigs, and chickens, leaving little for either white or black families to eat. But in their place the

---

52 Spencer Diary, ibid.

53 Mallett & Spencer diaries, ibid.

54 Sarah Debro, WPA, 11/2:249-251.

Federal soldiers left freedom. They told Sarah she was free and did not have to "slave for the white folks no more." An emotional confrontation in the coming days would put this new freedom to the test.

Sarah's mother had wept after her daughter was taken to work in the big house, and now she wanted her child back. Sarah found herself in the middle of a dramatic struggle, clinging to Polly Cain on the steps of the house while her mother tore her skirt off trying to pull her away. The white mistress pleaded for young Sarah to stay with her, but Sarah's mother refused. "You took her away from me an' didn' pay no mind to my cryin', so now I'se takin' her back home. We's free now, Mis' Polly, we ain't gwine be slave no more to nobody." As mother and daughter walked off, Sarah looked back and saw Mrs. Cain looking red-faced with rage.[55]

On the nearby "Fish Dam" plantation, the enslaved people celebrated the news of freedom as proof of God's power. It elicited tremendous exultation. "When the colored people found that General Lee had surrendered," Morgan Latta remembered, "they woke up at midnight praying out that their prayers might be answered." They prayed several days and nights for their deliverance and reunion with lost family members. The jubilation stayed with Latta for the rest of his life, and he never forgot the emotional responses of those around him:

> God has answered our prayers at His own appointed time; He has burst the bonds of slavery and set us all free. Some of the slaves would shout at the top of their voices, and some of them fasted three or four days, they were so glad that they were free from slavery. They went several days without eating or drinking, praising God for their freedom.[56]

Emancipation sparked a sublime emotion in all black communities. As rumors of another potential surrender reached their ears, they apprehensively looked to the future, guardedly optimistic that their long nightmare was finally about to end.

Union soldiers hoped it would end their suffering as well. The news of the meeting inspired hope throughout the army and lifted the spirits of the faithful for their Easter Sunday masses. Soldiers constructed a stage in an "old camp meeting style" with logs rolled together and boards laid across them as seats and a central platform for the ministers. Chaplains of the different regiments and faiths organized the meetings and the revival's message, one that would touch the hearts and free the souls of Sherman's hardened men. Each night during their occupation

---

55 Ibid.

56 M. L. Latta, *The History of My Life and Work* (Raleigh, NC, 1903), 114-115.

of Raleigh, soldiers seeking salvation met for religious services. More men came forward each night and joined their comrades to confess together their belief in the Scriptures. Religion attracted men who felt they needed forgiveness for their troubled souls. Most importantly, men sought to rediscover their humanity as the promise of a homecoming beckoned on the horizon. Religion's power helped Sherman's hardened veterans make peace with their war. Matthew Jamison attended a Baptist service and noted that "the sound of Sabbath bells and religious ceremonies came gratefully to our long-estranged senses." Victory and peace salved the wounds of war. Another soldier noted that with "the prospect of restoration all feelings of animosity are dispelled from the true soldier's breast and a warm feeling of fraternal brotherhood springs up." The coming days would severely test this spirit of forgiveness. Within hours shocking news would violently interrupt the transformational process men were experiencing, threatening to unleash the darkest emotions in Sherman's battle-hardened veterans.[57]

---

57 Samuel Merrill, *The Seventieth Indiana Volunteer Infantry in the War of the Rebellion* (Indianapolis, IN, 2008), 267-268; Matthew H. Jamison, *Recollections of Pioneer and Army Life* (Kansas City, 1911), 326-327; Greer, *Diary of Allen Morgan Greer*, 214; OR 47/3:234.

CHAPTER 6

April 17–18:
"O! how the great heart of the army
throbbed and swelled"

April 17

The most dramatic day of the campaign dawned gray and dreary. A group of nervous men huddled along a muddy road outside Chapel Hill and talked in hushed tones. At their center stood the stalwart former governor David L. Swain, who had assembled the group to meet the approaching Federal cavalry. Swain was heartened that, so far, the Yankees had spared Raleigh. He hoped they would also spare the university, but Swain had reasons to worry.

Just before 8:00 a.m., Union Brig. Gen. Smith D. Atkins, escorted by scouts, approached Swain and the committee. After introductions, Swain asked Atkins about his intentions. The general repeated his orders to respect the university and private property, except for forage and other supplies necessary for the army. The Southerners were relieved, but as they talked, several commissioners noticed soldiers breaking away from the column and dashing toward town. Swain quickly directed Atkins's attention to the men and urged him to establish guards quickly. The general ordered Col. George S. Acker to take his 9th Michigan Cavalry and ride ahead to protect the university and those houses that desired guards. It was a shaky start to a long occupation.[1]

---

1 Mallett, Diary, SHC/UNC.

The soldiers found a citizenry physically and emotionally worn down by war. The university remained open but the total student body in the class of 1865 was only two students. The students who made the town lively had been swept off to war and were replaced by frantic refugees seeking shelter. Each day news of a dead alumni or professor follow those of brothers, sons, and fathers. Mary Smith Hunter Mallett was the worst case of traumatic grief. While refugeeing in Chapel Hill with her five daughters, Mary's husband, Lt. Col. Edward B. Mallet was killed at the head of the 61st North Carolina at Bentonville. His last words ere, "My wife! My poor wife!" Mary had fallen into a catatonic depression after her husband's death and his corpse sent her into a fatal tailspin. Neighbors could see health rapidly declining and her weakening attempts to care for her children. Her hair turned gray and she became bedridden, dying nine months later at age 39. Anxiety and chronic depression physically changed women. Catherine Battle remarked on the state of her neighbors in a letter to her sister: "You . . . can sympathize with me in this doubt & uncertainty. I have fallen off 15 or 20 lbs & have but little sense left me. Mitz poor child grows paler & sadder as day after day passes." Catherine also noticed her neighbors' debilities. "Love Battle looks very badly—so does Laura Phillips in fact it seems to me ever body looks ten years older than they did three weeks ago." The passing of the Confederate army and Wheeler's trooper had stressed the community to its limits. Occupation by the enemy intensified their worry and apprehension.[2]

The university's library became an army stable and cows were evicted from barns to make room for soldiers' mounts. Union guards took over parlors and bedrooms throughout the town. Soldiers explored the school's library and observatory and went bowling in the dormitory halls. Despite his reputation as a notorious alcoholic, Acker kept infractions to a minimum in Chapel Hill, but Union foragers bedeviled the surrounding community. Every buggy and wagon, loaded with loot and forage soldiers brought into town were recognized as belonging to neighbors or friends being led away brought more anguish. Watching their neighbors' farms ravaged by foraging soldiers induced guilty feelings in the townspeople over the coming days. Catherine Battle felt sad for her friends and neighbors. "[A]ll around the village for miles around the country is laid waste & everything taken every horse, & a few old broken down ones were left in their

2 Spencer, *The Last Ninety Days*, 171; Catherine Lewis Battle to Emma Speight, May 5, 1865, John Francis Speight Papers, SHC/UNC; Bradley, *Battle of Bentonville*, 365-366; *The* [Raleigh] *Daily Conservative*, March 29, 1865.

places. What are people to do for support this year or next no one can see." Mary Smith's "Oakland," five miles outside of town, became a target for pillaging. One local reported bummers entering Smith's home "in advance of the guard, and in less than ten minutes the lower rooms, store-rooms, and bed-rooms were over-hauled and plundered with a swift and business-like thoroughness only attainable by long extensive practice."[3]

Reports of the severity of his soldiers' depredations moved Atkins to try and curtail the foraging. He ordered officers to supervise the collection of supplies and leave enough for families. To alleviate this stress on civilian food stocks, he ordered a detachment to the Morrisville depot to pick up supplies arriving by rail. But the confiscation of food and livestock continued. The loss of their horses and mules greatly concerned civilians who were starting to plant their crops. Without their draft animals there would be no fall harvest, and a winter without food. Thus fearing for their survival, they took matters into their own hands to protect themselves when squad of bummers terrorized the countryside in and around the town of Pittsboro.[4]

The bummers raided several homes and rode through the town "firing upon the citizens and returned soldiers." The townspeople returned the fire and followed the bummers, overtaking them near the Haw River. Two were killed and two others wounded, one mortally, in the shootout. Shocked residents of Chapel Hill feared retaliation but Atkins reacted with restraint, merely dispatching a detail to bring back the wounded and bury the dead.[5]

Other raiders faced similar dangers in the hostile countryside. Thirty miles to the south, along the banks of the Cape Fear River, XIV Corps officers sought to control their men during the surrender negotiations, urging them to "treat the people with all possible kindness." The local populace did not reciprocate, however. Franklin Yike of the 87th Indiana recorded that Sgt. Clayborn A. Eddy of the 105th Ohio had been "Shot by a bush whacker to day." This prompted a squad of 30 angry soldiers to head out in pursuit of the attacker. Two days later the detachment returned to camp with the suspect, whose fate is unknown.[6]

3 Catherine Lewis Battle to Emma Speight, May 5, 1865, SHC/UNC; Jones, *When Sherman Came*, 317.

4 William H. Brown, Diary, April 19, 1865, ALPLM.

5 *Semi-Monthly* [Pittsboro, NC] *Record*, June 15, 1866; Mallett, Diary, May 1, 1865, SHC/UNC.

6 Widney, *Campaigning with Sherman*, 355; Franklin Yike, Diary, April 16, 18, 1865, ISA; Morse and Morse, eds., *Civil War Diaries of Bliss Morse*, 199.

The anger the soldiers felt would soon be replaced by joy. The news of Sherman's meeting with the Confederates raised their spirits, and the possibility of peace ignited a nervous optimism throughout the army. They felt as if all their labors and sacrifices had all been for this moment. Victory meant a return to family and friends. Cornelius Platter reflected his hope in his diary, reporting that "everything [is] working favorable and he is confident of success. What a glorious Thing it will be if Johnston does surrender!" By day's end, Platter's emotions would make another wild change, from joy to extreme sorrow.[7]

At 8:00 a.m., Sherman and his staff prepared to leave Raleigh to meet Johnston somewhere between Durham and Hillsborough. As the general stepped aboard his train, a frantic telegraph operator rushed to his car and informed him of a coded message arriving over the line from Morehead City. He suggested the general should wait until it was deciphered; Sherman agreed and waited half an hour. The operator returned with a pale expression and handed the message to Sherman, whose face wilted after reading the paper. The general then swore the operator to secrecy and ordered him not to reveal the contents of the message. At depots along the way Sherman stopped and directed his commanders to meet him upon his return. At Durham's Station, Sherman disembarked and met with Judson Kilpatrick. Together they led an escort of 200 cavalrymen west toward the Confederate lines and his first meeting with his old adversary.

Seventeen miles to the west, Johnston also prepped for the meeting. Confederate soldiers who sensed the unfathomable moment of surrender at hand felt greatly pained; this was especially true among the 60 men chosen as Johnston's escort. The task of accompanying the general was the "most unpleasant day I have spent in all my life," recalled one trooper. The sight of Johnston riding out under a white flag confirmed the reality of surrender. One South Carolina lieutenant accepted the inevitable but resented the overt display, writing, "I would not show it so d[am]n plain."[8]

Around 1:00 p.m., Kilpatrick's scouts sighted Confederate horsemen coming down the road under a white flag. After a brief pause, the two generals rode forward and shook hands. This was the first time they had ever met, though both were West Point graduates who had served in the pre-war U.S. Army. They introduced their respective escorts, but Sherman, however, refused to

7 Platter Diary, April 17, 1865, UGA, 175.

8 Mildred K. Holman, "Civil War Diary of Lt. Jesse Roderick Sparkman," BP; Brooks and Rea, eds., *Stories of the Confederacy*, 306; Lindsley, *The Military Annals of Tennessee*, 896.

acknowledge Wade Hampton, whom he considered the embodiment of the haughty Southerner who had plunged the nation into war. The generals then retired to James and Nancy Bennett's modest farmhouse alongside the Hillsborough Road.

Once they were alone, Sherman handed Johnston the secret telegraph he had received in Raleigh. Beads of sweat burst from Johnston's head. The wire announced Lincoln's assassination. The Confederate commander instantly expressed his belief that the president's death was "the greatest possible calamity to the South." Both men understood the powerful ramifications of the assassination and its impact on their meeting. Sherman keenly anticipated the anger the news would elicit in the North and the demands that would be made for revenge on the South. But his immediate fear was his army's fury, which could only be assuaged by a Confederate surrender. He told Johnston he feared some "foolish" Raleigh citizen would anger his soldiers and bring about "a fate worse than Columbia" for the city. Sherman quickly demanded surrender, but Johnston demurred. Despite its deterioration, Johnston noted his army was two days' march ahead of Sherman and not surrounded like Lee had been in Virginia. Johnston, however, knew the Confederacy was finished and that both the people and the army had suffered enough. He also understood that continuing to fight in the wake of Lincoln's death would be disastrous. Instead of surrendering his army, Johnston made an incredible offer, suggesting that he could obtain authorization to surrender the entire Confederacy, end the war, and reunite the torn nation.[9]

Sherman hardly anticipated this but saw an opportunity. A total peace would temper both his army and the nation. Johnston assured him he could convince Jefferson Davis to surrender and suggested meeting the following day to discuss the terms. It was not what Sherman needed to pacify his men tonight but it could be a bigger deal tomorrow. He saw it as fulfillment of Lincoln's hope for the nation but Raleigh becoming another Columbia would poison the negotiation. He agreed and the two men shook hands. Sherman sped back to Raleigh, stopping long enough to share the news with his commanders and ordering them to keep their men in check. Reaching Raleigh, he doubled the provost guard and prepared for the worst.[10]

9 Symonds, *Joseph E. Johnston*, 356. Sherman, *Memoirs*, 349; Johnston, *Narrative of Military Operations*, 402.

10 Sherman, *Memoirs*, 349; Pippitt Diary, April 17, 1865, UTK.

Johnston returned to his downhearted army, which had grown distraught as news of his meeting spread. The idea of surrender unhinged some Confederate soldiers and sent them into a panic. Captain W. E. Stoney witnessed the collapse of Confederate morale and discipline that afternoon. "The wildest excitement seized the troops. . . . Colonel Rion immediately ordered the brigade into line and urged them not to leave." With the rumors flying about being surrounded on three sides, Johnston's men looked desperately to their officers. The idea of defeat panicked them. Stoney remembered their distraught condition:

> All the afternoon the cavalry were passing us saying they "were going out." The infantry soon become almost frantic, and in every direction were rushing to beg, borrow, or steal horses. Disorganization was complete. Horses and mules were everywhere taken without the least regard to ownership. Trains were openly carried off after plundering the wagons. The division supply train was thoroughly stripped. The flags of the brigade were burned by the men in the certainty of surrender. About dark an order came from army headquarters to keep the men together, but with that day the army perished—a mob remained.[11]

Thirty-seven years later musician William J. Worsham remembered the emotional shock upon hearing about the meeting between Sherman and Johnston. "We were anxious for the war to end, yet . . . hardly prepared for surrender. We had not calculated and looked into the depth of a surrender, the giving up as lost that for which we had fought for long and for which so many had given their lives, was indeed hard, and the idea grated like a harsh thunder, on our nerves."[12]

Officers blanketed the army with dispatches, hoping to gain any intelligence about what was taking place. Colonel Baxter Smith, asked Wheeler for any news about a surrender. Rumors were causing his men to desert, and he suspected more desertions during the night. Another of Wheeler's commanders, Brig. Gen. William W. Allen, admitted his command was "rife" with rumors, and desperately appealed for intelligence to share with his men. Allen admitted he wanted each of his troopers to "consult their own judgment whether to accept the terms or not," and urged the younger men in his command who did not want to lay down their arms to "attempt to join the Confederate forces in another quarter." General Hardee suspected a meeting had taken place and asked P. G. T. Beauregard for

---

11 Hagood, *Memoirs*, 369.

12 W. J. Worsham, *The Old Nineteenth Tennessee Regiment, C.S.A.: June 1861–April 1865* (Knoxville, TN, 1902), 176.

confirmation. Hardee felt he needed to know at once so he could quash any rumors before the situation got out of hand. Any acknowledgment of talks would be devastating, he warned. "The report, as you may well conceive, can do our troops no good." Beauregard refused to confirm any of the rumors.[13]

One Georgia officer considered surrender a forgone conclusion and believed it impossible for Johnston to back out of negotiations no matter what terms had been discussed; the army would not fight again, and the soldiers were already preparing to leave. "Thousands under pretence [sic] of not being willing to remain to be surrendered stole mules from wagons & horses from the Artillery and deserted their colors endeavoring to return home." Artillerist Charles Jones noted that a "spirit of dissatisfaction prevailed in the army in anticipation of its early surrender; and numerous desertions occurred, accompanied by constant thefts of transportation and artillery animals." Units were forced to set up camp guards to save what horses and supplies remained. One soldier in the 33rd Mississippi witnessed an emotional plea made by Maj. Gen. William W. Loring, who begged his brigade not to desert. Loring implored the men to "stand by their colors intact" and honor the flag under which they "had been fighting so gallantly during 4 long years." Loring's pleas fell on many deaf ears. Surgeon George W. Peddy struggled with the choice of staying with the army or heading home to his wife. "Honey, I am almost in the notion to be dropped from the roll and take the chances hereafter. What must I do, my dearest? . . . Now, my love, is far the darkest hour in our history that I have ever seen, but hope we will yet achieve our independence."[14]

Broomfield Ridley, a member of Alexander Stewart's staff, realized surrender meant dispersal of the army and with it the end of many friendships. His "heart [filled] with sorrow as I think of giving them up. The hardships, perils and dangers, that we have [faced] together ties the knot of friendship forever." Many officers and enlisted men throughout the army shared Ridley's sentiment.[15]

Feelings in the Union camps mirrored the intensity of those of their enemies. The death of Lincoln tore at the hearts of the soldiers. A few Union soldiers cheered Lincoln's death and were instantly arrested; most of Sherman's army, however, wailed in grief. Cornelius Platter, one of the first to hear the news after

---

13 OR 47/3:807-810.

14 W. W. Gordon, Diary, April 17, 1865, SHC/UNC; Jones, *Historical Sketch of the Chatham Artillery*, 216; Simmons, "The 12th Louisiana in North Carolina," 77-108; Albert Q. Porter Collection, LC; George P. Cuttino, *Saddle Bags and Spinning Wheels: Being the Civil War Letters of George W. Peddy, M.D.* (Macon, GA, 2008), 313.

15 Ridley, *Battles and Sketches*, 458, Webb Papers, SHC/UNC.

Sherman returned from the Bennett farm, told his diary: "I never saw such a gloomy set of men in my life as the soldiers were after the news came. . . . His loss is a great calamity—and the nation mourns his loss as she never mourned before."[16]

Lieutenant John G. Janke recorded one of the most heart-wrenching scenes of men's reactions to the news, which reached his camp at breakfast time:

A newsboy came running into our camp with a lot of Raleigh newspapers shouting: "All about the assassination! President Lincoln assassinated I buy a copy." Horror! The black border tells the truth! We drop knives and forks, and rise grief-stricken, and in solemn silence leave our breakfast. Lieutenant [William H. H.] Dooley is standing behind an oak tree crying, the tears falling from his eyes. Before I get through reading my bosom swells with painful emotion over the sad news. All is lost. My paper is sprinkled all over with tears. Officers and men feel thunderstruck. The camp is in mourning.[17]

Diaries and letters overflowed with the wrenching pain men felt. "No one knows the deep sadness that came over Sherman's army" wrote one Wisconsin soldier; "I saw old men weep and could hardly quiet them." A soldier in the 102nd Illinois expressed the irony of his loss at the moment of victory: "Had the bright omens of peace been suddenly swept away the reaction could not have been as violent as it was under the effect of this one harrowing thought—Lincoln slain in the hour of victory! O! how the great heart of the army throbbed and swelled; first with the wild thirst for vengeance, and then with a profound sorrow, that would heed no words of consolation."[18]

In some camps drummers beat the long roll to gather men for the official announcement. Brevet Brigadier General Harrison C. Hobart rode into the center and revealed the sad news, which had the "stunning effect of a thunderbolt from a clear sky. As it spread from one company to another the noisy chatter of our camp was followed by silence, then by whispers. We felt the ground slipping under our feet." M. D. Gage of the 12th Indiana also described the news in meteorological terms: "the astounding intelligence of the assassination of President Lincoln fell, like a clap of thunder from the clear sky, upon the hearts of our noble army. The

16 Platter Diary, UGA, 175-176.

17 Brown, History of the Fourth Regiment, 404.

18 Downing, Downing's Civil War Diary, 268; Sam Peck, Scrapbook, www.archive.org/details/SamPeakMemoir/page/n1/mode/2up, accessed June 3, 2017; S. F. Fleharty, *Our Regiment: A History of the 102d Illinois Infantry Volunteers* (Chicago, 1865), 166; Abel C. Stelle, *Memoirs of the Civil War* (New Albany, IN, 1904), 37.

shock was indescribable. Mixed emotions of grief, indignation, and horror thrilled every soul." Another soldier in Gage's regiment felt pain in his heart for Lincoln that inflamed his psychological wounds.[19]

Henry J. Aten of the 85th Illinois captured the depth and uniqueness of the men's pain, writing that "[a]t first the men were so stunned and dazed by the wanton and cruel murder that they wandered about the camps aimless and speechless, their sorrow too deep for utterance." A sadness that only soldiers could feel was "nearly, if not quite impossible, for those outside the army to wholly understand." Written 36 years after Lincoln's death, Aten's reflections capture the deep feelings Sherman's men harbored for their martyred president:

> In the darkest hours of the terrible struggle his firmness or purpose and his faith in ultimate success had been unfailing source of inspiration. To the rank and file "Father Abraham" was no unmeaning term. It was not a sentiment, it was a fact. It was the precise term that described the love and veneration they felt for him, whose courage rose in the darkest hours to the majesty of grandest heroism.[20]

The wave of sorrow flowing through the army changed many hearts. But the sadness soon soured and turned into searing anger. A soldier in the XX Corps admitted, "Our joy changed to sorrow; our friendship toward the vanquished to bitter hatred. . . . I must confess I begin to hate the scoundrels for the first time." Lieutenant Russell Tuttle noted the shift from "celebrating like beasts" over the surrender to feeling that "[h]umanity is shocked and the heart bleeds at the announcement." The simultaneous emotional crash of thousands of men created a dangerous, uncontrollable feeling that Tuttle and other soldiers struggled to understand. Tuttle could not "attempt to describe the overpowering grief and gloom that fell at once like a pall over the entire army." He watched as men gathered in groups and shared their feelings. Their collective reaction was "the instant desire for revenge . . . [which] seemed to pervade every heart." Another soldier in the 93rd Illinois summed up the ominous uncertainty. "The silence was painful. In whispers, on every hand, it was asked: 'Are murder and assassination, now, to follow the war? Is the history of the barbarous past to be repeated?'" The anger Sherman's men felt was captured in the words of one soldier who admitted

---

19 Widney, *Campaigning with Uncle Billy*, 355; Moses D. Gage, *From Vicksburg to Raleigh; or, A Complete History of the Twelfth Regiment Indiana Volunteer Infantry* (Chicago, 1865), 306.

20 Aten, *History of the Eighty-fifth*, 304.

the severity of any revenge, "cannot be doubted, had the army been led to battle against the enemy that day, it would have bathed the field in blood, without any compunctions of conscience then, nor stopped the slaughter until the 'last armed foe expired.'"[21]

Calls for unbridled destruction and punishment for the South intensified. Henry Aten noted the change that overcame many men: "a desire for vengeance took possession of them [and] they rejoiced in the thought that negotiations for surrender might fail, that hostilities might be resumed in order that they should have an opportunity to avenge the foul crime committed at Washington." The thought of Lincoln's assassination unlocked the intense rage stoked by years of battlefield trauma. The power of these emotions pushed men over their final moral boundary to the precipice of total war in its fullest meaning. "The army is crazy for vengeance," one noted. "If we make another campaign it will be an awful one." Bradford F. Thompson of the 112th Illinois angrily confessed, "We hope Johnston will not surrender. God pity this country if he retreats or fights us . . . [h]ad Sherman's army encountered Johnston's Confederate army, at that time, the latter would have been swept from the face of the earth like chaff before a cyclone." Another Federal soldier succinctly captured the mood of the army in one ominous phrase: "The whole army is ready to commit any act against the rebels."[22]

Major General O. O. Howard closely watched civilians' reactions to the news, hoping to discern their loyalties. "Even the people here believe that they have passed into severer hands, and have a sort of appreciation of the fact that they have lost a friend and not an enemy." Ohio trooper J. M. Culver noted the civilians' terror. "If there were any cheers by the rebels they did not reach our ears. However, they did not for they feared that we would feel so angry that we would burn, pillage and kill in revenge for such a dastardly deed and they came to our officers imploring protection from imaginary evils."[23]

21 Merrill, *The Seventieth Indiana Volunteer Infantry*, 268; Tuttle and Tappan, eds., *The Civil War Journal*, 210; Aaron Dunbar and Harvey Trimble, *History of the Ninety-Third Regiment, Illinois Volunteer Infantry, From Organization to Muster Out* (Chicago, 1898), 190-191.

22 Aten, *History of the Eighty-fifth*, 305; Wills, *Army Life of an Illinois Solider*, 372; Bradford F. Thompson, *History of the 112th Regiment of Illinois Volunteer Infantry, In the Great War of the Rebellion, 1862-1865* (Toulon, IL, 1885); Lawson Diary, April 19, 1865, AHSL.

23 Oliver Otis Howard, *Autobiography of Oliver Otis Howard, Major-general, United States Army* (New York, 1908), 159; Elliott B. McKeever, "Sketch of the 9th Ohio Cavalry," 28, Civil War Miscellaneous Collection, USMHI.

A fearful Kemp Battle readily offered a room to Capt. Benny Keeler and his wife as insurance against harm, nervously asking Keeler if the guard outside would protect them in case of a disturbance. "The guards are as angry as the rest of the troops," Keeler admitted. The captain returned to the Battle home later that afternoon with a dire warning: "There is danger of an outbreak tonight. The soldiers are greatly aroused. You must have every vessel on the lot filled with water. You and your wife must not take off your clothes. General Sherman has promised to protect you if possible and General Terry will aid of course. We will do our best." Others in town also followed this advice. Bessie Cain and other female students at St. Mary's School slept fully clothed with their most precious valuables stuffed in their pockets should a quick exit become necessary. Cain recorded the fear gripping her and other students: "We knew that on the least provocation the Yankees would do anything they wanted to us . . . we were frightened to death."[24]

By sunset the call to make Raleigh into another Columbia among inconsolable Union soldiers grew in volume. Guards of the 104th Ohio stood on corners, by stores, and in front of homes preparing for a difficult night. Nelson Pinney heard the growing cries "from every regiment along the line . . . a cry for vengeance, 'Burn the city, burn, burn, and spare nothing[!]' went up, and was carried along the line with lightning speed." The Ohioans spent a difficult night chasing soldiers through the capital's streets. They filled Raleigh's jail with men who had been arrested while trying to set fire to buildings. Chaplin George Bradley noted the arsonists as well as the powerful desire of many more men to destroy the city. "There was a most intense feeling." Writing years later, veteran Sam Peak still could not articulate the powerful emotions men felt; "[I]t is not in my power to express in words," but he did note the violent reactions the news elicited in soldiers. Rebel prisoners who expressed joy in the announcement "were killed instantly" because it "brought blood into the eyes of Sherman's army who were hoping to get a chance to wreak their vengeance out on Johns[t]on's army that had murdered so many of our boys in cold blood."[25]

Soldiers looked contemptuously at Raleigh considering it target for revenge. With each passing hour their anger rose until it boiled over. A mob of 2,000 of them grabbed torches and headed toward the city. Reports of the men reached Maj.

24 Battle, Memories, 194-195; Bessie Cain, Diary, Bailey Papers, SMS.

25 Pinney, *History of the 104th Regiment*, 82; McKean, *Blood and War*, 1048; Jabez N. Smith to Mother, April 27, 1865, Jabez Smith Papers, AU; Peak Scrapbook, www.archive.org/stream/SamPeakMemoir/Peak%20Memoir-reduced_djvu.txt, accessed Nov. 11, 2018.

Gen. John A. Logan, who intercepted them near the city limits. Logan ordered the troops to disperse and return to their camps. The enraged men refused and pushed past the general, branding the city a "Rebel hole [that] ought to be cleaned out." Logan rode ahead of the mob and again ordered the soldiers to disperse but his commands were fruitless. He then dashed ahead to the Union artillery emplacements that studded the city's earthworks, where he ordered two batteries to load their guns with the army's most lethal munition, double canister, and take aim at the advancing men. Logan approached the mob a final time with an ultimatum: Disperse voluntarily or be dispersed by artillery fire. Shocked back to their senses, the men stopped in their tracks. Amidst grumbles and curses the mob retraced its steps back to the camps. Disaster was averted for the moment.[26]

Similar angry reactions burst from men as word of the president's death reached distant commands. Simeon A. Howe recalled the shock he and his comrades felt in the XIV Corps' camps along the Cape Fear River. "[T]he news is awfull to think of it renders the army almost frantic for revenge." John Henry Otto of the 21st Wisconsin recalled the form this vengeance took:

[A]bout midnight the camp was suddenly illuminated as with a thousand electric lights. All the building of the plantation, the negro village included were burning brightly. It was a grand sight, and little was the pity lost at [the] sight of the holocaust. It was not found out, nor was it asked for, who were the originators of the grand display until after we were discharged at Washington. Then it was found that a few men of each Regt. of the brigade had secretly undertaken and finished the job thoroughly.[27]

Freedmen who came into the Union lines with blood chilling tales of their lives as slaves fueled the Federals' anger. Stories of Raleigh slave owner Jacob Mordecai were exceptionally cruel, and the soldiers organized a patrol to extract justice. They rode to Mordecai's farm, intent on hanging him, but discovered he had fled. One of the formerly enslaved, Essex Henry, remembered how the soldiers vandalized Mordecai's home and cleaned out two barns of corn. The Yankees were delighted to discover Mordecai's stashes of brandy, which fueled the looting.[28]

26 George Francis Dawson, *The Life and Services of John A. Logan* (Chicago, 1887), 119-120.

27 Simone A. Howe, Letter, April 18, 1865, MSU; David Gould and James B. Kennedy, eds., *Memoirs of a Dutch Mudsill: The "War Memories" of John Henry Otto* (Kent, OH, 2004), 359-361.

28 Essex Henry, WPA, 11/1:394.

Amid the chaos that night African American men and women around Chapel Hill seized their freedom and fled their former masters in a mass exodus. George Moses Horton, who had worked his entire life for freedom, now found it after wandering into town and meeting Union soldiers. Horton would come to play a unique role in the soldiers' lives, chronicling in poetic verse his liberators' pathos and his own emotions about emancipation.

Horton had grown up on a nearby plantation and rented out his time from his master. He walked eight miles each day to sell produce in Chapel Hill. In a time when slaves were not allowed to read, Horton, who was self-taught, learned the art of poetry from the university professor's wife. White students realized the black vegetable peddler could compose passionate love poems and commissioned him to help win the affection of local belles. Horton's popularity grew, as did his purse. He earned $3.00 to $4.00 every week for his poems. He published his first book, *Hope of Liberty*, in 1829 in hopes of buying his freedom. Unsuccessful, he continued to write his verses, which appeared in Northern newspapers. Though he published a second book, *The Poetical Works of George Moses Horton*, in 1845, he still was unable to win his freedom.[29]

When Horton arrived in Chapel Hill he found it overrun with Union soldiers. The poet struck up an acquaintance with men of the 9th Michigan Cavalry, who enjoyed Horton's ability to compose poems on any topic; but on this momentous night Horton's poetic talents particularly endeared him to the grieving soldiers. He seized upon their feelings and quickly produced a verse entitled, "Lincoln is Dead." Horton's eloquent lament captured their intense grief in a way the soldiers could not. One Federal copied the words and mailed them home to his family in Ohio. It was an incredible transmutation of feeling.

In the coming days, Horton's poems captured more of the thoughts and feelings about the horrors and hardships of war. Poems like "A Dying Soldier's Message," "The Terrors of War," and "The Soldier's Thoughts of Home at the End of the War" contained the emotions of white victors interpreted through the voice of a black freedman. Horton's own emotions of freedom eventually melded with those of his liberators in poems that filled a growing portfolio of new work.

29 *News and Observer* [Raleigh, NC], May 27, 1997; William S. Powell, *The First State University: A Pictorial History of the University of North Carolina* (Chapel Hill, NC, 1972), 48; Joan R. Sherman ed., *The Black Bard of North Carolina: George Moses Horton and His Poetry* (Chapel Hill, NC, 1997), 6-21.

These verses became an unprecedented record of the shared emotions of white soldiers and freedmen during a time of epic change.[30]

April 18

After a bumpy ride through the cool Carolina evening, a train pulled into the Hillsborough depot just after midnight on April 18. A group of men disembarked and made its way through the darkness to Alexander Dickson's house three miles outside of town. As they passed roadside campfires soldiers recognized Secretary of War John C. Breckinridge, Postmaster General John Reagan, and Governor Zebulon Vance and his clerk, Leo D. Heartt. The riders were headed to Lt. Gen. Wade Hampton's headquarters for a midnight conference to compose the Confederacy's obituary with General Johnston.

When they arrived, Hampton angrily confronted Vance about his treaty with Sherman, brokered by Graham and Swain. Although he stopped short of calling him a traitor, Hampton implied that Vance was disloyal. Vance stood in silence until Johnston stepped in and asked the governor to leave so they could discuss the surrender terms they would present to Sherman on the morrow. Vance left the house and found staff officer W. J. Saunders asleep under a blanket in the front yard.

Vance woke Saunders and said he had come to explain his letter to Sherman. Already distraught after losing his government and capital, the governor had taken Hampton's dismissive insult to heart. Saunders remembered Vance breaking into tears as he explained: "Me in communication with the enemy, me making terms for my State unknown to the authorities! Of all men, sir, I am the last man they can accuse of such infamy." Tears rolled down his cheeks as he covered his face with his hands. Saunders was greatly moved. "For four long weary years we had fought and struggled and given our all for the cause that now was lost—but God forgive me, as I gazed on this strong man in his agony of the shame put upon him, I felt all the bitterness or resentment, and for the first and only time, I, a soldier of the Confederacy, was untrue and disloyal to its colors." Before day's end, many more men would question their link to the Confederate cause.[31]

---

30 George Moses Horton, *Naked Genius* (Raleigh, NC, 1865), 48, 68, 147, 154.

31 W. J. Saunders, "Governor Z. B. Vance: Story of the Last Days of the Confederacy in North Carolina," *Southern Historical Society Papers* (*SHSP*), 52 vols., 32:168.

The rising sun spread its light over a troubled Rebel army. Men huddled around campfires, lost in thought. Nightmares of life after defeat made their sleep restless, and they struggled to understand the incredible changes they faced and the uncertainty of survival. The morning roll call revealed the distressing scores of unanswered names of men who had slipped away during the night. After reading the morning reports, General Hardee penned a sad dispatch to Johnston: "A large number of my command deserted last night. . . . I anticipate many more will go to-day and to-night." A battalion of Virginia troops appealed directly to Jefferson Davis for permission to disband and return home to protect their families. The flight of soldiers from the army fueled a rapidly deteriorating situation. Johnston worried that a swarm of hungry, armed men would cause problems for civilians, and he worked through the night with Reagan and Breckinridge to craft surrender terms that would end the suffering for them and all Southerners. But even as he prepared to meet Sherman, he worried if the assassination had ruined any goodwill they could expect.[32]

Sherman hoped the 24-hour delay had been worth it, and that Johnston was successful in obtaining permission to surrender the Confederacy. He had kept his men under control the previous night but worried about how long he could suppress their anger. Sherman slid a bottle of whiskey into his saddle bags and boarded his train for the journey back to Durham. Both Johnston and Sherman knew an agreement had to be reached. The volatility of both armies amid the rapidly evolving events underscored the need for joint action. They both worried about former Confederates igniting a guerilla war and the need to control angry Union forces threatening the unbounded devastation of total war. Each general clearly understood that an agreement was imperative to forestall even greater suffering and mass violence.

The generals met again in the Bennett home. Johnston, accompanied by Breckinridge, presented surrender terms they hoped Sherman would consider. Before negotiations began, Sherman offered the Confederates a drink of whiskey, which Breckinridge eagerly gulped down. The invigorated former vice president then launched into a speech about the merits of their self-proposed surrender terms. Realizing the Confederates were trying to dictate the terms of their own capitulation, Sherman exclaimed, "You would have me sending an apology to Jeff Davis." He then sat down to craft his own terms and started with another shot of whiskey. Breckinridge spat out his chewing tobacco expecting to get another drink,

---

32 OR 47/3:809-810.

but Sherman, lost in thought, did not offer him one. The offended Kentuckian later remarked, "Sherman is a hog. Yes, sir, a hog. Did you see him take that drink by himself? . . . He knew we needed it, and needed it badly."[33]

Sherman finished his terms and presented them to Johnston and Breckinridge. They were liberal and mirrored those the Confederates had proposed. In short, they stipulated that if the Confederates laid down their arms and went home, they would be unmolested by the Federal government and would have their constitutional rights restored. The Rebel leaders huddled in a corner to examine these terms and were relieved. They embodied the magnanimous spirit Lincoln had expressed to Sherman during their last meeting in March, and also reflected the benevolence Sherman always claimed was his goal: making a gracious peace in the wake of hard war. With a heavy sigh, Johnston returned to the table and signed the terms. The agreement ended the entire war and reunited the Union with a single pen stroke. Only the formalities of governmental approvals remained.

The monumental agreement had extraordinary consequences. Many believed peace had finally closed America's darkest chapter. Once again Sherman and Johnston shook hands and departed believing they had saved lives and the nation. But now Johnston had to rush back to his army and control his men as news of the agreement spread.

Johnston's surrender devastated the already downtrodden men of his army. For D. Augustus Dickert the idea of their surrender seemed inconceivable; "The thought of grounding their arms to an enemy never before entered their minds, and when the news came of a surrender the greatest apprehension and dre[a]d seized all. . . . The future made them shudder." The announcement unmanned even the most stouthearted. A soldier in the 11th Texas Cavalry remembered, "Our camp was turned into a camp of mourning . . . men and officers mingled their tears together. Old, weather-beaten and battle-scarred soldiers who had prided themselves on their six-shooters, horses, and valor as soldiers, threw their belts aside as something to get rid of, and wept like whipped children."[34]

---

33 John S. Wise, *The End of an Era* (Boston and New York, 1899), 450-451. Years later, Johnston remembered Breckinridge's fondness for liquor and the physical effects of sobriety on him in the days before the meeting: "Breckinridge had found it difficult, if not impossible, to procure liquor. He showed the effect of his enforced abstinence. He was rather dull and heavy that morning." More than a simple anecdote from the surrender negotiations, Breckinridge's thirst and reputation as a hard drinker affected his health; it failed eight years later and eventually led to his death from pneumonia and cirrhosis of the liver in 1875.

34 Augustus Dickert, *History of Kershaw's Brigade* (Newberry, SC, 1899), 529-530; *New Orleans Picayune*, November 9, 1902; Foster and Brown, eds., *One of Cleburne's Command*, 164.

Surrender meant the failure of their way of life, causing Southerners to conjure a future full of horrors. Artilleryman Charles Johnston confessed to his diary, "I am sick at heart. . . .The whole thing seems sometimes a fearful dream, too horrible to be real." William M. Pollard of the 1st Tennessee bluntly admitted, "Oh, the suspense! I am miserable thinking of our future. . . . I could scarcely keep back the tears." Jesse Sparkman could not express the pain at seeing fellow soldiers abandoning the army and the demoralized state of those who remained. "Will not attempt to picture the horrible condition of our troops. I will leave this for a more able pen than the feeble one which I wielded so weakly." The desperation that permeated the army over abandoning the Confederate cause had spawned widespread introspection in the ranks. "O, what will become of us all?" lamented Broomfield Ridley. "For Andy Johnson has about got us in his clutches, and Parson William G. Brownlow has said: 'Greek fire to the masses, but h[el]l fire to the leaders.'"[35]

Confederate officers desperately tried to retain order and keep the army together. "There was an appeal to soldiers today by General Loring to not take any ill-advised measures," a Mississippian wrote, "but to stand by the colors and that their officers would see that they have their rights. He begged them not to desert." Keeping discipline among the scared men was different. W. H. Andrews recalled that by night "howling mobs" of soldiers appeared at their commanders' headquarters and sought confirmation of the surrender. Andrews watched as officers made heartfelt pleas for order among their troops: "All of the officers tell the men to stand to their colors as they have always done and meet their fate like men." His brigade commander, Brig. Gen. George P. Harrison, spoke passionately to Andrews and his comrades, but "cried like a baby, begging his men to stand firm to the last." Captain Samuel T. Foster sadly admitted that he "[h]ad battalion drill today to see if the men would drill," but with the breakdown in discipline, it was a fruitless endeavor. Daniel Huger easily recognized that the negotiations broke the spirit of the Army of Tennessee and believed "the rank and file of Johnston's army did not intend to do any more fighting."[36]

35 Hutson Family Papers, Special Collection, UA; Dunkerly, *Confederate Surrender*, 86, 92; Colleen M. Elliott and Louise A. Moxley, *Tennessee Veterans Questionnaire* (Easley, SC, 1985), 17-45; Sparkman Diary, 16, BP; Dickert, *Kershaw's Brigade*, 529-530; Ridley, *Battles and Sketches*, 459; Francis Marion Jordan, *Life and Labors of Elder F. M. Jordan* (Raleigh, NC, 1899), 71-72.

36 Daniel, *Soldiering in the Army of Tennessee*, 167; Andrews and McMurray, *Footprints of a Regiment*, 180; Daniel Elliot Huger Smith, *A Charlestonian's Recollections: 1846-1913* (Charleston, SC, 1950), 106.

The rumors of surrender racing through the army caused chaos. Conflicting reports denying and confirming surrender circulated among the troops. Johnston issued a carefully worded circular to calm his men, which avoided calling his agreement with Sherman a surrender but instead labeled it an armistice. One commander noted how the announcement placated some: "[A]n order comes from Genl Johnston which is read out to all the troops announcing that an armistice has been agreed upon by the commanders of the two armies, but not for the purpose of surrendering this army—This seems to satisfy everybody." But for men in Johnson Hagood's brigade the order came too late. "Demoralization . . . is utter and complete; there is no spark of fight left in the troops."[37]

With the fate of the army and the Confederacy seemingly sealed, men's allegiances shifted to themselves. Since sacrifice for the cause was no longer required, survival of self became paramount. George Bussey of the 7th South Carolina was guarding a trainload of bacon when the news reached him; with the Confederacy about to die, he and others distributed the bacon to civilians and other soldiers. Bussey soon joined a rioting crowd "and got me three splendid pairs of shoes" from a government storehouse. A day later, Bussey and a few others walked miles after hearing a rumor that boxcars of food were parked down the track. They instead discovered barrels of whiskey buried under some brush. Bussey remembered men coming from every direction with canteens and water buckets in order to collect a share of the alcohol. "Before I could reach the spot, it was reported that it was all gone. There were a great many drunken men in camp that day."[38]

For a fellow South Carolinian, Diedr Nordmeyer, thirst and dependence on alcohol would eventually help end his life. Nordmeyer, who had enlisted in August 1861, successfully managed his trauma until he started evincing emotional problems with fits of anger in June 1864. The violence of these episodes forced the commander of Nordmeyer's battery, Capt. William H. Bachman, to bring him up on charges. But Bachman withdrew the charges after Nordmeyer distinguished himself in action and repented for his angry outbursts. It would take 14 years, but the war finally claimed Nordmeyer. While working as a bar keep in Charleston, Nordmeyer decided he had had enough of wrestling with the war's memories. In

---

37 Foster and Brown, eds., *One of Cleburne's Command*, 164; Hagood, *Memoirs*, 369; Bradley, *This Astounding Close*, 182.

38 George Bussey, "Memoirs of Reverend G. W. Bussey," in *Recollections and Reminiscences*, 12 vols. (South Carolina Division, United Daughters of the Confederacy, 1991), 2:442-443; Dunkerly, *The Confederate Surrender*, 55.

July 1879, after bathing, shaving, and dressing himself, the former artilleryman lay on his bed and used a mirror to shoot himself through the temple.[39]

Another soldier who left the army in Greensboro with the goal of surviving, Arthur Ford, reached Salisbury with a group of comrades and found train cars waiting for Jefferson Davis and his cabinet. The soldiers jumped aboard and threatened to throw the conductor off unless he carried them farther south. He reluctantly took them about 20 miles down the track until they reached a section torn up by George Stoneman's troopers on an earlier raid. Ford and his gang jumped off, and the engineer returned to meet an angry Breckinridge, declaring that the leaders should "be seized and severely punished." Days later, Ford's wayward band discovered another train awaiting the cabinet. This time, though, Samuel Cooper, the Confederate adjutant general, and the local home guard caught them. Cooper threatened "blow [them] to hell" if they did not get off his train.[40]

Desertions began to increase and the discovery of absent men offended some Confederate officers. Lieutenant Colonel Joseph Waring, for instance, indignantly recorded the names of those who left his Jeff Davis Legion, griping about this being the unit's first instance of desertion. "It is the first & only disgraceful desertion from this regiment. God grant it may be the last." But Waring was struggling to cope with his own feelings about impending defeat and tried to rationalize the cost. He believed blame for the loss rested on the heads of others: "[A]ll our sacrifices are in vain. . . .We shall be betrayed by our own leaders." Waring, however, felt compelled to be positive, writing that the "army will again live. The South will yet be free." His zeal was not matched by his men, who continued to leave.[41]

The news of the negotiations deeply touched civilians, who became conflicted over what peace would bring. Many could not see the future past the specter of famine that stared them in the face. With hungry soldiers scouring the landscape for food and stealing animals to ride home, ordinary citizens faced a bleak future. The issue drove the indefatigable former governor Swain into action yet again. He penned a desperate appeal to Sherman for help to stave off mass suffering: The "slow lingering death of famine, is eminent to thousands—not only to men but helpless women and children." He begged the general to halt his army's

---

39 *Compiled Service Records of Confederate Soldiers*, NARA; *The* [Anderson, SC] *Intelligencer*, July 24, 1879; *The* [Baltimore] *Sun*, July 19, 1879.

40 *OR* 47/3:818-819; Ford and Ford, *Life in the Confederate Army*, 67-68.

41 Waring Papers, SHC/UNC, 38.

impressment of horses, lest the fall harvest be prevented; quite simply, if they had no horses, there would be no crops. General Atkins approved Swain's request the following day, saying he would happily return the animals if ordered. An unmoved Sherman replied three days later; he refused to concede to Swain's request and said it was the price to be paid for forcing the nation into war. Sherman agreed, however, to honor the request when peace arrived, which seemed imminent with the terms inked at the Bennett farm. But as the surrender process dragged on, the crisis civilians faced only tormented them more. Fear of starvation and Yankee retribution remained as well. All this weighed heavily on the minds of a heartbroken people.[42]

Soldiers in Sherman's army bedded down that night with many powerful feelings racing through their minds. They felt joy at the war's conclusion, but their celebrations were half-hearted. Despite the glorious the news the emotions caused by Lincoln's death crippled the troops. The grief left dedicated diarists at a loss for words and many journals went unfilled for the day. The words of those who did express themselves reflected the emotions of stupefied men and how these feelings evolved into impulses of hate and revenge. J. F. Culver of the 129th Illinois expressed his wildly swinging emotions in a letter to his wife. He confessed his "heart was too sad to write much," but he wanted to relate the news of the Confederate surrender and Lincoln's death. "Yesterday the [surrender] news would have been received with wild acclamations of joy, to-day there would be no outburst at all." Culver tried to explain the deep state of mourning that filled himself and his fellow soldiers: "This is a sad day in the army. The news reached us officially this morning of the assassination and death of President Lincoln. . . . I never saw so much sadness manifested. The whole army is silent as the grave." But the consuming grief Culver described gave way to anger. "Groups are gathered here & there discussing the sad event. I have heard only one sentiment expressed, & it seems to be universal throughout the army. Woe to the South if this Army is compelled to pass through it again. Woe to the Rebel Army that compels us to fight longer."[43] These hardened veterans could express their emotions through violence, an equation they knew well. Despite both the continued religious revival among Sherman's men and the prospect of peace, the troops expressed the kind of anger that threatened to erode whatever morals remained. Soldier Francis M. McAdams warned, "if we move against the enemy, the worst deeds of the past will be humane

42 *OR* 47/3:248, 279-280.

43 J. F. Culver to wife, April 18, 1865, UI.

in comparison with what will follow. Every heart is sad, all heads are bowed in mourning, and every mind is filled with thoughts of the awful crime." Tens of thousands of Union soldiers shared this reaction. Charles Brown thought he had never seen a "more exasperated set of men" and believed that new men will "stop from committing any outrage or crime they may choose to." He hoped the negotiations between Johnston and Sherman would fail. "I would like to see Wm. T. turn his army loose over what is left of the S.C. [Southern Confederacy]."[44]

Captain William Calkins of the 104th Illinois recalled the dramatic transformation among his men:

> Such a time I hope never to see again. Habitually profane men forgot to swear, tears ran down from eyes unused to weeping. Everywhere men wept who had never flinched in the white heat of battle. The calamity in Washington touched the recesses of every soldier's heart. The soldiers declared that they did not want peace and would take no more prisoners.

"Hard, indeed," another officer told his diary. "After four years of bloody trial and bloody war and just as the harbinger of peace was returning he goes to his long home. The soldier's friend, the country's second father. What a gloom must hang over the country."[45]

The agreement signed at the Bennett farm came at a critical moment; it forestalled a wave of violence, and an uneasy peace settled over the land as the armies waited for the terms to be ratified by the Union and Confederate governments. The rest gave soldiers time to wrestle with their conflicted feelings. Their belief that their war was at its end tempered their urges for revenge. But this fragile peace would not last and the surrender would be rejected. The whipsaw emotions the resumption of hostilities threatened to unleash the anger of soldiers and usher in the darkest chapter of the war.

---

44 Francis McAdams, *Every-day Soldier Life, or a History of the Hundred and Thirteenth Ohio Volunteer Infantry* (Columbus, OH, 1884), 152; Charles S. Brown to Mother & Etta, April 18, 1865, Charles S. Brown Papers, DU.

45 Calkins, *One Hundred and Fourth Illinois*, 314; Eaton, *Diary of Federal Officer*, 252.

CHAPTER 7

April 19–24:
"You cannot begin to imagine the feeling—
it is fearful."

April 19

Confederate soldiers talked late into the night about the surrender and their unknown fate. They agonized over their gloomy prospects: should they stay with the army until its end or escape with their health intact? For many the choice was easy: leave the army and go home. Soldiers said good-bye to each other in hushed tones and melted away into the darkness. The army's morning reports revealed the impact of the agreement had on the minds of Johnston's men. The number of desertions during the night pained the general, and he expressed his disappointment in a circular to the army. Johnston knew he had to confirm the rumors of surrender, so he published the agreement with Sherman. To soften the blow for his men, the general referred to it as "a suspension of arms" rather than a surrender.[1]

The grim news spreading throughout Johnston's widely scattered army elicited a spectrum of wild and deep emotions. Dumfounded and confused men cornered their commanders, asking what the announcement meant. Generals Alexander P.

---

1 OR 47/3:810, 813.

Stewart and William W. Loring addressed a large assembly and tried to explain the armistice. They urged the troops to complete their duty and stay with their units until they were discharged, but the news erased what discipline that remained. Stewart appealed directly to a group of deserters who "laugh[ed] and mock[ed] him." Soldiers in the 9th Mississippi Consolidated expressed a different reaction when they rejoiced and wept: "The glorious news came this evening that peace is made. . . . Some seem delighted at the idea of peace while others are very sad." One soldier, though glad about peace, confessed an aversion "to return home (with the rest) a whipped people." Lieutenant General Stephen D. Lee and his staff, along with a crowd of soldiers, surrounded Johnston's headquarters that afternoon to learn the particulars of their fate. But when the general emerged from his tent to address them, he was unable to speak. He handed Lee a copy of the terms and motioned for him to read it aloud. As Lee spoke, Johnston's eyes began to well up with tears that then "burst bounds and trickled down his cheeks."[2]

Since Johnston's command was spread across central North Carolina, the news traveled slowly. Some men learned of the disaster in Virginia and their impending surrender simultaneously. "This news came as a great shock to us," wrote one; "We none of us ever dreamed of such a thing as Genl Lee ever being forced to surrender." He confessed to a compatriot, "I don't know; I believe Mars Joe will do what is right but if he has to surrender I just wish I had a barrel of whiskey. I never was drunk in my life but if that is true I would like to go out in the woods & die drunk & bury all my sorrows."[3]

The trickle of men leaving the Confederate ranks swelled to a flood that night, and over the next week many more followed. Johnston estimated his army lost "not less than four thousand in the infantry and artillery, and almost as many from the cavalry" between April 19–24. Soldiers' frantic departures led to widespread lawlessness. According to one officer, "Our army is getting demoralized. A band of marauding soldiers visited our camp this morning and coolly helped themselves to some leather and goods that we had quietly secured from the Quartermaster's Department." Arthur Ford, who witnessed the roadside court-martial execution a month earlier, continued his marauding streak by stealing whatever he could in Salisbury. He joined a mob of around 300 paroled men from Virginia in ransacking a Confederate storehouse. "I joined in the crowd to get my share," he said, despite a dozen home guardsmen protecting the food and clothing. The guards "protested

2 Bradley, *This Astounding Close*, 182-183, 202.

3 McNeill, "Survey of Confederate Soldier Morale," 19.

violently," Ford remembered, "but were just swept [to] one side, and the door broken open." he grabbed a handful of Confederate money, a pair of shoes, socks, flour, bacon, and a small roll of jean cloth that he carried on his shoulders back to Aiken, South Carolina, and traded for food to feed his family. Another South Carolinian, Daniel Huger, made off with "a bag of flour on the pommel of my saddle; a side of bacon strapped behind; two canteens of molasses; [and] two pairs of shoes" from the naval commissary in Greensboro.[4]

Mobs emptied store houses along the railroad from Haw River to Greensboro. Reports of looting at McLean's Station prompted Governor Vance to ride out and see for himself. He found Confederate officers standing by as their men grabbed whatever they could carry and wandered off into the woods. "The Cars had just been emptied as I got there and the road side [was] crowded with soldiers staggering under heavy loads of plunder. It seemed to be an understood and permitted matter, as officers of nearly all grades were standing quietly around." Reports continued to reach Vance about the extent of the looting. Barrels of alcohol were dumped "for fear the Yankees" or demoralized Rebels would steal it. Other supplies were destroyed as well: a carload of shells was burned, and barrels of molasses and alcohol were overturned and the contents formed pools on the ground. One witness remembered that the "[h]ungry women dipped up molasses from the gutters in buckets. Hopeless men lapped up the liquor like dogs."[5]

Vance angrily accused Johnston of not protecting state property. North Carolina's treasury, the state archives, and other valuables removed from Raleigh before it fell were at risk. Vance said he would rather take this valuable property back to Raleigh where, at least, Sherman promised its protection. State treasurer Jonathan Worth, who was in charge of the wagons carrying the state's treasure, arrived at the village of Company Shops in the wake of the looting. Worth's harrowing journey from Raleigh had included many encounters with stragglers and deserters. "Lee's army being destroyed," he told friends, "would have dissolved" Johnston's army "but for the commencement of hostilities." The exasperated Worth admitted that "vast stores on this road have been destroyed, stolen, and wasted and the army is subsisting by ruthless impressment." In a panic he decided

4 Ridley, *Battles and Sketches*, 459; Johnston, *Narrative*, 410; Final Confederate paroles issued 27,719; Ford and Ford, *Life in the Confederate Army*, 66; Smith, *A Charlestonian's Recollections*, 107.

5 Barrett, *Sherman's March Through North Carolina*, 89; OR 47/3:815; Sallie Walker Stockard, *The History of Guilford County, North Carolina* (Knoxville, TN, 1902), 66.

to hide the bags of gold and recover them later, rather than take a chance of being robbed.[6]

But Vance was correct. Sherman had maintained a tense calm in Raleigh, and hoped to preserve this peace by having the city's printers produce copies of his special field order announcing the Confederate surrender. Sherman ordered these broadsides widely distributed in hopes of tempering his men's anger. It proclaimed "peace from the Potomac to the Rio Grande," and invoked the idea of returning home as victors. He hoped it would convince his troops to avoid sullying their well-won reputation by further destruction or depredations, "The fame of this army for courage, industry, and discipline is admitted all over the world; then let each officer and man see that it is not stained by any acts of vulgarity, rowdyism, or petty crime."[7]

Sherman's subordinates published their own decrees in order to keep their men under control. General Oliver Otis Howard issued General Order No. 15, which halted foraging and addressed the reluctance of his troops to adhere to orders limiting confiscations from civilians. Howard directly addressed the disobedience of his men and the damage their actions would have civilians: "Great disregard has been shown in many instances to the orders heretofore issued on this subject." Thus, "many of the poor people of the surrounding country are entirely deprived of their provisions and of their animals, which are worthless to us, but are invaluable to them to enable them to raise crops for the subsistence of the people." He urged his officers to take "extraordinary precautions" and threatened to hold them accountable for any infractions. Another of Howard's circulars charged quartermasters with inspecting "trains, camps, quarters, and knapsacks" for unauthorized properties such as "ladies' wearing apparel, watches, jewelry, shotguns, silver plate, & c."[8]

Maintaining control meant busying idle men and reminding them they were soldiers. Reenforcing military regulations and practices both helped Sherman reassert his authority and realigned his men's judgment. He set the tone by ordering a review of his army. The XXIII Corps was reviewed on April 21, the XX Corps on April 22, and the XVII Corps on April 23. The successive parades encouraged the troops to spruce up their appearance and reassume a soldierly bearing. "The men were much in need of clothing, caps, hats and shoes," one soldier wrote, and a

6　OR 47 3:810-811; Worth, *The Correspondence of Jonathan Worth*, 382.

7　OR 47/3:250.

8　Ibid., 251.

"good pair of shoes could hardly be found, while socks were a reminiscence of earlier days." With the repair of the railroad, supplies flowed into Sherman's army and a distinct change began when the men donned the new clothing. Uniforms, guard duty, drill, and camps were again the focus of the soldiers' daily lives. William Belknap and the men of the 15th Iowa felt pride at their return to military bearing; he boasted that his brigade had "one of the finest looking camps laid out during the war, [and] it was becoming a topic of curiosity and an object of newspaper illustration."

Camps bustled with men reacquainting themselves with the rules of being a soldier. They spent hours polishing, shining, and cleaning, as well as undertaking drills and knapsack inspection. One Yankee remarked on their drastic transformation from dirty, hairy animals to soldiers "with closely cropped hair, cleanly shaven faces, arms and accoutrements cleaned and polished, looking as fresh, smart and tidy as militia." This return to military order and easy duty, as well as the possibility of peace, helped ease the weight of war these men felt. A member of the 3rd Wisconsin noted how they "reveled" in the stressless rest. "There was every prospect that the strain of nerves and strength in bloody, arduous war was to cease; and none rejoiced at this . . . more heartily than the veteran soldier." [9]

That night, the men who initially marched on Raleigh bent on destruction instead marched in peace. They held a mass meeting to acknowledge the impending end of the war and to silently mourn for those who had been lost. Sherman's order provided some relief for those whose hearts still ached. Officers made speeches and "[t]hree cheers were given for Genl. Sherman & the Union restored." Peace brought consolation; the shadow of death that doggedly followed the soldiers began to fade, and they started to grieve for the dead. The Union soldiers felt the need to emote and express their pent-up feelings as one.[10]

9 Ibid., 251, 268, 289; William Worth Belknap, *History of the Fifteenth Regiment Iowa Veteran Volunteer Infantry* (Keokuk, IA: 1887), 483; Downing, *Downing's Civil War Diary*, 269; Peter Eltinge to Father, April 20, 1865, Eltinge-Lord Collection, DU; Lawson Diary, April 19, 1865, AHSL; Edwin A. Bryant, *History of the Third Regiment of Wisconsin Veteran Volunteer Infantry 1861-1865* (Madison, WI, 1891), 329.

10 Culver, Culver, Dunlap, and Bearss, *Your Affectionate Husband*, 437; Widney and Girardi, eds., *Campaigning with Uncle Billy*, 356; McAdams, *Every-day Soldier Life*, 153; Brown, *History of the Fourth Regiment*, 407.

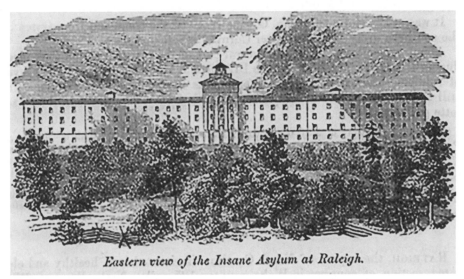

Eastern view of the Insane Asylum at Raleigh.

The North Carolina Insane Asylum admitted its first patient, a veteran of the Mexican War, in 1856. After the capture of Raleigh in April 1865, Union soldiers flocked to the grounds of the asylum to jeer at the patients. Ironically, many of those same men would be institutionalized themselves in the years to come. *North Carolina State Archives*

April 20

The cool morning brought more rain for the thirsty spring blossoms, but no news from Washington. Many believed the terms of surrender must have reached the capital and that their final approval was no more than a day or two away. Union soldiers spent their idle hours touring North Carolina's capital city and discovered it to be the birthplace of the new president, Andrew Johnson. They found his father's tombstone in the city cemetery, which one soldier called "a lovely city of the dead." Other men visited the Deaf, Dumb and Blind Asylum located in the heart of the city; the asylum's president, Willie J. Palmer, gave several of them a tour and demonstrated the "proficiency of the pupils." Fellow soldiers mocked the 4th Minnesota band after it serenaded the school's deaf patients.[11]

Many Federals visited the North Carolina Insane Asylum, which sat on a bluff overlooking the city. The hospital had opened its doors in 1856 after a successful campaign by Northern activist Dorothea Dix. Its first patient, Andrew M.

---

11 Diary of E. P. Burton, April 28, 1865; Brown, *History of the Fourth Regiment*, 401, 407; Pepper, *Personal Recollections*, 388-389; Hatcher, *The Last Four Weeks of the War*, 244-245.

Holderly, was a Mexican War veteran whom doctors believed was suffering from sunstroke. With the onset of the new war, the hospital faced operational challenges such as lack of funding and overcrowding. The growing toxicity of war filled more hospital beds with troubled Confederate soldiers and civilians broken by the conflict. By April 1865, 171 patients peered from the asylum's windows at the 12,965 men of the XX Corps camped on the hospital's expansive grounds. H. Page Martin of the 123rd New York described the asylum as a splendid building of stone with separate wings for male and female patients, and remarked on their behavior: "[W]e are not allowed to go inside but from the outside we can see them looking through the iron grates at us . . . some are crazy as loons, others appear half rational and others quite rational." Many patients interacted with the soldiers gathered outside. One woman would sit by the window and eye the sea of men gathered below until she picked out one and screamed, "There is the man who sent me here! He is the father of my child. Bring him here and I will scratch his eyes out!" Another patient professed to be the ruler of the world and addressed the soldiers as "cousins." He urged them to treat the ladies kindly but would suddenly erupt in anger and yell, "Kill all the men!" Officers established their headquarters in the hospital and wandered the wards. "I could but pity many of the Lunatics I saw," remarked one, "and then laugh at the ridiculous capers & sayings of others." The shouts and screams of the inmates haunted soldiers. Captain Robert Cruikshank wrote that he could hear the inmates "screeching night and day" at his headquarters a quarter of a mile away. Cruikshank admitted he was glad to be a soldier rather than a nurse in the asylum. Some soon started taking advantage of the inmates and playing cruel jokes upon them, necessitating the placement of a guard.[12]

Uriah H. Farr and other members of the 70th Indiana stood guard duty at the hospital. Once, while they paced the hospital's front veranda, a general and staff officer brushed past Farr to confront hospital administrators who refused to admit a black soldier "who had lost his reason." Though the staff protested over treating a black patient, Sherman's commanders left them no choice. The army forcibly integrated the hospital by compelling this man's admission, along with those of several other local African American civilians.

During their daily gathering outside the asylum, Sherman's men encountered a patient named Rainey, who became their favorite due to his Union sentiment and

12 H. Page Martin to mother, April 15, 1865, Author's Collection; Strong, *A Yankee Private's Civil War*, 198; Robert Cruikshank to Wife, April 15, 1865, OSU; Strong, *A Yankee Private's Civil War*, 198-199.

the "shows" he performed. The soldiers came to hear the inmate sing and enjoy the entertainment. "He was a good singer, knew a lot of rebel songs, and could tell stories to perfection. . . . He professed to be a Union man and begged to be released. He had a violin and knew how to use it." Rainey lowered a basket, and soldiers filled it with food. He gained such popularity with the men that calls for his release grew louder. The idea of a professed Unionist wrongly confined angered the soldiers; they became obsessed with freedom for this patient and planned to force his release.[13]

Rainey, whose real name was likely Alston Lavender, hailed from a prominent North Carolina family. Though an intelligent child growing up, his family described him as "peculiar." The young man developed serious issues with his mother, which forced his father to remain constantly close. With the outbreak of war, Lavender claimed his father placed him in the insane asylum for his political views, but some suspected he was indeed mentally unbalanced. Lavender became a favorite of the hospital staff and would often accompany doctors on their rounds, until one day he attacked an attendant with a piece of glass. Thereafter he was confined to his cell. With the approach of Sherman's army, Lavender saw his chance to escape with help from the Yankees. Indeed, sympathetic soldiers helped him get a letter to Sherman asking for his freedom.[14]

The soldiers' demands for Lavender's release increased, and a crowd of them gathered at the hospital's doors on the afternoon of April 20, growing increasingly rowdy and boisterously calling for the patient's release. This growing agitation unnerved Farr, who walked with his musket and bayonet pointed toward the crowd to keep it at bay. As the hours wore on, the men became more aggressive and surged at Farr, shouting and cursing. Just as the sentry prepared to call for help, Maj. Gen. Joseph A. Mower rode his horse into the mob while swinging his sword and shouting, "Back! Back!" The men fell over each other to avoid being trampled. This was the second time Federal officers had to threaten their men to keep them under control. Mower sat astride his mount amid the crowd and exclaimed,

> Soldiers, I am surprised at you. Here you have been imposing on this sentinel, who had a right to shoot you down, but he forbore to do it. You all know the duty of this sentinel, for I see [by] your bronzed faces that you are veterans. Shame on you for so far forgetting yourselves as to impose on the good-natured forbearance of a sentinel, one of your own

13 Samuel Merrill, *The Seventieth Indiana Volunteer Infantry* (Indianapolis, 1900), 269.

14 T. F. Maguire, Sr., to C. C. Crittenden, March 9, 1940, Alston Lavender Papers, NCDAH.

comrades. Now disperse to your quarters, and do not assemble here again. Sentinel, load your gun and shoot down the first man who attempts to press on your beat again.[15]

Upon hearing reports of the rowdy soldiers and their case for the professed Unionist in the asylum, General Sherman decided to see for himself and took a tour of the hospital. He spoke to Lavender and several other lucid inmates. Convinced of their unwarranted confinement, Sherman warned the hospital administrators that unless they wanted their facility to be burned to the ground, they should consider releasing Lavender. Union doctors examined the patient and found him sane enough to be released; he walked out the asylum doors and followed Sherman's army north. In the coming months, Lavender's place in the asylum would be taken by many traumatized by the war, as Confederate soldiers and civilians who had been in the path of the armies would inundate the struggling hospital.[16]

The causes of civilians' issues were directly related to the occupying troops of both armies. War increased the stress of North Carolina civilians and exhausted the few, essential resources that remained. Delphina Mendenhall, who lived near Jamestown, wrote that "[t]here is much suffering for bare bread in the country—women & children just ready to perish—I have very little to spare them." Mendenhall had also provided food and shelter for Union prisoners released from Salisbury prison who appeared at her doorstep. Confederate soldiers occupying her neighbor John Hiatt's farm ruined 150 acres of his wheat and oats, leaving only a dozen acres for his family to survive on. Another neighbor, Mana D. Foust, avowed that her "troubles . . . have almost pushed me into the earth." Worrying for her family made her almost manic: "I feel that I can bear but few more [trials] and but for my two unprotected daughters I would pray to be at rest, but for their sakes I try to live." Surveying the destruction wrought by both armies made their trauma understandable.[17]

15 Merrill, *The Seventieth Indiana*, 268-271.

16 Charles Harding Cox, "'?Gone for a Soldier': The Civil War Letters of Charles Harding Cox, 1862-1863," *Indiana Magazine of History* (March 1972), 68/1:236-237; Merrill, *The Seventieth Indiana*, 270-271; Statement of Mrs. T. F. Maguire, 1940, Allston Lavender Papers, NCDAH.

17 Abbie Rogers, "Confederates and Quakers: The Shared Wartime Experience," *Quaker History* (Fall 2010), 99:2, 5; Mary A. Browning, *Remembering Old Jamestown: A Look Back at the Other South* (Charleston, SC, 2008), 116; Letter from Delphina E. Mendenhall to John L. Ham, February 1, 1879, Paul W. Bean Civil War Papers, University of Maine; Mana D. Foust, Letter to daughter, April 20,1865, GHM.

Union soldiers realized the extent of their destruction by riding through the army's path of the previous weeks. Oscar L. Jackson of the 63rd Ohio led a wagon train back to Goldsboro and found himself shocked at the destruction he saw. "I never before had an idea of how desolate our army leaves a country and we thought we were letting North Carolina off easy. It is terrible the wretched, suffering condition the people are in." A soldier in the 3rd Wisconsin admitted the amount of death and the destruction the Federals had inflicted on the Confederacy: "The punishment that the South has already endured is like Cain's 'greater than they can bear.' The destruction of life in this war in the South has been terrible." Many soldiers reflected on the devastation and how it made them feel, an emotion that would stay with some forever. [18]

Union officer Peter Eltinge tried to sort out his feelings about this destruction. He admitted being troubled by conflicting emotions over Lincoln's murder, and said promising news of peace had tempered his grief over the assassination. Questions swirled through his troubled thoughts, and he wondered if the traitorous South had paid a high enough price for its treason. "I begin to fear that our Government will have a disposition to be too lenient to these outlaws and traitors," he wrote. Eltinge knew he could not kill all Southerners but strongly believed they should be prosecuted, especially those who served as Confederate generals or politicians. He was convinced that fully enforcing the Emancipation Proclamation and Confiscation Act "to the letter" of the law was important. Though forgiveness reflected moral superiority, Eltinge believed a price had to be paid: "It is a very good thing for the victors to be lenient and forgiving but don't carry it to extremes."[19]

The emotions that washed over Sherman's army were intense and dangerously powerful. Captain Thomas R. Keenan of the 17th Massachusetts tried to express the intensity of the anger of the men, revealing how dangerous and ruthless hard war had made them. The magnitude of their rage, and its potential for destruction, scared him:

> [I]t is awful! I never saw such a desperate set of men in my whole life, as I see in every company. Go where you will, nothing but the most fearful curses and cries for revenge can be heard. As soon as the news reached General Sherman he moved all his army away from

---

18 David P. Jackson, ed., *The Colonel's Diary: Journals kept Before and During the Civil War by the Late Colonel Oscar L. Jackson* (Sharon, PA, 1922), 208-209; Julian W. Hinkley, *A Narrative of Service with the 3rd Wisconsin Infantry* (Madison, WS, 1912), 174.

19 Peter Eltinge to Father, April 20, 1865, Eltinge-Lord Collection, DU.

the vicinity of the city, fearing the men would break through all bounds and destroy the whole concern. It was a merciful thing, for the place is crowded with women and children. As it was, the utmost vigilance had to be used to prevent the guards themselves from firing the buildings. If Johnston had not given up as soon as he did, I actually think that our men would have attacked him without orders. Another fight would be a scene of horror. The men would not take a prisoner. You cannot begin to imagine the feeling—it is fearful.

Keenan's realization, and reaction to, the devastation that the army had unleashed disturbed him. "If fighting had continued, no one knows how it would end. Apart from the closing of the war, it is a mercy few of us yet appreciate. The South would have been deluged with blood; fire and sword would have laid a heavy mark on this once fair land. Nothing would have been left." Keenan described the anger many soldiers felt at Lincoln's death and tried to explain how the hardships of war had endeared the president to his men:

If I should speak my real feelings, I should say that I am sorry the war is ended. Pray do not think me murderous. No; but all the punishment we could inflict on the rebels would not atone for one drop of the blood so cruelly spilled. I would exterminate them, root and branch. They have often said they preferred it before subjugation, and, with the good help of God, I would give it them. I am only saying what thousands say every day. Our army is sorry that they have done their work; they have a deep-seated love for Abraham Lincoln, and when they see no chance for further chastisement of our enemy, they give vent to their feelings in other ways. I do hope you won't think me violent. I cannot help it. You, at home, little know the trials and dangers we have passed through in four years of war.[20]

Keenan's dark emotions, a product of his own violent war, shamed him: "The more I think of it the worse I grow." Like many soldiers he paid dearly for his service. Keenan enlisted in June 1861 and fought until May 1864, when he suffered a near-fatal wound at the battle of the Wilderness. He returned to service, but the trauma and physical damage never healed, and led to his early death in 1868.[21]

20 Lydia M. Post, ed., *Soldiers' Letters, from Camp, Battle-field and Prison* (New York, 1865), 466-468; *New England* [Boston] *Farmer*, November 21, 1868.

21 Thomas Kirwin and Henry Splaine, eds., *Memorial History of the Seventeenth Regiment Massachusetts Volunteer Infantry* (Salem, MA, 1911), 304-305.

April 21

Raleigh's *Daily Progress* ran the chilling notice that two black soldiers had been "shot near this City on Wednesday last for crimes the penalty for which is declared by Gen. Sherman's order to be death." Readers could infer the nature of these crimes by the punishment issued. The Union Army was forced to deal with crimes involving sexual assaults committed over the past weeks. Prosecuting the cases through courts-martial reenforced discipline and reestablished the moral line men could no longer cross, especially black soldiers.[22]

Two more black troopers were condemned for their crimes but survived. John Cornish of the 30th United States Colored Troops (USCT) was convicted of rape and sentenced to death, but President Johnson commuted his sentence, and he was freed. James Lee of the 4th USCT, also convicted of rape, survived as well. Lee deserted from his regiment in Smithfield, stole an ox, and shot at its owner. But he allegedly committed four sexual assaults, including the attempted rape of 15-year-old Alice Mitchner. Lee was convicted and condemned to hang, but the sentence was commuted to ten years in prison because the rape had not been completed.

Others in the Union ranks were put on trial for similar offences. Enoch George of the 5th Ohio Veteran Volunteers faced a speedy trial that started only 18 hours after he raped an African American woman named Nisa Grimes in Raleigh. A surgeon testified that Grimes was distressed and physically ill after the attack, which convinced officers to sentence him to life in prison for the crime. Major General Henry W. Slocum reviewed the facts and returned George to duty. Slocum noted the need to "punish all outrages" but felt the victim did "not indicate a degree of resistance on her part." Apparently, this decision was based on the fact that Grimes had drawn a bath for George before the assault. Soldiers of the 117th New York stood trial after they attacked a 16-year-old African American girl outside Wilmington. She testified that the soldiers tried to "take my maidenhood." Only one soldier, John Murray, was court-martialed, but he was acquitted in May.[23]

Perhaps the most shocking trial was that of Peter Hickey of the 3rd New York for assaulting a young boy. Hickey found 11-year-old Charles Manley and an African American companion leading an ox cart outside Raleigh. Posing as a paroled Confederate, Hickey climbed into the wagon with Manley. Two miles from

22 [Raleigh] *Daily Progress*, April 21, 1865.

23 Lowry, *Sexual Misbehavior*, 130-134.

the city, Hickey exposed himself and forced the boy to rub him. When Manley started to cry, the soldier threatened to shoot him, and then forced the boy to perform oral sex on him. Hickey was convicted, discharged from the service, and sentenced to a year in prison. Other accused soldiers were acquitted after hearsay evidence cast doubt on the victims.[24]

Sexual violence and the fear it fostered traumatized women. The constant terror of sexual assault forged a deep enmity in white women toward Union soldiers, and this grinding emotional pain sometimes erupted into angry outbursts. Orville Chamberlin of the 74th Indiana stayed at the home of Duncan McRae, a former Confederate colonel and newspaper editor. McRae treated Chamberlin civilly during his stay, but his wife despised the man. "If you or any other Yankees was lying at the point of death, and I could save your life by giving you a cup of water . . . I would not give it. I would not even give it to you to alleviate your dying agonies." After spending time with Chamberlin, Mrs. McRae approached him and revised her opinion—but only slightly. "After thinking the matter over," she told him, "I have concluded that if you were all mangled and torn to pieces by a Rebels missile, I would give you a cup of water to soothe your dying agonies, and, as you are a Yankee, I wish I had the opportunity to do so."[25]

Women also faced continued stress over their survival and that of their families. Many North Carolinians looked to the dying Confederacy for help, but found little. Just as David Swain had begged Sherman to save his livestock, Governor Vance asked Johnston for help to ease the suffering of the state's citizens. Vance urged Confederate officers to rapidly turn over "200 unserviceable animals and . . . a number of unserviceable wagon, harnesses, &c." for distribution to needy civilians. Johnston, who was struggling to take care of his starving men, refused to spare the animals. This reluctance or inability to help led desperate citizens to take matters into their own hands, which ultimately doomed the dying Confederate Army.[26]

In spite of these setbacks, Johnston continued fighting for the lives of his men. He sent orders to warehouses in South Carolina and Augusta, Georgia to forward all provisions to Greensboro. "This matter is pressing," he stressed. The next day, April 22, Johnston's hopes were dashed after he learned that paroled soldiers had

---

24 Ibid., 134-135.

25 Orville Chamberlin to Joseph Chamberlin, April 21, 1865, Joseph and Orville Chamberlain Papers, IHS.

26 OR 47/3: 820.

pillaged several of the trains heading for his army. To stretch what rations remained, the distressed general gave orders for his cavalrymen to fend for themselves off the countryside. Confederate quartermasters feverishly looked for any available rations. Johnston wrote quartermasters in Charlotte admitting that he had only four or five days' worth of food for his troops. He considered distributing government stores so the men could feed and clothe themselves but feared this would only lead to further attacks by soldiers and civilians.

If he could not give his men food Johnston hoped to provide them with anything else that could help them survive. He wrote to Secretary of War Breckinridge, asking what funds remained in the treasury to pay his men. "I have heard from several respectable persons that the Government has a large sum of gold in its possession. I respectfully and earnestly urge the appropriation of a portion of that sum to the payment of the army, as a matter of policy and justice." Thanks to Beauregard, Johnston knew the treasury was in Greensboro and that it was supposed to be given to the army in order to attend to "its most urgent wants." He reminded Breckinridge that these soldiers "have stood by their colors with a constancy unsurpassed—a constancy which enables us to be now negotiating with a reasonable hope of peace on favorable terms." Johnston believed the Confederacy owed his men *something* for their sacrifices. Payment from the remaining treasury funds would be critical to their survival.[27]

Dissemination of the details of Johnston's terms lessened the fears of Confederates remaining with the army. Major General Robert F. Hoke returned to his command and shared the specifics of the surrender proposal in hopes of easing his men's duress. Soldiers feared they would be exiled, imprisoned, or possibly executed by a vengeful North; but hearing the particulars left men relieved, if not hopeful, that all had not been lost in the war. General Johnson Hagood recorded in his diary the terms, as he understood them: take an oath, march home under arms, and return to the rights they had before the war, including property as defined by the Constitution. Hagood took "all rights restored" to specifically mean "negro slavery untouched." Union authorities in Washington drew this same conclusion from Johnston's and Sherman's terms and were not pleased.[28]

Grant was shocked to read the Bennett farm agreement when it reached Washington. Obviously, the terms went far beyond what Sherman was authorized

---

27 Ibid., 801, 820; Johnston, *Narrative*, 408-409; Joseph E. Johnston, "My Negotiations with General Sherman," *The North American Review* (August 1886), 143:192.

28 Hagood, *Memoirs*, 370.

to offer. Grant reluctantly recommended to Secretary of War Edwin M. Stanton that he assemble the cabinet to review the terms. Each line was read aloud, the anger among the cabinet members rising with each sentence. President Johnson and others asked by what authority Sherman could make such awful concessions. Some suggested Sherman's mental faculties might explain the horrible terms. A furious Stanton even questioned Sherman's loyalty as he dictated the official reply rejecting the terms and ordering Grant to Raleigh to take over negotiations. Soldiers on both sides and civilians caught in the middle were about the have their hopes and emotions whipsawed once again, making another painful memory.[29]

April 22

The Carolina sky slowly dawned upon anxious Confederates who had spent a long, worrisome night contemplating their fate. They had distracted themselves by visiting friends, exchanging addresses, signing autograph books, and discussing the return home. One distraught Rebel remembered the demoralized state of the army, with "[d]iscipline very loose. . . . Everyone doing pretty much as he pleases." Men seized upon every hopeful rumor. In fact, "rumor yet walks majestically through the army," one South Carolina soldier observed; "Plenty of grapevine [rumors] afloat but nothing reliable, but it serves to make the men worse and worse." These rumors took their mental toll on the men, who sought any distraction.[30]

Wade Hampton's troopers used the racetrack next to their camps outside Hillsborough to hold a "tournament," which drew women from far and near to watch them joust. Lieutenant Colonel Waring, however, could not enjoy the strange festivities. "I am glad the men can enjoy themselves," he wrote, "[b]ut my heart was too sad to enjoy anything. It looked so like mockery." For some, distraction from the painful reality provided the best tonic, but clearly, the army was dying.[31]

Some soldiers refused to admit the war was over; defeat had negated everything they believed about themselves. None took defeat harder than the members of the Southern elite who filled the officer ranks of the Confederate Army, who had the most to lose. Surrender meant the loss of status, power, and

---

29 OR 47/3:263.

30 Foster and Brown, eds., *One of Cleburne's Command*, 164; Dunkerly, *The Confederate Surrender*, 60, 91, 96.

31 Waring Diary, SHC/UNC, 39.

wealth, while ideals of self, community, and faith were called into question. It was a future General Hampton refused to consider. He fired off a dispatch to President Davis warning of the horrible fate awaiting them: "A return to the Union will bring all the horrors of war, coupled with all the degradation that can be inflicted upon a conquered people. We shall be drawn into war with Europe, and under a rigorous conscription we shall, alongside of our own negroes, be forced to fight for the Yankees under Yankee officers." Hampton admitted he could not abide by the surrender and would seek a way to go to Texas or Mexico. He started making plans to escape from Johnston's army and keep the war alive.[32]

Thousands of men agonized over what course of action to take. Rumors that several brigades in Hoke's division were contemplating desertion reached Lt. Col. James H. Rion, who quickly conferred with his fellow officers and compiled a circular that reaffirmed that the soldiers' duty was to stay with the army until the end. Men gathered around Rion's headquarters and he addressed them at length. He began by sharing what he knew of the surrender terms. Their desertion, he told them, would not only be a violation of the signed agreement but would also compromise their commander, their personal safety, and, above all, their honor. Rion's words won over many officers, but his troops continued to melt away in increasing numbers.[33]

The disintegration of the Army of Tennessee was obvious as Rebel soldiers continued streaming into Greensboro looking for provisions and answers. "In little, sad groups," one chaplain observed, "they softly talked of the past, present and the future." Captain Nicholas Schenck noted the torturous decision they faced: "That ugly future torturing men's minds had motivated them to leave before the final terms were approved." None knew if they would be sent to Yankee prisons like Point Lookout, Johnson Island, Elmira, or other "Death Hotels." Schenck believed it was better to die fighting than endure the horrors of prison life, "scant food," the "death line," and "freezing to death"—the fate of thousands of captives.[34]

Broken-hearted, heavy-spirited Confederates continued to flood roads that led away from Johnston's camps. While taking a rest near Salisbury, Arthur Ford recognized President Davis in an approaching party. Ironically, Ford and his comrades had hijacked the president's train days earlier. "He was sitting gracefully

32 OR 47/3:829-830.

33 Hagood, *Memoirs*, 370.

34 Schenck, "Reminiscences," 41.

erect on his horse, and courteously returned our salutes," Ford remembered. As the party clopped across the wooden bridge over the Yadkin River, a captain from Davis's escort rode up and asked the group "if we were willing to go on across the Mississippi and continue the war there?" Ford and others volunteered, but of course "we heard nothing more of it."[35]

Veterans trying to make sense of the war also began assigning blame for defeat. M. J. Tolly of the 24th Alabama wrote of his sadness: "When I think of the many noble soldiers that has been slane and for nothing . . . and who was the cause of it skulkers Cowards extortioners and Deserters not the Yankees that make it woss [worse]." Major George P. Collins blamed the people for not supporting the soldiers: "Everything seems to indicate a speedy termination of the Confederacy & a restoration to the old state of affairs which though it is very humiliating to us still has its pleasant features—everyone is worn out with war, & I am almost inclined to believe that our people scarcely deserve freedoms as they would stand up better." Still others in the Confederacy blamed the Army of Tennessee for the defeat. John Kennedy Coleman passed through Greensboro after his parole from Lee's army and directed his anger toward the western soldiers. "They will [surrender] in a few days. If they had done their duty, how much better off we would have been[.] They are undoubtedly all to be blamed for it all."[36]

As the army waited to hear about the final terms, the crisis of dwindling rations grew dire. Dispatches reached Johnston's headquarters concerning the lack of transportation needed to deliver what little food remained. The commander sent an uncharacteristically angry message to the supply train's commander in Augusta: "You will starve us if you don't get the wagons back immediately. Use all dispatch to do this, and do not move them again without orders[.] Bring supplies across country as rapidly and regularly as possible. You should have reported immediately on withdrawing the wagons. Time is important." Adding to Johnston's misery was the destruction of the Catawba River bridge, which had further hampered rapid delivery of food. He ordered his pontoons north from Chester, South Carolina, to the site of the burned bridge, hoping to ensure that provisions reached his starving

35 John William Jones, *Christ in the Camp: or, Religion in the Confederate Army* (Atlanta, 1904), 596; Ford and Ford, *Life in the Confederate Army*, 65.

36 A. D. Betts, *Experience of a Confederate Chaplain, 1861-1864* (Greenville, SC, 1900), 78; J. M. J. Tolly to James A. Hall, April 22, 1865, Bolling Hall Family Papers, ADAH; George P. Collins to Anne Cameron Collins, April 22, 1865, SHC/UNC; John Kennedy Coleman Diary, USC.

army. This lack of food and supplies forced an increasingly unstable army to live off civilian farms, which were facing their own dire shortages.[37]

Rural neighborhoods were on high alert for days after passing Confederates soldiers plundered several homes, and again after the XIV Corps arrived. Nervous and anxiety-ridden families spent hours hiding food, livestock, and valuables. Reverend Johnson Olive recalled that when Union soldiers finally came, men filled his home from sunrise to sunset, "taking everything they desired, from a common brass pin to a horse or wagon, plundering most uncivilly every drawer, private room and outhouse all through the live long day, killing fine cattle (sometimes for a mess of steak), and leaving the remainder to waste. . . . Such are some of the hardships of cruel war."[38]

In one of Olive's congregations, Mt. Pisgah Baptist Church, Deacon P. H. McDade recorded church business in the minute books. His simple inscription relating the state of earthly and spiritual affairs seemed out of place in the records. "Owing to the two contending armies passing through the neighborhood about this time there was no conference held for this month. The four years of bloody war between the North and South have closed to the defeat of the South, and as Christians we will still say, let the will of the Lord be done."[39]

The daily religious services in the Union camps continued to grow and gain converts. J. F. Culver and others, hoping to share religion's ability to absolve and inspire, formed a brigade church. The previous week, the congregation had numbered 160 souls, including eight who joined in Goldsboro. The message of divine guidance and forgiveness continued draw men to the sermons. Culver kept his family informed: "Everything bears the impress of the Holy Sabbath. We had an excellent meeting this morning. Genl. Class at 9-1/2 & preaching at 10-1/2." Five days later the soldiers' church had grown to 195 members, with "ten joined to-day." Culver surmised that the church played an important role in helping the men grieve over Lincoln. Ohioan Bliss Morse confirmed to his diary the poignant

---

37 *OR* 47/3:829-830.

38 Johnson Olive, *One of the Wonders of the Age; or The Life and Times of Rev. Johnson Olive* (Raleigh, NC, 1886), 236.

39 Mt. Pisgah Baptist Church Records, Z. Smith Reynolds Library Special Collections and Archives, WFU.

sermon and its attempt to assuage the men's sorrow. "Chaplin Morton preached a discourse concerning President Lincoln. Text, 'A great prince has fallen.'"[40]

The increased interest in religion and the prospect of peace notwithstanding, the anger of some Union soldiers kept the hard war alive. General O. O. Howard learned of soldiers committing "crimes of a heinous character" in the town of Franklinton, north of Raleigh. Howard immediately blamed his men and issued Special Order No. 97, authorizing a detachment to the area to arrest all men who were there without written authority. He also called on civilians to help them in capturing the marauders, whom he termed a "disgrace to our army and our country." John A. Logan also issued orders for a shakedown inspection to find and confiscate loot taken during the march. A day later the patrol confirmed that bummers were responsible for the attacks on civilians. Despite Howard's orders specifically curtailing the foragers, the patrol's report noted that "men belonging to authorized foraging parties" had perpetrated "many of the outrages."[41]

Soldiers in both armies spent long hours lost in thought. For the first time since their war began, they let themselves think about surviving and going home alive, an important emotional step in deconstructing their soldier selves. Most hardened men on both sides found this transition especially difficult. Changing this mindset meant breaking down the emotional walls they had built, and this left men vulnerable and exposed. News that would disturb this process and jolt them back into their hardened casts was heading to North Carolina from Washington.

April 23

The prospect of peace and the beauty of the Carolina spring enlivened the spirits of many Federal soldiers on the morning of April 23. Soldiers found themselves moved by the rebirth of trees from their winter slumber and the invigorating sounds of nature that surrounded them. "The morning of the 23d dawned with all the beauty God could bestow. The mocking bird sang in the tree tops, and not a sound was heard save the singing of the birds, and the merry laugh of a joyful soldier," wrote Henry Morhous of the 123rd New York. J. F. Culver woke to the same symphony. "The first sound that greeted my ear on awakening this morning was the sweet warbling of a bird. I heard several sing very sweetly this

---

40 Culver, Culver, Dunlap, and Bearss, *Your Affectionate Husband*, 435; Morse, *Civil War Diary*, 199-200; Jamison, *Recollections*, 328.

41 *OR* 47/3:280-281, 288.

morning. During the few years of war, the birds have been very scarce [near] the Army, at least, & to hear them again is a great treat." It seemed to some soldiers as if Mother Nature had blessed the fruits of their labor. The serene moment led Culver to confess, "It seems as if the war was over."[42]

Culver and other soldiers turned their anger toward Northern traitors as the final triumph over the Rebels neared. He believed rumors that Confederate sympathizers in the North had been accomplices in Lincoln's assassination. The usually restrained Culver ominously predicted that after four years of "honorable warfare" traitors remained, and that Sherman's army would fix things upon its return. "[M]any innocent will doubtless suffer with the guilty. But the issue must be met, & the Army is preparing for it." Sherman's men especially hated "Copperheads," Northerners who openly sympathized with the South. Rumors circulated that they could be responsible for the long delay in approving the surrender terms. As they waited, soldier's thoughts turned to home and they considered what their return would entail.[43]

Union chaplain William Hyde noticed an uneasiness in himself and in the men, who could not understand the lengthy surrender process. With peace so close and home within reach, each passing hour seemed ominous. "I never was so restless myself and never saw the regiment so restless as they are now," Hyde told his wife. As peace approached, soldiers and civilians began considering what shape the new nation would take under the reins of Andrew Johnson. Many feared the new president was unsuited for the delicate and mammoth task at hand. According to one Federal, "Considerable anxiety prevails in the army for the administration of Pres. Johnson. He is deemed as too passionate dissipated and unstable for so responsible a position at such a critical a period." Harvey Reid of Wisconsin also bemoaned the situation: "Every man felt that he had lost a dear personal friend, while another depressing feeling is an utter want of confidence in that poor drunken wreck, Andrew Johnson. We fear that he may yet tear open anew the breach that Abraham Lincoln's honest sincerity and real kindness was fast healing." Grief still hung heavy over the army and filled men's thoughts, diaries, and letters home. W. B. Emmons recalled comrades who "deeply felt" Lincoln's death:

---

42 Henry C. Morhous, *Reminiscences of the 123d Regiment, N.Y.S.V., Giving a Complete History of Its Three Years' Service in the War* (Greenwich, NY, 1879), 179; Culver, Culver, Dunlap, and Bearss, *Your Affectionate Husband*, 439.

43 Culver to wife, April 23, 1865, UI.

[A]ll praise him; all regret the loss of what is considered to have been the strongest pillar & brightest ornament in the temple of American fame and patriotism. Deep are the curses that men utter against the wretch that murdered our Commander in Chief. But we hope & firmly believe that our great loss was his great gain. He has gone to a far better world where no fiend can steal his great life from him again & cause angels to weep at the loss, as men now do.

Citizens could clearly see and feel the discontent of the soldiers, and they were careful to avoid any comments or actions that would upset the emotional men. A stream of nervous locals overcame their fear and poured into the capital, hoping to find a horse or mule to help them plant a spring crop. But even if they were lucky enough to find one, it was often a substandard animal unfit for the critical duty required of it. The effects of sustained foraging by both armies were having a devastating effect on civilians, and scores had been forced to go to Raleigh in search of food. Captain James L. Burkhalter wrote that he had "been troubled a great deal with repentant citizens who are constantly hovering about headquarters for begging purposes." The question of food, not to mention their overall safety, also gnawed at the minds of residents who had good reasons to be uneasy.[44]

Lieutenant William Collin Stevens of the 9th Michigan Cavalry related a tragic incident involving a new recruit, Henry Anderson, who was court-martialed for "murdering a citizen" and sentenced to be shot. As he wrote, Stevens listened to the firing squad practicing their deadly task. Anderson and two other soldiers had been out in the countryside and got drunk. Meeting two citizens in a buggy, Anderson demanded their money. When they refused, Anderson shot one while the other escaped into the woods. Stevens recounted the scene of the execution, at which the condemned man warned his comrades of alcohol's dangers. It was a vice that affected the enlisted men as well as the officers. Eventually the rising frustrations of officers in the 9th Michigan Cavalry boiled over and they met to draw up a set of resolutions accusing their commander, Col. George S. Acker, of severe intemperance. To the disgust of his staff, Acker was on a bender while in Chapel Hill. The men drafted a letter "earnestly requesting him to abstain from the use of intoxicating liquor," and if that were too much for him to do, then they encouraged him to "resign his commission." When the letter was delivered, Acker

44 Charles S. Spencer Collection, April 23, 1865, SHSW; Burkhalter Diary, April 23, 1865, KCA; Harvey Reid, *The View from Headquarters: Civil War Letters of Harvey Reid* (Madison, WI, 1965), 243; W. B. Emmonds, Diary, April 23, 1865, UI.

was drunk, and charges eventually were proffered against him.[45] Alcohol threatened to destroy the discipline Sherman hoped to rebuild in his men.

Johnston also struggled to maintain the rapidly deteriorating discipline of his men, but the idea of defeat made this endeavor impossible. Hardee's corps received orders to move that morning and marched nine miles toward Greensboro, but the breakdown of discipline in its depleted ranks hampered the movement. Desertion in the camp had been endemic. One Confederate noted the collapse: "Seven men of the Seventh battalion and fifteen men of the Twenty-seventh regiment left for home yesterday and today. The division is being rapidly reduced in this way. They are going in large bodies and at all hours without an effort being made to stop them." General Laurence S. Baker's command continued to unravel, causing deep emotions to cascade from the men. "I started to cry," Henry Webb admitted:

> I was more than ever saddened to part with them, for not only were they the most estimable & good boys & pleasant company but they were the last links in the chain which bound me to my late company. We shall never[,] never all meet again this side of eternity. Oh sad, sad reflection. My brave, my excellent men. You know not, nor ever will, how much your Caption has loved you.[46]

Some commanders tried shore up their men's shaky nerves by trying to reinforce military discipline and keep their units together. These attempts were seen as ludicrous to many who considered the army practically finished. Outside Maj. Gen. William B. Bate's headquarters, a group of officers observed a commander drilling his division as if the war were just starting. "Who is that fool officer?" one asked. The effort to reinstall military bearing on demoralized men had little success. For some soldiers their psychological state interfered with their ability to comply. One soldier who showed signs of mental collapse was Neal Story, who enlisted as a teenager in the 46th Georgia in August 1863. A month later the young soldier found himself embroiled in combat at the battle of Chickamauga and it quickly took its toll on him. Soldiers noted Story developed "peculiar" behaviors. When he returned home after the war and tried to return to normal life, he could not do so. By 1872, he had grown violent and threatened to kill his family members and burn down their house. Story's family built a log cabin expressly to confine

---

45 William C. Stevens to father, May 13, 1865, W. C. Stevens Papers, UM.

46 Lewis Henry Webb, Diary, April 23, 1865, Webb Papers, SHC/UNC; OR 47/1:1083-1084; Hagood, *Memoirs*, 370.

him, which failed. Listless and lethargic, Story died in the Georgia lunatic asylum in Milledgeville.[47]

As Story lay down for a troubled sleep that night, he had no way of knowing events soon would add to his unbalanced state of mind. A dispatch arrived at Sherman's Raleigh headquarters announcing Maj. Henry Hitchcock's arrival in Wilmington with the administration's reply to the Bennett Place agreement. The note informed the commander that Hitchcock would be at his headquarters in the morning. What the dispatch did not mention was Hitchcock's traveling companion, Ulysses S. Grant, who was along to personally bring the bad news to Sherman of his terms' rejection.[48] This news would create a dangerous crisis for soldiers and civilians who were already contemplating peace. The resumption of hostilities amid the emotional storm that swept through both armies threatened to take the war to tragic depths heretofore unexperienced.

April 24

Union soldier George W. Whetstine missed morning roll call. When his messmates could not find him, they formed a search party and soon discovered him dead. Whetstine, who had been drafted into the 33rd Indiana, suffered greatly during his short time in war. Sent to North Carolina, he had to leave his wife and three children in Morgan County, Ohio. He arrived in Goldsboro on April 9, the day before the campaign began. Separation from his family and being thrust into the harsh world of hardened soldiers was evidently unbearable for him. Comrades remember Whetstine complaining of a headache the previous evening; nothing else seemed concerning, but something happened during the night that led him to take his own life. He took off his suspenders and threaded the end through the buttonhole to make a noose and ended his life. It was nine days past his thirtieth birthday.[49]

As Whetstine's comrades tried to make sense of his death, Hitchcock and Grant arrived at Sherman's headquarters in Raleigh. Sherman was shocked but pleased to see his old friend, but his mood quickly changed. The generals found a secluded room in the Governor's Palace, where Grant showed Sherman the official

---

47 Guild, *Narrative of the Fourth Tennessee*, 147; Diane Miller Sommerville, *Aberration of Mind: Suicide and Suffering in the Civil War-Era South* (Chapel Hill, NC, 2018), 155.

48 *OR* 47/3:287.

49 McBride, *History of the Thirty-third Indiana*, 236-237.

George W. Whetstine hoped to avoid the war but found himself drafted in the winter of 1865. He was torn away from his family and sent to join Sherman's army in North Carolina. His comrades noted that Whetstine struggled and brooded over army life. On April 23 he complained of a headache and went to bed. During the night he strangled himself with his suspenders. *James C. Murphy, descendant*

rejection and explained the cabinet's reasoning. Sherman was badly shaken by the egregious reaction of the new administration. Grant pointed out that the terms Sherman had offered the Confederates went far beyond the general's authority. Unbeknownst to Sherman, anger directed at him had resulted in an order being issued for his removal. Grant kept this, as well as the directive to takeover of the negotiations, to himself. Out of respect for their close friendship, Grant advised Sherman to contact Johnston and inform him of the terms' rejection, as well as the expiration of the armistice in 48 hours. The dumbfounded Sherman, who believed he had honored Lincoln's wishes and saved the nation from further tragedy, nevertheless immediately telegraphed Kilpatrick at 6:00 a.m. and ordered him to relay two messages to Johnston. The first announced the rejection of the terms and the resumption of hostilities in 48 hours. The second demanded the Confederate army's surrender on the same terms Grant had given Lee. Next, Sherman sent out movement orders and announced a return to active operations.[50]

Sherman's unsuspecting men, of course, considered the war over and were preparing to return home. A soldier in the 2nd Iowa waxed wistfully on the feeling of victory: "the Rebellion is over and the starry Banner yet waves without a single Star being erased once more it waves triumphantly over a whole United States bidding T[r]aitors, beware how they undertake to trample upon it with impunity it now waves triumphantly over the Giant Rebellion and bids defiance to the whole

---

50 Sherman, *Memoirs*, 358-359; Cox, "Johnston-Sherman," 498-499; Ulysses S. Grant, *Personal Memoirs of U.S. Grant*, 2 vols. (New York, 1886), 2:488; OR 47/3:293-294.

world." Over the past week the emotions of Sherman's men had swung between anger and grief to happiness and relief, and they anxiously awaited news of the surrender's approval and the order to march home. The news of a resumption of hostilities came as a horrible shock to soldiers eagerly longing for peace.[51]

The news staggered men already starting their transition from soldier to civilian. Hardened soldiers who had let down their guard and allowed themselves to believe they had survived the war suddenly faced a return to combat. This shock made nightmares of the men's dreams of family and home. All the grief, rage, disappointment, and hate that boiled in their hearts spilled over. Sherman's disappointed, dejected, and furious troopers found themselves preparing to unleash an apocalypse on the enemies before them. The stage was set for true total war.[52]

Major General John A. Logan prepared to start his command in pursuit of Johnston. Officers assembled and pickets returned to their regiments. Without their guards, local families began to panic. Alarm bells rang at "Will's Forest," the Devereux home, and slaves rushed in announcing the arrival another Yankee column. Margaret Devereux hurriedly grabbed her children and headed to her bedroom. As she passed the sitting room, she met a half-dressed houseguest hysterically fleeing Union soldiers who were climbing through her window. Margaret quickly locked the door and flew upstairs. She burst into the bedroom where the refugee Burgwyn family, oblivious to what was happening, was dressing. Together they looked out of the window and saw a "sea of upturned faces; not just by the house, but away down the slope, as far as the eye could reach." They could see men climbing up the exterior of the house. As the group of terrified women huddled in the room, Anna Burgwyn's already frayed nerves snapped at the ravaging she feared was about to befall them. Rather than face horrors at the hands of the Yankees, she preferred suicide: "We can throw ourselves from the window," she whispered darkly. Their salvation came when a Union officer begrudgingly gave his word that they would not be harmed. The experience was too much for Anna's husband, Henry King Burgwyn, Sr., who had suffered a stroke that left him partially paralyzed after the death of their son, Henry, Jr., who fell while leading the 26th North Carolina at Gettysburg on July 1, 1863. The hardships of refugeeing

51 Powell Diary, DU.

52 Jennifer Cain Bohrnstedt, ed., *Soldiering with Sherman: The Civil War Letters of George F. Cram,* (DeKalb, IL, 2000), 166.

and the anxiety of occupation caused another stroke, which rendered Burgwyn unconscious. He would linger another 12 years before his death.[53]

Unlike Andrew Johnson's rejection of the surrender terms, Jefferson Davis eagerly approved of them and notified Johnston of his acceptance. The general took comfort in his belief the great conflagration would officially be over and both his men and fellow Southerners would be spared further pain. But a range of emotions roiled through Johnston's mind as he contemplated how the Confederacy's final chapter had played out. He felt he had been recalled to command to achieve the impossible against Sherman's army and was set up to suffer embarrassment as the scapegoat for surrender. Despite fulfilling his own prophecy, Johnston had demonstrated great skill in getting the best terms for his men and the rest of the South in the wake of Lincoln's murder. Most of all, he believed he had saved the nation from further suffering by ending the entire war.

Whatever calm Johnston felt was shattered when one of Hampton's horsemen dashed into his camp that afternoon with Sherman's announcements. Learning of the rejection of the terms fulfilled his prediction that Lincoln's death would prove a calamity for the South. The Confederate commander clearly saw that the North would offer his people no quarter, leaving him few options. If the armies marched again, everyone would pay a tremendous price.

Johnston dispatched couriers to General Stewart announcing the rejection and ordering preparations to march when the armistice expired at 11:00 on the morning of April 26. Dumbfounded commanders exchanged worried looks as they considered how to enforce the order; others cheered the news, which confirmed their belief that the Confederacy had not yet been beaten. Men in the ranks received the tidings with mixed emotions. Some were happy to continue fighting, but many others had accepted defeat and had already begun their own metamorphosis from battlefield to home front. To be thrust back into harm's way for what seemed a hopeless cause tore at the hearts of many of the men. "Every man had his eye turned homeward," Broomfield Ridley wrote, "and this suddenness of a proposed continuation of the struggle is more saddening than the first news of a possible surrender." William Andrews of the 1st Georgia watched the army decompose around him after hearing the news. That night he heard the tramp of men's shoes on the railroad crossties as they left the army under the cover of darkness. When tasked with forming a guard detail, Andrews found that every company in his

---

53 Devereux, *Plantation Sketches*, 165-167.

regiment refused to fall in for the duty: "the boys had decided they had done their last guard duty and stuck to it."[54]

A stunned Johnston fired off a telegram to Secretary of War Breckinridge informing him of the rejection of terms and the resumption of hostilities, and he frantically requested instructions. The general had no illusions about what renewed fighting would do to both his army and the South. He believed Sherman and his men would spare nothing and no one after Lincoln's assassination, and his own famished troops would have little sympathy for starving civilians. To avoid more suffering, he suggested to Breckinridge that he should "disband this small force to prevent devastation to the country." Johnston summoned A. P. Stewart and his lieutenants to his headquarters the following morning to discuss the decision they faced.

Late that night Johnston's telegraph jumped to life with a reply from Breckinridge that embodied the desperation felt by the fleeing Confederate cabinet. Aides handed the bleary-eyed general the message, and he grew angry with each word he read. The secretary seized on Johnston's idea to disband his force but added some caveats. He urged the general to send the infantry and artillery home, with instructions to reunite in the future. Breckinridge also suggested ordering the cavalry and a few pieces of artillery to join the cabinet heading south as protection for himself and the executive party. Breckinridge noted, "Such a force could march away from Sherman and be strong enough to encounter anything between us and the Southwest."[55]

Johnston poured indignation and disdain into his curt reply. The order was "impracticable," he told Breckinridge, and believed it to be a selfish ploy by the Confederate cabinet members to save themselves to the detriment of both civilians and the army: "We have to save the people, spare the blood of the army, and save the high civil functionaries. Your plan, I think, can only do the last." He nevertheless allowed Hampton's troublesome cavalry to join the presidential entourage, as most of it had already headed to Charlotte to do just that. Johnston also informed Breckinridge that his commanders believed their men would not fight again. Allow me to make terms for the army, Johnston entreated. In a final reply, Breckinridge ignored the issue of renegotiating and insisted on Johnston

54 Ridley, *Battles and Sketches*, 464; Andrews and McMurray, *Footprints of a Regiment*, 180-181.

55 OR 47/3: 835-837.

sending the cavalry and any man who wanted to join them. Johnston coolly agreed to forward the names of such men, but he never complied.[56]

April 25

Johnston spent a long night deep in thought, worrying about the fates of his army and the people of the South. Surveying his situation, the general found few options. With the Confederate government in flight and his army melting away, he considered how they, as well as North Carolina's civilians, would fare as Sherman's angry forces began to march. He weighed these concerns against his commitment to duty and his honor. At 11:30 a.m. Johnston wrote Breckinridge a final time, sending him just a single sentence: "I have proposed to General Sherman military negotiations in regard to this army." Major General Mathew C. Butler carried Johnston's new offer to Sherman for another meeting. But Johnston still felt he needed to negotiate and suggested only amending the agreement the two had forged on April 18, rather than Sherman's insistence on the same terms Grant gave Lee.[57]

Considering his position, it was a bold presumption, and Johnston worried that Sherman would reject the new offer. Out of caution Johnston issued movement orders for the following day; this announcement devastated men who already were struggling with the idea of defeat and survival. "The eagerness of the men to get to their homes now is beyond picture," one officer declared; "Do believe they would sacrifice everything except honor. Old Joe say continue the fight though, and his orders are the gospel of the Army of Tennessee." But even reverence for "Old Joe" could not impel traumatized men to rally to the Confederacy's dying cause. Though marching orders had arrived, wrote an officer in Hagood Johnson's South Carolina brigade, the troops were "still leaving in crowds." The Army of Tennessee had come unglued.[58]

The possible restart of hostilities also caused emotional upheaval among the Federal troops. The reaction of one soldier was simple: "[W]ithout . . . any explanation of the cause [there arose] a savage spirit." The indignation could be seen on every face and heard in every voice. "Our men could be seen and heard . . . muttering vengeance . . . on man or beast or property that should henceforth be

56 Ibid.; Johnston, *Narrative*, 411.

57 OR 47/3:836.

58 Ibid., 836-838; Ridley, *Battles and Sketches*, 464; Hagood, *Memoirs*, 371.

found in our path." George F. Cram recorded the radical shifts in his emotions in a letter home: "I have never in my life seen such intense disappointment nor experienced it," he told his family. "[J]oy was quickly changed to gloom and sorrow and a great black cloud [hung] over us all." But Johnston's request for another meeting reignited their hopes for peace.[59]

Relieved that his adversary still wanted to discuss surrender, Sherman welcomed another chance to end the war without more bloodshed or a chase across North Carolina. He agreed to meet the Confederate general at the Bennett farm the following day. Had he read Johnston's dispatch more closely, however, Sherman would have suspected their conference would not be as cut and dry as he hoped. Johnston's idea of amending the original terms sought to prevent another wave of parolees from swarming over the South, as the "disbanding of . . . Lee's army has afflicted this country with numerous bands having no means of subsistence but robbery." Despite these suggestions of "other terms," Sherman knew Johnston was right, but also realized he had no room to negotiate. Peace, and under what terms it would be made, still hung in the balance.[60]

Sherman confirmed the meeting and issued orders countermanding the movement of his agitated army. To his men, this suggested that peace might yet be possible. Washington Vasburgh of the 115th New York viewed the timeliness of the surrender proposal as beneficial to the Southern citizenry: "It is well for the people of the south that the war is so near over. For the soldiers would have but little mercy for any of them even the non-combatants."[61]

With disaster averted for the moment, the morrow's negotiations became crucial. Johnston still felt obliged to bargain for the benefit of his men and the Southern people. Sherman was barred for striking any deals and needed his foe to surrender on terms identical to those at Appomattox. Uncertainty still ruled the hour and people on all sides held their breath waiting to see what would come of this final meeting.

59 Widney and Girardi, eds., *Campaigning with Uncle Billy*, 356; Bohrnstedt, ed., *Soldering with Sherman*, 166.

60 *OR* 47/3:303-304, 312.

61 Washington Washburn to Ella, April 25, 1865, Nina Ness Collection, UM.

CHAPTER 8

April 26–30:
"The war took something of the boy out of us."

April 26

What remained of the 11th Texas Cavalry huddled around campfires outside Chapel Hill. Many in the regiment had left and those who remained sank deeper into melancholy. The quiet morning was interrupted by a joyous shout of "Apple jack!" The men hurried out from under their blankets, cups in hand, and rushed to the barrel of whiskey discovered in the underbrush. Soldiers dipped whatever was handy—cups, kettles, and buckets—into the treasured liquid and liberally passed them around. Suddenly, the pickets began firing. Not wanting to waste the glorious discovery, soldiers guzzled what they had and stumbled toward the gunfire. The command divided itself into two 50-man squadrons and deployed alongside their pickets. A heavy mounted Union force was probing the Texans' line and threatening the camp. The Rebel cavalrymen waited for the Federals to charge and emptied their revolvers into the attackers. They retired behind the second squadron in their rear. Trooper David Sadler noted the ferocity of the skirmishing: "The enemy came up vigorously, swift, and strong, in charge after charge—for we did not have to wait long for them. . . . Business was good."

The "fairly lubricated" Confederate cavalry fought hotly by forming up and repeatedly countercharging the Federals. After an hour of skirmishing the fighting diminished, and the men were awaiting the next Union charge when they heard a shout. "Hello, Johnny; don't shoot!" yelled a Yankee who stepped into the field.

"We want to make peace with you." The blue-clad soldier then asked who they were and why they were fighting so hard. "[T]he Eleventh Texas," came the retort. "We are drunk and reckless, and if you want to fight come over!" The Federal replied, "I thought there was something the matter, for we never saw you boys so lively before; go to camp, the war is over for to-day." Then he turned and disappeared into the trees.[1]

The rest of the disheartened Rebel army started its day with shock and dismay. Both officers and men were chagrined when orders arrived instructing them to move when the armistice expired. Many considered the prospect of renewing the conflict worse than surrender. "Received orders to be ready to move at that time," wrote an officer in Hagood's South Carolina brigade; but "[m]en were still leaving in crowds. Our brigade lost thirty-nine, all from the Seventh battalion." "May I ever be spared such a sight as I witnessed when the order to move was given," Hagood sadly admitted. "Whole regiments remained on the ground, refusing to obey."[2]

Few men answered the roll calls this day, and those who did slowly and painfully loaded wagons. Columns formed up for the last time and with the final "Forward, march," they left their camps. Norman Brown thought the talk of peace made it hard to go back to soldiering, but he believed discipline could be restored after a few days of "hard marching and some fighting." Rumors of another conference of the commanding generals conflicted with Brown's optimism, but he understood the importance of achieving a surrender: "our fate depends on it."[3]

Johnston once again left his headquarters in Greensboro and headed to the Bennett farm with that goal in mind. Along the way, he received troubling reports that the Union VI Corps was approaching Greensboro from Virginia. If true, the move posed a serious threat to the safety of his army. At 11:35 a.m., Johnston paused long enough in Company Shops to send a request to Sherman that should stop their advance. Johnston continued his journey, but a train accident further down the tracks threatened to derail the important rendezvous.[4]

With the armistice expired and without confirmation of a new agreement, the armies may soon have found themselves in a new death struggle if Sherman left before the meeting. Johnston fired off another dispatch, intended for immediate

1 *Charlotte* [NC] *Observer*, October 19, 1902.

2 OR 47/3:837-838; Hagood, *Memoirs*, 367-373; OR 47/1:1083-1084.

3 OR 47/1:1083-1084; Jones, *Historical Sketch of the Chatham Artillery*, 216; Foster and Brown, eds., *One of Cleburne's Command*, 168.

4 OR 47/3:313.

delivery to Sherman, announcing the delay and his intention to make the conference.[5]

At 8:00 a.m., Sherman left Raleigh and retraced his path back to Durham's Station and the Bennett farm. The vehement rejection of the terms disheartened Sherman, and the letter he had penned the previous evening to Secretary of War Stanton rattled around his mind as the train rolled along the tracks. "I admit my folly in embracing in a military convention any civil matters," Sherman wrote, "but, unfortunately, such is the nature of our situation that they seem inextricably united." The general recalled that while occupying Savannah, he thought Stanton had authorized him to "control all matters, civil and military." He expressed his belief that the Federal government had made a mistake, but acidly noted "that is none of my business—mine is a different task." Sherman ended by voicing his dissatisfaction with Stanton's backstabbing after his four years of "unremitting, and successful labor." He knew the meeting with Johnston would have to be the last, and hoped for the South, and the nation, that it would result in an agreement of peace.[6]

Fortunately, Johnston's dispatch announcing his delay reached Sherman, who then waited an hour at the Bennett home until the visibly worn general arrived. Stress was taking an obvious toll on the 58-year-old Confederate commander. Though he knew he had little to bargain with, Johnston was determined to negotiate for all he could for the sake of his men. Seated again at the Bennett family table, Sherman offered Johnston the same terms that Grant offered Lee. Johnston balked; he needed more. He explained the pending starvation of his men and the fact that some lived as far away as Texas and needed help getting home. Sherman understood his adversary's predicament and believed that closing the war without help would "drive a people into anarchy." But he also realized that his hands were tied and shied away from promising any deviations from the terms he had been authorized to offer. The generals found themselves at a foreboding impasse.

Frustrated, Sherman summoned Maj. Gen. John M. Schofield, whom he introduced as the new commander of the Department of North Carolina, to help facilitate an agreement. After listening to the generals discuss the current crisis, Schofield struggled to find a solution. Johnston exclaimed, "I think General Schofield can fix it." He explained that Sherman could not change the terms he offered, but Schofield could augment them with supplemental terms that promised

5 Ibid., 317.

6 Sherman, *Memoirs*, 362; OR 47/3:312.

rations and transportation. Sherman paced the floor considering this new proposition. At one point he stopped and asked Schofield to write down the additional terms he would dictate. Schofield did so and handed them to Sherman, who read them aloud. The supplemental terms supplied 250,000 rations and permitted use of Federal trains and boats for paroled Rebels. This kind act cemented the bond of friendship between the opposing army commanders, an affection that would last throughout the rest of their lives. With the supplemental terms finished and attached to the original ones, Sherman signed the terms and passed them across the table to Johnston. After a final glance, Johnston sighed and admitted, "I believe that this is the best we can do," and signed the surrender. As the men prepared to leave the Bennett farm, Sherman and Johnston shook hands for final time, both hoping they had finally forged a lasting peace.[7]

Sherman returned to Raleigh and showed the terms to Grant for his approval. To avoid any more political problems, Sherman insisted that Grant inscribe his approval on the document. He then turned over to Schofield the responsibility for completing the surrender and demobilization of the Rebel army. Johnston tapped Maj. Gen. Mathew C. Butler with the task of administering the appropriate paperwork for the Confederate paroles. Butler would later refer to the job as "one of the most painful duties of my life, and I never recur to it without a feeling of sadness and gloom."[8]

The news of the surrender dealt a final emotional blow to Johnston's exhausted men. One Tennessean remembered that "excitement ran high and all the first night the men moved around in great unrest." Few slept and "the only topic discussed during the night was surrender." Johnny Green told his diary, "This was the blackest day of our lives . . . [a] great gloom settled over the command; all was lost . . . there seemed to be no hope for the future." Broomfield Ridley wrote of widespread confusion and unrest; "the stern realization that we are subdued, and ruined, is upon us. The proud Southern people, all in a state of the veriest, the most sublimated sorrow." Ridley took comfort in Confucius's wisdom: "our greatest glory is not in the never falling, but in rising every time we fall." Lieutenant Edwin

---

7 Johnston, *Narrative of Military Operations*, 418; OR 47/3:334; *Military Order of the Loyal Legion of the United States, In Memoriam, Companion Lieutenant-General John McAllister Schofield* (Washington, DC.,1908), 54-55; Brooks, *Butler and His Cavalry*, 476.

8 Sherman, *Memoirs*, 363; Sparkman Diary, 17, BP; Schofield, *Forty-six Years*, 352; Brooks, *Butler and His Cavalry*, 477.

Reynolds of the 5th Tennessee vividly remembered his fellow soldiers' reactions, which had a deep impact upon him years after the war:

> I have never witnessed such a scene as that which presented itself, when it became fully known that we were to lay down our arms. All phases of human feeling were exhibited. Some raved and swore that they would never submit to it. Some paced back and forth like caged lions. Some seated themselves on logs and buried their faces in their hands. Some wept like children, and the faces of others took on a look of stolid and stoical submission, and others still looked on at this unusual exhibition of emotions with feelings of wonder and astonishment.[9]

James W. Brown tried to explain his comrades' feelings. "The report of our having to capitulate is now believed, and [there] is immense desertion to avoid the humiliation . . . men are terribly depressed, and since dark have been calling on all their comd'g officers for speeches to tell them the situation."[10]

Soldiers from Kirkland's North Carolina brigade marched to Col. John H. Nethercutt's headquarters tent for comfort and guidance. Stroking his long beard, the colonel stepped from his quarters. "[M]y Brave soldiers whom [sic] Has never turned their Backs on the Enemy in time of Battle[.] Little did I thinke that Bentonville would Be our Last Battle." But he gave his men an honorable way to escape. From his perspective, since the command had officially been part of Lee's Army of Northern Virginia, his men were at liberty to escape and make their way home or remain and possibly become prisoners.[11]

Nethercutt's talk confused Henderson Dean as he wandered back to camp. Sitting down beside an oak tree, he struggled to decide what to do. He opted to run after an officer told him that the plank road from Greensboro to Fayetteville was open, and that a determined party could get around Sherman's army. Dean quickly hid his Springfield musket and cartridge box under the bottom rail of a fence and headed home.[12]

9 Brooks, *Butler and His Cavalry*, 476-477; Worsham, *The Old Nineteenth*, 176; McNeill, "Survey of Confederate Soldier Morale," 20; Ridley, *Battles and Sketches*, 466; Edwin Hansford Reynolds, *A History of the Henry County Commands Which Served in the Confederate Army* (Jacksonville, FL, 1904), 116.

10 Dunkerly, *The Confederate Surrender*, 90.

11 Smith, *A Charlestonian's Recollections*, 107.

12 Henderson Dean Diary, April 26, 1865, SHC/UNC.

Some soldiers, however, could not let the war go. Texans and Arkansans of Harrison's Brigade decided not to surrender and pledged to fight on with Kirby Smith's army west of the Mississippi River. As they parted, the troopers appealed to their counterparts in the 4th Tennessee Cavalry to join them. Lieutenant James M. Hough and the skeletal remains of the 6th South Carolina Cavalry agonized over the decision but ultimately chose to ride away with the horsemen. Lieutenant Colonel William Stokes dismissed the troopers of the 4th South Carolina Cavalry to return home rather than "go through the formality of surrendering."[13]

The Union Army erupted in jubilation when Sherman returned to Raleigh. The news of final surrender overwhelmed the ranks. Upon lining up and hearing the good news from Bvt. Maj. Gen. John E. Smith, the "whole army went wild with rejoicing." John C. Arbuckle remembered that "flags and banners were all unfurled; the drum corps were called out; guns fired; bonfires were kindled," and "it was a night never to be forgotten; not until the small hours of the morning did we lie down to dreams and sweet sleep." Moved by the moment, Smith rode down the line, hat in hand, saying, "God bless you all!" Soldiers sat down to record how the news moved their hearts. "We consider the Rebellion virtually at an end," Lucius Barber joyfully informed his diary, "and peace, sweet peace, will now fold her wings over us, and joyful shouts and anthems will ring out over all our land, welcoming back to home and friends, our country's preservers."[14]

Brigadier General Charles C. Walcutt learned the news before other Union officers who were camped further from Raleigh. Overjoyed, Walcutt ordered his brigade commanders to make as much noise as possible throughout the night. William Oake remembered, "Permission was given the troops to celebrate the event by firing all the blank cartridges we wished in honor of the occasion." Oake said the celebration lasted for hours with the night "lit up as with electricity by the rapid fire of musketry supplemented by the roar of the numerous pieces of artillery." Thousands of muskets booming guns shattered the silence of the spring evening, creating the roar of a major battle that carried 10 miles to the surprised ears of Bvt. Maj. Gen. Absalom Baird. Recognizing what he thought was the sound

13 George Guild, *A Brief Narrative of the Fourth Tennessee Cavalry Regiment, Wheeler's Corps, Army of Tennessee* (Nashville, TN, 1913), 146; Brooks and Rea, eds., *Stories of the Confederacy*, 307; Lloyd Halliburton, ed., *Saddle Soldiers: The Civil War Correspondence of General William Stokes of the 4th South Carolina Cavalry* (Orangeburg, SC, 1993), 199.

14 John C. Arbuckle, *Civil War Experiences of a Foot Soldier Who Marched With Sherman* (Columbus, OH, 1930), 153-154; Brown, *History of the Fourth Regiment*, 409; Lucius W. Barber, *Army Memoirs of Lucius W. Barber, Company "D", 15th Illinois Volunteer Infantry* (Chicago, 1894), 205.

of battle, he frantically dispatched two brigades to help while the third started building breastworks. After marching three miles, a jubilant soldier from Walcutt's command met Baird's column and explained the commotion. The false alarm angered Baird and "for a time the air was sulphurous" with curses, but the ensuing celebration quickly tempered the general's ill demeanor.[15]

Surgeon John Bennett of the 19th Michigan sat down to write to his wife and weighed the Federal victory against its sinful cost. "God leads us in a way we know not, and I feel and know that all will be for the best—that He will make this affliction work out good for this nation." Bennett admitted, "We have been very wicked and *would* not see our own national and individual depravity and wickedness till God should by chastisement remind us that Sin bringeth sorrow and woe." For Bennett that sin was the existence of slavery. His experiences in the South had changed his view of African Americans. He now considered them an ascending race, loyal to the nation, that would soon "be much more intelligent and learned than the present generation of whites." For Bennett the weight of the sin slavery had wrought suggested that "history has shown the Black race at times superior. Why not again? Especially if we sin so deeply toward them, God will cast us down and raise them up." J. F. Culver realized the prohibitive cost the South had paid for secession and the war. "I begin to think we have accomplished much more than we ever anticipated in this war, i.e., the subjugation of the South. Their spirit is certainly broken."[16]

Moved by the emotion of the moment signal officer Lt. George Round crawled up the stairs to the roof of the capitol. From his signal post high above Raleigh, Round watched as tens of thousands of men celebrated, listened to the myriad of bands playing, and heard endless cheers of joy. Round knew the concert was coming to its end with the opening sad notes of "Home, Sweet Home." The melancholy song that reflected the deep sadness of homesick soldiers like no other had become popular with the armies of both sides. Shrill bugles followed echoing "Taps" from one camp to another, marking the close of another day and the end of war.

Stirred by the magnitude of his emotions, and of those that swirled around him, Lieutenant Round sought permission around 11:00 p.m. to fire off his rockets.

---

15 Oake, *On the Skirmish Line*, 319; Calkins, *The History of the One Hundred and Fourth*, 317.

16 John Bennitt, *I Hope to Do My Country Service: The Civil War Letters of John Bennitt, M.D., Surgeon, 19th Michigan Infantry* (Detroit, 2005), 368-369; Culver, Culver, Dunlap, and Bearss, *Your Affectionate Husband*, 440-442.

"They were of beautiful colors, some of them changing many times as they floated in mid-heaven" wrote a soldier gazing skyward. The rockets revealed the first word of Round's message "P-E-A-C-E." Round reached down to light another rocket and continue his message when it ignited and shot up, "casting its hot and hellish blast of cinders and flame full into my upturned face." The shock of the blast blew him backward and through the glass top of the rotunda, and the thin wire screen strung beneath the rotunda was all that saved him. After a quick self-check revealed only a burnt face and some singed hair, Round, "resembling a boiled lobster," continued firing his rockets. Despite his pain the message he felt compelled to send captured the relief felt by men in the army. "Peace on earth, good will to men."[17]

April 27

Ringing church bells broke Raleigh's morning silence and greeted the first sunrise without war in four years. Union soldiers breathed the cool air with new vigor and envisioned their return home. With the sweet echo of birds singing amid the chimes, the morning seemed much more beautiful than any other to George Cram. "I never heard them sing so sweetly, and never saw them flit about so merrily. The green ground in which we are camped had a peculiar beauty and freshness and as the sun rose above the city steeple it seemed as if we could float right up with it." With the dawn of peace, soldiers grasped the fact that they had survived. "The great American insurrection is now a matter for history to deal with," Thomas Osborn confided to his diary. Harrison Randall of the 100th Ohio wrote joyfully to his father, "Oh is it not glorious news to the army and their friends[?] I saw this news in an extra published here in this town we have been looking for it a long time and at last it has come[.] Hurrah Hurrah now what do you think of it and I am here just where it is ended[;] little did I think I should be so near the closeing scene as I was but so it is[.]"[18]

Grant bade farewell to Sherman and left Raleigh with the revised surrender terms in hand. En route to Washington, he stopped in Goldsboro, where he saw copies of the latest newspapers brimming with outrage over Sherman's original terms with Johnston. Grant knew this angry criticism would hurt Sherman and felt for his old friend, "I fully realized what great indignation they would cause him."

17 [Washington, DC] *National Tribune*, July 23, 1903.

18 Bohrnstedt, ed., *Soldiering with Sherman*, 166; Osborn, *The Fiery Trail*, 218; H. E. Randall to Father, April 27, 1865, UND.

He sympathized with Sherman's emotional state and regretted the agitation it would cause: "I do not think his feelings could have been more excited than were my own."[19]

Sherman spent the day preparing to leave the army for Charleston, South Carolina. The general urged his officers to take great care "that all the stipulations on our part be fulfilled with the most scrupulous fidelity, whilst those imposed on our hitherto enemies be received in a sprit becoming a braver and generous army." Sherman made good on his promise to David Swain and gave his commanders the option to loan spare horses, mules, or equipment to needy civilians so as to encourage "friendship among our fellow citizens and countrymen." General Orders No. 31 reiterated the olive branch, announcing the end of the war and halting foraging, except under necessity, upon which compensation would be paid. It also urged ex-Confederate soldiers and civilians to work together to bind up the nation's wounds.[20]

Sherman also issued Field Order No. 65, officially announcing the suspension of hostilities in the Eastern Theater. He sent a copy of the order to Johnston along with a letter that both underscored his benevolence and issued a warning. Sherman reiterated his orders to his subordinates, fulfilling what both generals desired: "the return to their homes of the officers and men composing your army." He restated his pledge to help rebuild the war-torn nation. "Now that war is over, I am as willing to risk my person and reputation as heretofore, to heal the wounds made by the past war, and I think my feeling is shared by the whole army." But Sherman also predicted violence as the South adjusted to their new world, speculating that it would be produced by some "unthinking young men" and warning that "if forced to deal with them, it must be severely."[21]

Schofield issued his own order announcing of the end of hostilities and pledged rations and animals for those in need. But he omitted one important point; this forced the immediate issue of General Order No. 32, which clearly declared slavery dead, adding that "all persons in this State heretofore held as slaves are now free." Schofield recommended that white Southerners hire their former slaves at reasonable wages, and urged freedmen to stay on their farms and "labor faithfully so long as they shall be kindly treated and paid reasonable wages." But he ended his

---

19 Grant, *Personal Memoirs*, 488.

20 OR 47/3:330.

21 Ibid., 322; Cox, "Sherman-Johnston," 501.

order warning freedmen not to gather in towns or around military camps, and he assured whites that "they will not be supported in idleness."[22]

For the 8th Indiana Cavalry the horrors of war had not yet ended. Gruesome accounts reached them as they marched back toward Raleigh from Durham Station. The unit had seen its ranks swell with new recruits and convalescent soldiers. One of the returnees was Joshua H. Waddell, a former prisoner in the Confederate prison camp in Andersonville, Georgia, who had escaped and made his way back to his regiment. Waddell recounted the unearthly horrors of the prison and showed his comrades his scars on his legs, which had been torn by the teeth of bloodhounds. He described his experience as a fate worse than death, with the suffering of the prisoners as "beyond human description." Hearing of the tortures at Andersonville stoked the fires of hate in the soldiers, leaving them even more emotionally conflicted as the war approached its final days. The joy of returning home was tempered by anticipating the painful experience of talking to families of the dead, which meant reliving horrible events. "How many would enquire at home," asked returning Capt. John H. Otto of the 21st Wisconsin, "after father, husband, brother or sweetheart: how they died, and where they rested?"[23]

Sherman's men turned their eyes homeward once again and prepared to march to Washington D.C. Some portions of the Union Army would remain in the South to keep the peace during reunification. The X Corps, XXIII Corps, and portions of Kilpatrick's cavalry faced the daunting task of establishing and maintaining order. This duty further aggravated the strained nerves of the men. One of these regiments, the 203rd Pennsylvania, was recruited in late September 1864 and sent south in January 1865 to take part in the attack on Wilmington's Fort Fisher. The regiment rendered short but fierce service. Twenty-one-year-old immigrant Augustus Grosch served with the regiment until mustering out in June, after which he returned to Pennsylvania and tried to pick up his life. Unable to work, Grosch became increasingly despondent over the ensuing years. On the morning of November 22, 1888, he walked into the alley behind his house and hanged himself with a rope from a child's swing. He stuck a brief note in his house's keyhole: "I am

22 Schofield, *Forty-six Years*, 368; OR 47/3:331.

23 Williamson D. Ward, Diary, April 27, 1865, IHS; Gould and Kennedy, *Memoirs of a Dutch Mudsill*, 364.

tired of living . . . Don't take me into your house. Let the city officers take charge of me. From your crazy uncle."[24]

Oliver O. Howard, still concerned about the conduct of his men even with peace restored, issued Special Field Orders No. 102 to his Army of the Tennessee as they prepared for the march home. The order halted foraging and required reimbursement for supplies taken from citizens. This entire process would be conducted under the supervision of a provost guard "selected with the greatest of care and sent ahead, so that every house may be guarded, and every possible precaution . . . taken to prevent the misconduct of any straggler or marauder." "Entering or pillaging houses" would incur "severe and immediate" punishment.[25]

Howard was facing the difficult task of turning off the war spirit he and others had fostered in the men. He stressed the new rules directly to corps commanders John Logan and Frank Blair, imploring the former to control his destructive corps. Howard wanted this movement to be "a model one for propriety of conduct, showing to our people that when there is no war we can obey the laws and respect private rights with jealous care." He warned of swift, severe punishments for infractions. The general also appealed to the troops' pride in order to hold them in check. Every officer should keep "the honor of the army at heart. . . . This army is very proud of its record. Let . . . every officer and man do his best to keep it unsullied." Minding the army's reputation required a sense of pride—a quality that some men valued but others ignored.[26]

Peace brought a consuming confusion to the Confederate camps. The nagging uncertainty wore on the men's frayed nerves, and messages from commanders seeking information about the surrender bombarded Johnston's headquarters. Johnston's adjutant, Col. Archer Anderson, snappishly responded to Maj. Gen. Robert H. Anderson, who wrote asking for news: "There has been no surrender.

---

24 *Harrisburg* [PA] *Telegraph*, November 22, 1888. Carlton Stevens of the 23rd Michigan had similar struggles. He joined the army on September 12, 1862 at age 28 with his older brother Edward. Five days before the regiment mustered out on June 22, Stevens put a bullet through his forehead. "It is generally believed he was partially deranged," another soldier observed. Wendell D. Wiltsie Diary, June 22, 1865, UI.

25 *OR* 47/3:324-325.

26 Ibid., 327. Other corps received identical orders with the same threats and appeals. Henry Slocum issued Special Order No. 57 to the Army of Georgia headquarters outlining the rules for the march north. Under pain of severe and summary punishment no soldier could enter "a dwelling or house." The order urged commanders that "every effort should be made to prevent lawless and dishonest men from bringing disgrace upon us, as we are about to return to our homes."

There has been a convention, the terms of which will be shortly announced. All private property will be respected." By 8:00 a.m. on April 27, Johnston had issued General Order No. 18, which provided details of the surrender terms and ordered the soldiers of the army to lay down their arms and cease fighting against the United States until "properly relieved from that obligation." In return, the men would not be bothered by Federal authorities. After signing paroles, they would march home under their officers with a small number of arms, and there disband. Johnston closed by trying to justify the reasons for surrendering his army. "Events in Virginia, which broke every hope of success by war, imposed on its general the duty of sparing the blood of this gallant army and saving our country from further devastation and our people from ruin." Unfortunately, in a consequential oversight, Johnston offered no guidance to his men about appropriation of rations and transportation for their return, which he had fought so hard to gain. [27]

Despite Johnston's surrender, some refused to admit the war had ended. Wade Hampton could not allow himself to honor the terms and, deciding to fall back on his exchange with Breckinridge a few days earlier, asserted that he was not included in Johnston's agreement. Hampton sent a final copy of the note to Johnston, claiming he was now under orders to join the Presidential convoy. "If I do not accompany [the president], I shall never cease to reproach myself, and if I go with him I may go under the ban of outlawery [sic]. I choose the latter, because I believe it to be my duty to do so." The question of whether to honor the terms vexed many in the cavalry. Lieutenant Colonel Joseph F. Waring and his subordinates in the Jeff Davis Legion all felt "bound in honor to take the fate of the army" and advised their men to do the same. As Hampton prepared to depart, he delivered a moving farewell address to his men that left "not a dry eye." Hampton and Johnston exchanged barbed dispatches over the former's claim of exclusion from the surrender. Hampton's flight angered Johnston, who saw it as endangering men for a futile cause and worse, personally dishonorable. Joseph Wheeler pushed for permission to follow Hampton, which Johnston peremptorily refused: "You must obey my orders, unless you have contrary orders from higher authority."[28]

The Confederates dealt with a welter of intense emotions, expressed in the thoughts of many men. "I was glad and sorry too," Carroll Henderson of the 1st Tennessee Consolidated said. "Glad the war was over and sorry we had to give it up." For others, the evening darkness cloaked their struggle with the emotions that

27 Ibid., 843-844; Jones, *Historical Sketch of the Chatham Artillery*, 219.

28 Joseph Frank Waring, Diary, SHC/UNC, 41; *OR* 47/3:845-846.

the realization of defeat wrought. Norman Brown spent "a dreadful night" with his comrades reviewing the painful past and pondering a cloudy future. The dreadful task of recounting the war and its campaigns and battles saddened him intensely. His fellow soldiers felt the same as they recounted the names of the dead and shared stories of the wounded around the campfire. "We had a dreadful night," Brown wrote, "all hands up and talking over the situation. . . . They go over the war gain, count up the killed and wounded. . . . It is too bad! If crying would have done any good, we could have cried all night."[29]

Samuel Foster echoed this sentiment: "[W]e feel relieved from war's onerous burdens and lifted by the prospect of returning home. No more picket duty, no more guard duty, no more fighting, no more war. It is all over, and we are going home." But he also struggled with more fundamental questions. "Who is to blame for all this waste of human life? It is too bad to talk about. And what does it amount to? Has there been anything gained by all this sacrifice? What were we fighting for, the principles of slavery?" In their bewildered state Foster and others clung to the tangible. Their officers reaffirmed their "undiminished confidence and esteem" for Johnston, who had showed them compassion, and expressed solidarity with his decisions—"fully sympathizing with him in the present unfortunate issue of our affairs." A trooper in the 8th Texas described the mental struggles consuming him as "the blankest part" of his life. An officer in Stewart's Corps signed his name in the back an autograph book that was making its way through his headquarters, recording their names and addresses as a memento. He added a poignant line from a poem by Ebenezer Elliott: "This day we pass beneath a portal wide, Whose opening gates reveal an unknown sphere."[30]

April 28

Presses churned throughout the night, printing thousands of paroles. Confederate officers signed for their men and took stacks of blank forms back to their commands. The paroles were one of a pair of souvenirs they would be handed to remind them of the long war. Johnston, in a final gesture toward his men's

---

29 Dunkerly, *The Confederate Surrender*, 108, 111.

30 Foster and Brown, eds., *One of Cleburne's Command*, 169; John R. Lundburg, *Granbury's Texas Brigade: Diehard Western Confederates* (Baton Rouge, 2012), 243; OR 47/3:848-849; Bradley, *This Astounding Close*, 242; George D. Wise, Diary, The North Jersey History & Genealogy Center Digital Collections, www.cdm16100.contentdm.oclc.org/digital/collection/p16100coll2, accessed September 2013.

well-being, ordered the army paid. He finally managed to obtain $39,679.96 of what remained of the Confederate treasury, most of it in Spanish silver coins. The final accounting numbered 32,174 soldiers in the Army of Tennessee; each man therefore received $1.17 as final payment for his service. Captain W. E. Stoney intended to have his silver coins made "into a medal to keep and value as received from the dying hands of my government. It is the greatest earthly satisfaction and my only consolation now, that I entered her service on the day of the inauguration of this war." Broomfield Ridley gave a dime and a nickel to his body servant and kept the rest, hoping to have them engraved as an heirloom. After receiving their few coins and paroles, "the once grand army bent their steps toward their desolate homes."[31]

A large map of the United States was tacked to a wall of Greensboro's courthouse. Men huddled around measuring the distances of their routes home with straws and sticks. Knowing that roads would be clogged with hungry men eager to eat everything they could get their hands on, many decided to break away and travel by alternative routes in hopes of surviving the journey. After their final, sad farewells, the men drifted into the woods. Some stuck together for safety; others set out alone. Companies remaining together marched off with their arms and colors. This blatant defiance could not last: many such groups disbanded within a few days.[32]

Desperate to find transportation, Capt. George Miller gathered his dismounted cavalrymen and searched for horses to ride back to Alabama. Stumbling upon a regimental commissary officer driving a six-mule team, they demanded the wagon, but the officer refused. They would have to take the horses by force if they wanted them, he said. Miller's men obliged him and cut the mules free while Miller stood by with his "hand on [his] pistol holster." With their captured mules under them, they started the long journey home.[33]

As the army disintegrated and soldiers headed west toward Charlotte, some generals feared the damage the men would cause in the city. Adjutant General Samuel Cooper worried especially about Wheeler's lawless troopers. As they approached, Cooper wrote to Wheeler in Concord and ordered him to bypass

---

31 OR 47/3:850; Hagood, *Memoirs*, 37; Ridley, *Battles and Sketches*, 460.

32 Charles W. L. Hall, *Plowshares to Bayonets in the Defense of the Heartland: A History of the 27th Regiment Mississippi Infantry, CSA* (Bloomington, IN, 2012), 80; Dickert, *History of Kershaw's Brigade*, 531.

33 Reminiscence, George Knox Miller Collection, SHC/UNC.

Charlotte. Eventually, given the cavalrymen's dire straits, Cooper relented and suggested that Wheeler allow only a few men into the city to collect provisions.[34]

Rural towns and farms braced for more suffering as parolees left the army. Civilians facing starvation already were begging Union authorities for provisions. One of Fayetteville's prominent citizens waited days to see Brig. Gen. Joseph R. Hawley to plead for rations for the 2,000 or so destitute people who had been stripped clean by the passage of armies in March. "There is undoubtedly suffering which the authorities don't know how to relieve," Hawley wrote in forwarding the petition, "and to grant these requests would have a good effect on a wide region." Good effects did come about: steamers soon brought barrels of corn meal, salt beef, bacon, flour, and hard bread to Fayetteville. A squad of Wheeler's cavalrymen did try to grab the shipment but aroused civilians, with their survival at stake, chased them off.[35]

Union soldiers noticed the spectrum of Confederates' emotions, ranging from jovial to distraught. William Bircher saw one emotionally wrecked Rebel, who seemed overcome by deep sadness. "'I reckon Sherman didn't leave us any homes to go to. What are we poor fellows going to do, going back into our country without a dollar in our pocket, our homes destroyed, stock driven away, and our families scattered, God only knows where? Oh, war! it is horrible! Horrible.' And the poor fellow cried like a child."[36]

Throughout these sufferings, Sherman continued to show compassion and urged his army to do the same. The benevolent sentiments he conveyed to his former adversary through an exchange of letters touched Johnston. Despite the ferocity of their recent history as opposing commanders, both men wanted to relieve the pain of the country and its people. "The enlarged patriotism manifested in these papers," Johnston wrote in a heartfelt reply, "reconciles me to what I had previously regarded as the misfortune of my life—that of having you to encounter in the field." Johnston knew how the vanquished had been treated in wars past. This made Sherman's benevolence meaningful and appreciated: "The enlightened and humane policy you have adopted will certainly be successful. It is fortunate for the people of North Carolina that your views are to be carried out by one so capable of appreciating them." Finally, Johnston expressed his appreciation of his former enemy's honor as a soldier. It was their common values of order, honor, and

---

34 OR 47/3:852.

35 Ibid., 343, 377.

36 William Bircher, *Diary of William Bircher, April, 1865* (St. Paul, MN, 1889), 185.

comradeship that helped shaped their understanding of national reunion. "The disposition you express to heal the wounds made by the past war has been evident to me in all our interviews." But the kindness Johnston showed Sherman would not be replicated by an angry North.[37]

In Raleigh, the caustic newspapers that Grant had read finally arrived in Raleigh and found their way into Sherman's hands, and he flew into a rage after reading Edwin Stanton's scathing criticism of his surrender terms in the *New York Times*. The paper listed all of Stanton's reasons for disapproving the terms and the even more damning truth that Grant had been ordered to take over negotiations with Johnston. The unkindest cut of all was Stanton's inference that Sherman was placating the South and that his patriotism should be questioned. Stanton went so far as to suggest that Sherman had been bribed with Confederate gold to let Jefferson Davis escape. One general delicately described Sherman's reaction as showing "that he had felt their conduct very sorely."[38]

Sherman's anger exploded that night in the Governor's Palace. Carl Schurz and twelve other generals stood mute as their commander paced the floor "with his 'excitable temper' . . . wrought up to the highest pitch of exasperation" as he expressed his disappointment "with the utmost freedom." Schurz noted Sherman's "eloquence of furious invective" and the riveted attention he received. Stanton, Sherman raged, was a "mean, scheming, vindictive politician, who made it his business to rob military men of credit earned by exposing their lives in the service of their country." He considered his critics a "mass of fools, not worth fighting for," and blasted the press as "an engine of vilification" that enjoyed "too much freedom." Maybe severe laws and punishments would curtail their vile practices Sherman angrily reckoned.[39]

Once calm enough to write, Sherman penned an angry letter to Grant. He justified his initial agreement with Johnston: it was a measure designed to avoid subjecting the people to complete lawlessness, "I did not desire to drive General Johnston's army into bands or armed men, going about without purpose, and capable only of infinite mischief." The accusation that he intentionally let Davis escape had wounded him deeply. He was astounded that his deeds, tireless service, and patriotism were being questioned. To confound the charge of being a traitor,

37 Cox, "Sherman-Johnston," 501; Bradley, *This Astounding Close*, 226; OR 47/3:336-337.

38 Cox, "Sherman-Johnston," 505.

39 Frederic Bancroft and William A. Dunning, *Reminiscences of Carl Schurz 1863-1869*, 3 vols. (New York, 1907), 3:116-17.

Sherman urged the Washington cabinet to come see what he did to the South. "I invite them to go back to Nashville and follow my path, for they will see things and hear some things that may disturb their philosophy."[40]

Sherman thought his punishment of the South proved his patriotism. If the Northern public but knew the depth of his soldiers' suffering and sacrifice, their experience reaping vengeance on the slave owners, politicians, and civilians who started the war, they would quickly realize that the price of secession had been paid in full and his reunion terms were adequate. Reminding Grant of the divide between soldier and civilian, he quipped that only ignorant men who "sleep in comfort and security" and knew nothing of the realities of war comprised the cabinet. The armies, though, knew what the battlefield looked like and the brutality men were capable of. Washington civilians could not understand the extent to which the South suffered, which made reunion, on any terms, desirable to anyone who loved the nation. If a vengeful administration believed further pain should be inflicted on the South beyond what he had already made it suffer, Sherman believed it would only deepen Southern bitterness and hamper reunification.[41]

That night Sherman's men paid him a final respectful visit to say goodbye. Thousands of soldiers strode the streets in a torchlight procession, which resulted in a nerve-fraying exhibition for Raleigh's residents. Soldier Jesse Bean remarked on the grandness of the vigil: "We had torches and the scene was beautiful to all." The nocturnal parade ended at General Howard's headquarters on the grounds of St. Mary's School. "A torch light procession and a band came into the grove and formed a circle at the front gate. The officers were sending up fire rockets at the same time," student Bessie Cain remembered. Fireworks set off across the city bathed the night sky in showers of light. The sounds of the band lofting through the dazzling spring night left Bessie momentarily conflicted between the awe of the spectacle and her bitter disillusionment; she and her friends enjoyed "this splendid, beautiful sight" with "sad, sad hearts," but despite the distraction, the reality of defeat dumbfounded her. It was a common shock across the South. "[A]fter fighting four years in a noble cause, and after gaining so many brilliant victories how we could have been defeated?"[42]

40 Sherman, *Memoirs*, 365-367.

41 Barrett, *Sherman's March Through North Carolina*, 100.

42 Jesse Bean, Diary, April 28, 1865, SHC/UNC; Bessie Cain, Diary, April 29, 1865, Bailey Papers, SMS.

April 29

Dawn brought another day of deep reflection for the defeated Confederates who struggled to make sense of the war's cost and what their future held. Campfire conversations repeated the same question: "What does it amount to?" This was uppermost in the minds of many men, especially Govan's Brigade when they gathered to receive their paroles. The unceremonious end seemed unreal; no Union soldiers were present, nor did the men formally stack arms to end their war. "We boys all walked up to the place designated," Lt. Robert M. Collins solemnly remembered and "signed some sort of a document, got our parole, and one dollar apiece in silver." Many simply left their muskets where they lay and walked out of the war. Collins boasted that he drove "his little Confederate sword out of sight into the earth" rather than surrender it, "and it is there yet if some North Carolina farmer has not plowed it up." Colonel Charles Olmstead of the 1st Georgia wrestled with a complex set of emotions. Weary of war and longing for home, mere survival uplifted his spirits, but he could not shake the reality of defeat. Thoughts of the dead haunted him: "The faces of many dear friends who laid down their lives for the Cause, were present with me too."[43]

Confederates also noticed dramatic changes in their own hearts and minds wrought by war. After days of deep reflection, Norman Brown admitted his wonder at defeat's power to reshape himself and those around him. "[M]ens minds can change so sudden, from opinions life long, to new ones a week old." He spoke to his comrades, some of whom were slave owners, and was shocked to discover their sudden realization that the institution of slavery was wrong and "for that abuse this terrible war with its results, was brought upon us as a punishment." But Brown quickly caught himself. Rereading his unguarded thoughts, he went back and scratched out "for that abuse." Brown revealed his changed mind was a product of the deep contemplation of his inner self and the dramatic changes he and others were experiencing. "These ideas come not from the Yanks or northern people but come from reflection, and reasoning among ourselves."[44]

As Johnston's army fell apart, violence threatened to erupt. Unsure of their futures, anxious soldiers demanded answers from officers who had none. Johnston finally issued an order distributing transportation among the various units, but

---

43 Foster and Brown, eds., *One of Cleburne's Command*, 171; Collins, *Chapters from the Unwritten History*, 301; Dunkerly, *Surrender at Greensboro*, 137.

44 Foster and Brown, eds., *One of Cleburne's Command*, 171.

officers found it ambiguous. General Stewart tried to clarify Johnston's explanation and quell tempers and fears, admitting that the loss of control was an "embarrassment" for his officers. "Unless the point is settled" he added, "a good deal of trouble is anticipated." Fellow corps commander Stephen D. Lee echoed Stewart's concern and confessed his own anxiety about the matter. He asked Johnston for information to pass on to his soldiers, saying that an order from the commander would help calm the men down. Lee also indicated that the spreading demoralization was rapidly eroding any remaining military discipline, and he feared for the safety of himself and his headquarters. Lawless men, he wrote, would "lay claim to everything, and it is my belief that they will strip most of the generals of their wagons." One Confederate captain simply stated that the "stern reality of accomplished defeat is upon us. Famine begins to threaten us." Johnston knew this and stressed the need for the rations that had been promised at the Bennett farm should be sent as soon as possible. Replying to Schofield's plan to bring up his men and take control over surrendered property, Johnston quietly reiterated the need for rations: "Our forces are a good deal dispersed to procure forage."[45]

Johnston believed he had fought for his men's survival at great personal cost to his honor, and he felt obliged to defend his role in the Confederacy's death in dispatches sent to the rest of the South. He penned correspondence to the governors of Georgia and South Carolina and explained that he had made his choice to spare his men more suffering, "to spare the blood of the gallant little army committed to me," as he put it, and "to prevent further sufferings of our people by the devastation and ruin inevitable from the marches of invading armies." Johnston claimed duty led him "to avoid the crime of waging a hopeless war" had compelled him to surrender. His benevolence, not his generalship, had brought him to the negotiating table. Johnston's explanations all went for naught. His self-defense proved useless once the "Lost Cause" rationalization evolved and blamed him for defeat when the fight was, in some minds, far from over.[46]

Joseph Wheeler urged his men to remain loyal to the cause and fight on. He told them he would defy the terms of the surrender and encouraged his horsemen to follow him and find Jefferson Davis's fleeing caravan. Wheeler's defiance fractured an already splintered command. About 600 men pledged to ride with him

---

45 OR 47/3:349, 853, 857; Hagood, *Memoirs*, 372.

46 OR 47/3:855. Johnston's note to Governor John Milton of Florida never made it to his hands. Milton committed suicide on April 1. Daisy Parker, "John Milton, Governor of Florida: A Loyal Confederate," *The Florida Historical Quarterly*, Vol. 20, No. 4 (1941), 361.

west, away from the crumbling army. Those staying with Johnston had little use for Wheeler and his diehards. One Georgia officer, William W. Gordon, declared, "I would not cast in my fortunes with Wheeler & his Texans, for I regarded the latter as no better than pirates." Others sneered at Wheeler for leaving the army under the guise of caring for Davis's safety.[47]

As Johnston struggled justify his actions Sherman and his staff boarded a train for Wilmington. He would not see his triumphant army again until he arrived in Washington for the grand review of the victorious Union armies in late May. Elements of army also prepared to leave for that reunion. Howard's Army of the Tennessee packed up tents, strapped on backpacks, and began its first march as victors. The reality of peace set in as men turned in all their ammunition except for five rounds. The fighting had ended, but the journey home would be emotional.

All morning long, wagons and men lurched northward accompanied by the deep echo of cannon fire; blasts were let loose every thirty minutes to honor Lincoln's memory, each one a reminder of the scars the president's death left on their hearts. Visible signs of the pain soldiers felt for Lincoln were everywhere. Sherman had ordered officers to don black armbands on their uniforms, symbols of mourning, for six months.[48]

Men of the XVII Corps soldiers noticed one huge change as they started their trek: they saw few soldiers who tried to forage on the countryside or destroy property. George P. Metz of the 99th Indiana confirmed this improved behavior in his diary: "Instead of going for chickens and Rails we had perfect order. . . no Foraging of no kind nor burning of Rails is allowed. Quartermasters are sent out and are paying cash for all."[49]

Charles Wright felt proud as he stepped off toward home. "We have the best set of men in the world," he told his diary. "When it is in order to raise h[ell] they have no equals in destructiveness and ability to hate and worry, or superiors as to fighting Rebels, but now they have none, and they are perfect lambs." The men, he observed, "don't pretend to love our 'erring brethren' yet, but no conquered foe could ask kinder treatment than all our men seem disposed to give these Rebels."

47 William C. Dodson, ed., *Campaigns of Wheeler and His Cavalry, 1862-1865* (Atlanta, 1899), 359; W. W. Gordon, Diary, Gordon Collection, SHC/UNC; Bradley, *This Astounding Close*, 224.

48 J. F. Culver to wife, April 29, 1865, UI; J. W. Gaskill, *Footprints Through Dixie: Everyday Life of The Man Under A Musket, On The Firing Line And In The Trenches, 1862-1865* (Alliance, OH, 1919), 179.

49 Geer, *Diary of Allen Morgan Geer*, 217; George Metz, Diary, April 29, 1865, George P. Metz Papers, DU.

Their exodus from North Carolina took them a step closer to family and friends and farther away from war and Lincoln's death. Now they faced a new challenge: the change from soldier back to civilian.[50]

April 30

Outside their tents along the Neuse River, the men of the XV and XVII Corps cooked bacon, brewed coffee, and enjoyed a leisurely Sunday morning. Oliver Otis Howard, a devout Christian, always rested his men on the sabbath. The pause gave them a chance to let the reality of peace to continue sinking in. Charles Wills tried to explain his conflicted feelings and the changes peace had brought about. He admitted it would take more than a mere week to adjust to no more guard duty, entrenching, skirmishing, and combat. Despite the cruelties and hardships, war had been exciting, something the civilian world could not offer. Wills admitted the dread men first felt at the charges, attacks, and the mere anticipation of battles. But they soon looked forward to war with a "feverish eagerness [a part of] (human nature)." War had supplied thrilling excitement, and now it was over. Wills felt astonished as he contemplated his experience: "It is all over, thank God, but it seems impossible."

As Wills and comrades mulled peace, a salesman bound for Raleigh with a cart of newspapers rolled into their camp. Soldiers anxiously snatched up papers and read the news, amazed to discover the details of Sherman's first armistice with Johnston and its rejection. They felt conflicted and confused about the man who led them through so much of the war. Even loyal soldiers questioned Sherman's judgment and motives. "I am very sorry for him," Wills admitted, "but we have thought for a year, and it has been common talk in the army, that he was ambitious for political honors, etc. I have often heard it said that he was figuring for popularity in the South." Reactions across the army speculated about the placations Sherman had afforded the South, especially in the shadow of Lincoln's death. The North's reaction to Sherman's terms shocked them even more. Colonel David Palmer, commander of the 25th Iowa, noted that the Northern populace was "down on Sherman, [but] I think they do not understand it at all." The army certainly still harbored love and affection for its commander. "I'd rather fight under him than Grant, and in fact if Sherman was Mahomet [Mohammed] we'd be as devoted Musselmen [Muslims] as ever followed the former prophet." Soldiers were

---

50 Wright, *Army Life of an Illinois Soldier*, 373.

yet to realize that this difference in opinion was but the first of many they espoused that put them at odds with the civilian world to which they were returning.[51]

The men of Henry Slocum's Army of Georgia prepared to start their journey home, little suspecting it would be one of the worst marches of the war. The XIV Corps mustered to received pay and mail before breaking camp. Henry F. Perry of the 38th Indiana wrote, "The 'piping times of peace' had come, and the excitement and zest of army life was gone; but thoughts of home animated every breast, and spurred the weary limb to renewed effort in the long and toilsome march." "Peace and happiness reigned over the land," noted William Bircher, and even the "song-birds in the woods seemed to know it." The soldiers, proud of their victory, sprang from their camps under flying flags and stepped off to patriotic songs. But within the ranks of the 125th Illinois was one deeply troubled soldier who felt only pain and confusion.[52]

Fellow soldiers knew war had ruined Owen Flaherty's mind. His decline began after the battle of Stones River in December 1862. Shaken by his first combat, Flaherty had requested a furlough to deal with the shock of battle. Upon its denial he grew depressed and his behavior began to change. Fellow soldier remembered he became wild eyed, nervous, and delusional. Flaherty's mental health worsened dramatically during the march through North Carolina. Just after the battle of Bentonville, he ran into camp screaming about imaginary attacking Confederates. Flaherty returned from the war into the arms of a family that soon realized his broken and violent behavior could not be controlled. With any mention of the war or army life, he would fly into a rage. During one lucid moment, Flaherty blamed "those cannon balls" when asked what caused his problems. The old soldier's delusions grew steadily wilder; his behavior forced his family to commit him to an asylum in 1876. In the years to come more of Flaherty's fellow soldiers would succumb to their own mental breakdowns and fill asylums across the country.[53]

The tents of the XX Corps disappeared rapidly from the grounds of Raleigh's insane asylum. Men lined the streets to bid their comrades farewell as they marched in lockstep cadence. One joyful Wisconsin soldier spoke for many: "They were going home—and what was meant to those campaigners by the word 'home'? It

51 David Palmer, Diary, April 30, 1865, David J. Palmer Papers, UI; Wills, *Army Life of an Illinois Soldier*, 373-374.

52 Henry Fales Perry, *History of the Thirty-eighth Regiment Indiana Volunteer Infantry* (Palo Alto, CA, 1906), 233; William Bircher, *A Drummer Boy's Diary* (St. Paul, MN, 1889), 186.

53 Dean, Shook Over Hell, 1-3.

never had a sweeter, holier significance to any mortal man than to those toilers through the swamps and forests of the Carolinas." Another echoed the exuberance of the moment: "Every step was light, and every heart beat quick at the thought of going home."[54]

But as the columns left the city and their speed increased to a breakneck pace, their victorious mood was soon tempered. The rivalry between the corps took an ugly turn after Sherman's departure. Commanders made grand wagers on which corps would make it to Washington first and the ensuing race proved to be fatal. "And as there never was a very large amount of Love between the two corps," noted a New York officer, "our Corps the 14th Determined to win the race at all hazards."[55]

Generals speculated they could march as many as 35 miles in a day, a dangerous feat made more so in the humid spring heat of the Carolina pine barrens. Men staggered under both their heavy packs and the grueling pace. Several soldiers suffered heat stroke and died of dehydration. The sight of corpses littering the route of march angered Robert Strong. "When our own boys fell down, we would pull them into the shade, pour water on their heads, and go on and leave them. We lost no men by death on this march, but we saw dead men lying in fence corners or under trees every day." To Strong, it was "simply murder." The deaths embittered him and stirred his rage long after the war was over. Officers inflicted further damage by enforcing the strict rules of the march. When several sick men fell out of the ranks, they were ordered to walk around the formation as it marched, which killed several of them. One lieutenant declared, "This brutality should be investigated," while another proclaimed, "We have never made a much harder march and some of our Generals deserve to have their necks broke for such 'Tom foolery' after the war."[56]

Five miles north from Raleigh, troops of the XIV Corps met the same newspaper wagon that the XV Corps had encountered earlier in the day. Again the men read Stanton's scalding attack on their beloved commander and were infuriated. General Slocum noticed a group of soldiers on the side of the road setting fire to the newspaperman's cart and sent a staff officer to investigate. "Tell

54 OR 47/1:745; Bryant, *History of the Third Regiment*, 330; Samuel H. Hurst, *Journal-History of the Seventy-third Ohio Volunteer Infantry* (Chillicothe, OH, 1866), 180.

55 Will to Dear Friend, May 4, 1865, Will Fisher Collection, NYSL.

56 Strong, *Yankee Private's Civil War*, 203; Metz Papers, DU; Barrett, *Sherman's March Through North Carolina*, 100.

General Slocum," came the answer from the group, "that cart is loaded with New York papers . . . filled with the vilest abuse of General Sherman." Soldiers expressed their deep devotion for their commander, "We have followed Sherman through a score of battles and through nearly two thousand miles of the enemy's country, and we do not intend to allow these vile slanders against him to be circulated among his men." Slocum thereupon approved their behavior, noting it "was the last property burned by the men of Sherman's army."[57]

After their anger subsided, the men were left confused and discouraged over what they had read. Many admitted that Uncle Billy had "put his foot in it, though he 'meant well.' A man of his character, temperament and position, given to much talking, and writing, as he always was, will do such things occasionally." Officer Peter Eltinge could not "account for this strange conduct of Gen. Sherman. He has certainly lowered himself much in the opinion of the whole Army and a majority of Loyal citizens. . . . [T]he credit and renown that he had won by his great campaign has nearly all been lost by his attempting to make himself a great Peacemaker." The unfortunate agreement with Johnston would be remembered as a defeat for a general who usually knew only victory on the battlefield, and it would leave a blot on both Sherman's reputation and the memory of his victory in North Carolina. The marching troops would experience more moments to stir deep and profound reflection as they struggled to comprehend what peace meant.[58]

Along the road, soldiers met citizens who demonstrated a Union spirit, and greeted their arrival with a powerful pulse of patriotism. The scene made many men proud; loyal Southerners acknowledging the power of the Union raised their spirits. But for some soldiers, peace, victory, and the patriotic displays failed to lessen the deep anger they felt toward the South. "Some of the boys" declared themselves sorry the war was over. "[T]hey would like to have a chance to forage." Evidently peace, victory, and liberation would take time, if ever, to soften the souls of men hardened by war.[59]

Thomas Ennis, who slipped away from the 6th Iowa's camp to inflict one last wound on the South, was one of them. Assuming the alias of John W. Dodge, he met a civilian, Richard Madden, stole his horse, and found his way to the Warren County home of Caroline T. Neal. Caroline and her mother, Mary T. Harris, stood

57 Johnson and Buel, eds., *Battles and Leaders*, 4:757.

58 Calkins, *The History of the One Hundred and Fourth*, 315; Peter Eltinge to Father, May 5, 1865, Eltinge-Lord Collection, DU.

59 James D. Crozer to family, May 2, 1865, NCDAH.

terrified when Ennis rode into their front yard. Mary begged the soldier to take pity on their poor family. Ennis, however, walked silently into the house, broke the family's shotgun hanging over the door, and demanded to know where the pistols were hidden. After determining the house was safe, he "then came out on the piazza," according to Caroline's subsequent court-martial testimony, "and said if any of us would supply him with what he wanted that would save us." They knew he wanted sex. Mrs. Harris quickly informed him she was an old woman and had a heap of kids. Turning his gaze toward Caroline, Ennis said, "if that young woman there would, it would do." Caroline protested that she was a married woman, but Ennis ignored her protests and took her by the shoulders, saying that she must come with him. The more she resisted and begged, the angrier he became. He grabbed her in a headlock and dragged her into an adjacent room, shut the windows, locked the door, and set down his gun. "He put me on the bed then and had connection with me—he came out—took up his gun and knapsack and left." Later convicted, Ennis received only two years at hard labor for the rape he had committed. Caroline Neal's encounter with the war and Union soldiers, on the other hand, forever scarred her.[60]

As Sherman's grand army marched away from war, its members experienced a dramatic realization that their soldier lives were ending. The intimate bonds with their mess mates, forged under the very worst of conditions, would soon be torn asunder. Men who once held each other's lives in their hands would soon disappear. The thought of the dissolution of their powerful brotherhood elicited a deep melancholia. "Soon, all our long and weary marches would be over, and we looked forward with joy to again see our friends [in] the North," William Royal Oake recorded. "Then again, our thought would revert back to the many bloody fields through which we had passed, and we again imagined we could see the cold and mangled remains of beloved comrades as we last saw them ere we consigned them to their last resting place."

These visions of lost friends who would never share in life's sweet rewards conflicted and haunted Oake. "As those thoughts forced themselves upon us even amidst our great joy at the thought of home and friends a great lump would arise in our throats, and it was impossible to check the falling tears." Only those who had been there could understand. As the Yankees left North Carolina they met some of their former enemies and realized these men also understood what war was. They pitied the "ragged" Rebels who "had nothing to eat and no blankets," and "invited

---

60 John Brown Papers, NCDAH; Lowry, *Sexual Misbehavior*, 134.

them to sleep with us, and at such time talked over the events of the war till far into the night. We always found these ex-rebels friendly and glad the war was over, and the parting in the morning would be like leave-taking of old friends."[61]

But unbeknownst to soldiers on both sides the worlds to which they were returning did not and could not understand or relate to the veterans. The bonds between soldiers were different and dissolution of these relationships was virtually impossible to understand. The love of families and friends could fill them to bursting, but it was not a soldier's joy. With each step closer to home men pondered what this meant and what their return to civilian life would be like. "I hope I shall be able to be home so as to help father with his work," Jabez Smith told his family, "but I don't know how farming would sute [suit] me now I haven't worked at it for so long I don't think I could content myself to settle down to farming." Simeon H. Howe wrote home expressing his pride in his army service, at the same time wondering how compatible he would be with civilian society. "I think I shall bring home a suit of Soldiers Clothes with me as I am not ashamed of Uncle Sam's clothing and I think I shall have a perfect right to wear them. So, I dont think I shall buy any citizens clothes when I come home." Charles Willison of the 76th Ohio also acknowledged his upcoming transition to civilian life and pondered how the men would weather the change. "The putting off the panoply of war to assume the garb and avocations of peace; the end of war's turmoil and excitement and settling down to the monotony of civilian life—a new start to many of us." One Union soldier spoke about the coming change in terms of removing the psychological "mask" many soldiers had created to protect themselves in war. "The Chaplin delivers a farewell address and Ritchey discards the mask he has worn during nearly three years of trials and tribulations and rejoices with comrades." Soldiers found themselves at the end of the conflict and reflected on the change they experienced and the men they had become. With their innocence long torn away, one soldier grasped the essential change he and his comrades had endured: "the grim experiences of war took something of the boy out of us."[62]

---

61 Oake, *On the Skirmish Line*, 319; Merrill, *The Seventieth Indiana Volunteer Infantry*, 271.

62 Jabez N. Smith to Mother, May 16, 1865, Jabez Smith Papers, AU; Charles A. Willison, *Reminiscences of a Boy's Service with the 76th Ohio in the 15th Army Corps, Under General Sherman, During the Civil War* (Menasha, WI, 1908), 125; Simon Howe to wife, April 8, 1865, Simon Howe Letters, MSU; Gaskill, *Footprints Through Dixie*, 183; Hosea W. Rood, *The Story of the Service of Company E, and the Twelfth Wisconsin Regiment Veteran Volunteer Infantry in the War of the Rebellion* (Milwaukee, 1893), 438.

CHAPTER 9

May 1–4:
"It was impossible to check the falling tears."

May 1

Reverend
John B. M. McFerrin looked over the worn faces of the men who sat before him on the forest floor. The Methodist minister held aloft a bible and preached a sermon meant to comfort the exhausted soldiers of Palmer's brigade, who had seen the worst of war. McFerrin's stirring words had a great effect for the troubled Confederates he ministered to. He hoped to prepare them for their perilous future: "Be thou faithful unto death, and I will give the[e] a Crown of life." For an hour McFerrin held the hardened veterans "spellbound." The soldiers sang each hymn with conviction and sank to their knees with each prayer. "It was a time to be remembered," wrote one emotional soldier. The minister's words were a beacon for troubled souls searching to regain the hope that defeat had destroyed. God's word provided an anchor when beliefs of honor, duty, and tradition had faded with the war's end.[1]

This loss of identity was felt the hardest by men like those in the Chatham Artillery. Originally formed on May 1, 1784 to protect the citizens of Savannah, the unit dissolved on its 79th birthday in North Carolina. The hundred men still with their unit pulled their cherished cannons unceremoniously into a field and left them

---

1 Foster and Brown, eds., *One of Cleburne's Command*, 172.

there. The soldiers then collected their paroles and their allotments of Spanish silver coins and began their trek back to Georgia. Cannoneer William R. Talley remembered feeling a deep sadness after surrendering his guns. "That was the first time in three years that our gun had gone and I was not to go with it and as I watched that gun roll away I felt a loneliness and grief down in my heart and the tears streamed from my eyes. I was sad and sorrowed as if I had lost a loved one." South Carolina cavalryman Daniel Dantzler remembered: "We were lined up and stacked our guns in a field and left them there. But not yet formally disbanded. We take up a line of march, in regular order, homeward bound." After marching a hundred miles from Greensboro, the company received its paroles and said its final goodbyes. But as the army melted away desperation overwhelmed what reason remained.[2]

Men fearful of their lives continued grabbing whatever food and supplies remained to ensure their survival. As resources dwindled the situation grew increasingly dangerous. "No right acknowledged now except might, no property safe which is not defended with pistol and rifle," wrote an officer in Hardee's Corps.[3]

Joe Johnston fought to maintain discipline to the very end. He issued a final decree designed to foster order among those still with the army and those preparing to march home. He told his brigade commanders to withhold paroles until the men reached the end of their marches. Johnston believed it would protect his men and civilians. The general still felt deeply connected to his men and believed the Confederacy and its leaders owed much to those who had made the greatest sacrifices and suffered most grievously. What most irritated Johnston was the lack of concern for the common soldier he sensed in Davis and the rest of the Confederate government. For instance, he replied to one commander, who had inquired about the war department's location, that he knew "of no War Department nor other branch of civil government." He condemned the cabinet in another dispatch: "[T]he civil government seems to have left this part of the country, taking with it all means of supporting troops." It was help Johnston knew his men sorely needed if they were to survive the demobilization and return home.[4]

2 Jones, *Historical Sketch of the Chatham Artillery*, 221; Reverend William R. Talley Memoirs, GDAH; Dunkerly, *The Confederate Surrender*, 138.

3 Hagood, *Memoirs*, 372.

4 OR 47/3:861.

From Hillsborough, R. H. Anderson dispatched riders to Confederate headquarters begging for food for his starving cavalrymen and their mounts. He received a reply promising that help was on the way. When a supply train finally arrived from Greensboro, Anderson's hungry men found only salt, cloth, and yarn—barter goods to be traded with local civilians for food. But Anderson's men knew the countryside had been stripped bare after weeks of foraging, and could buy little from locals living in fear of their own starvation. A desperate Anderson appealed directly to the enemy for help. He sent two dispatches to General Schofield, decrying his predicament and admitting his troops "have been without food for three days" and "are in a starving condition." Anderson admitted that he was "extremely anxious to get my command away from this place as soon as possible, being unable to subsist my men and horses without subjecting the citizens to suffering and want." The general tried to hold his men together until they received their paroles, but Union officers bypassed him, heading directly to Greensboro to sign paroles there.[5]

Before his division marched away, Gen. Robert F. Hoke delivered a heartfelt farewell address to his men. In an attempt to boost their pride, Hoke said they should have no shame for executing their duty, which won them glory fighting with the Army of Northern Virginia. Hoke noted the special bond they now shared with fellow soldiers both alive and dead in what he called "that holy brotherhood whose ties are now sealed by the blood of your compatriots who have fallen." As for that "sad, dark veil of defeat" hanging over them, "fear not the future," he urged, "but meet it with manly hearts."[6]

On their homeward march Union soldiers experienced feelings opposite of their Rebel counterparts. Marching north the XIV and XX Corps encountered a moving scene. Around 4:00 p.m., at the crossroads community of Wilton, they watched a considerable gathering of citizens raise an American flag. One woman had kept the banner hidden, resisting the warnings of her secessionists friends that she would live to regret it. A regimental band struck up a jaunty song as they passed, and women waved their handkerchiefs. Soldier John Henry Otto felt "proud . . . that the Nation was saved from disgrace and ruin, that liberty and popular souvereignity [sic] henceforth be the ruling power in the coming great."[7]

---

5 OR 47/3:366-367, 860-861.

6 Daniel W. Barefoot, *General Robert F. Hoke: Lee's Modest Warrior* (Winston Salem, NC, 1996), 319-20.

7 Gould and Kennedy, eds., *Memoirs of a Dutch Mudsill*, 365.

Besides great pride, victory elicited other emotions less joyous. Sherman's men experienced an incredible sadness which overwhelmed many hearts. Those who could step away from being hardened soldiers unlocked feelings they had suppressed for years. Iowan William Royal Oake's discordant emotions brought him to tears:

> Soon, all our long and weary marches would be over and we looked forward with joy to again see our friends [in] the North. Then again, our thoughts would revert back to the many bloody fields through which we had passed, and we again imagined we could see the cold and mangled remains of beloved comrades as we last saw them ere we consigned them to their last resting place.

The visions of lost friends who would never share in life's sweet reward haunted Oake, just as it would other men. He felt as "those thoughts forced themselves upon us even amidst our great joy at the thought of home and friends a great lump would arise in our throats, and it was impossible to check the falling tears."[8]

Freedmen flocked to meet the army and expressed a deep, sometimes uncontrollable, joy as they welcomed freedom. "Saw lots of darkies all along, whom we told were free," one soldier remembered; "One old fellow just stood and yelled all the time. Another said 'much obliged to you gemmen [gentlemen] for the undertaking.'" Black men and women were "wild with excitement" noted one soldier and commented on how thunderstruck they were by freedom, "some do not know what they are doing." In Warrenton, soldiers encountered crowds of freedmen eager to glimpse their liberators. "[I] saw the most Negros here I ever saw together at one place. They had all gathered in from the country to see the Army," George Metz wrote. Captain James Crozer also noted the former slaves' excitement. They were "nearly wild [they would] jump shout roll in the dirt pull their wool & everything you could think of. One wanted the lord to give him wings so he could fly." A member of the 4th Minnesota remarked, "The negroes are all loyal and often clap their hands and shout, 'Bress de Lord! We's glad to see ye!' and like expressions of joy." Near the town of Louisburg Colonel David Palmer was struck by the beauty of the land and the feeling of the people who lined the road to

8 Oake, *On the Skirmish Line*, 319.

watch them pass. Former slaves they met were "wild with excitement," with some so thunderstruck by freedom that they "do not know what they are doing."[9]

Union commanders understood their soldiers wildly shifting emotions and worried about their ability to abide by the new rules of peace. General Howard assured the citizens of North Carolina of their safety and informed them of the limits he had imposed on foraging by his men. "Every sort of precaution will be taken by our officers to render the march orderly; and, it is hoped, that the great terror that prevailed during active operations will now cease." Soldiers of his XV Corps passing through the town of Louisburg witnessed Howard's wrath at those breaking his promise: Three soldiers were tied to a fence with the label "PILLAGER" pinned to their jackets.[10]

May 2

Under the spreading leaves of a maple tree shading Ralph Gorrel's yard in Greensboro, General Johnston sat by his tent listening to a serenade by the 37th Georgia band. Musician Z. W. Anderson recorded their final number for the general in his song book: the "Kate Polka." It was an odd choice of a lively tune in dour times, but the song was played as an homage to Johnston's alma mater, West Point. Underneath the pencil notes and bars of the song, Anderson recorded a near-universal sentiment, "All are very anxious to get home."[11]

Johnston addressed his men a final time from Gorrel's shady grove. In General Order No. 22, Johnston bade them farewell. He urged his men to observe the surrender terms and, if they did that as well as they performed on the battlefield, they would "best secure the comfort of your families and kindred, and restore tranquility to our country." The general expressed his belief that their commitment to the end had earned them the admiration of the entire South. He then thanked them for the most important trait he appreciated in his soldiers. "I shall always remember with pride the loyal support and generous confidence you have given me." Then he said goodbye. "I now part with you with deep regret, and bid you farewell with feelings of cordial friendship, and with earnest wishes that you may hereafter have all the prosperity and happiness to be found in the world." The

---

9 Brown, *History of the Fourth Regiment*, 412; David Palmer, Diary, May 1, 1865; May 3, 1865, IA.

10 Joseph A. Saunier, ed., *A History of the Forty-seventh Regiment, Ohio Veteran Volunteer Infantry* (Hillsboro, OH, 1903), 444.

11 Z. W. Anderson, Band Book, Special Collections, DU.

address stirred the men's already heightened emotions. One soldier felt Johnston's words which "sank like lead into the hearts of the brave men."[12]

Johnston had laid down his sword, but he soon picked up his pen and continued to fight the war. He tried to write a memoir of the conflict that kept his honor untarnished used the pages of magazines and newspapers to defend his actions during the war. The general recognized the value of the Confederate archives would be to his endeavor and contacted Schofield and told him to expect a collection of records that he was "anxious" to preserve. Johnston turned over 10 tons of records he hoped to use in the future. His deputy in command, Gen. P. G. T. Beauregard, also wanted to protect materials that could secure his postwar legacy. At 7:00 a.m., Beauregard telegraphed Johnston and alerted him that the records of the engineering department had been spotted in an open train car, and he suggested that they be included with other war department archives for safe keeping. Beauregard carefully noted that "[p]apers of [the] siege of Charleston are among said records." These were evidence of Beauregard's finest hour, which he dearly wanted to preserve; doing so would be important to his deflection of questions of blame for losing the war.[13]

But even stalwarts like Beauregard succumbed to war's stresses and hardships. One of his officers recalled, "The worst whipped man—of the entire army—that I saw—was Gen. Beauregard," and he remembered him "sitting on a crosstie—with hands at his face—and an expression of despair." Gloom affected other Confederate generals as well. Braxton Bragg wrote to Secretary of War Breckenridge that the supplies sent to purchase food from locals were already gone, and they needed more. Bragg specifically asked if hard currency could be sent along to help, adding in a postscript a personal note about his own plight. "My own means, all in Confederate paper, are very limited."[14]

With each passing hour Johnston's army continued to crumble. Hagood's Brigade formed for the last time and prepared to march to Lancaster, South Carolina, where it would disband. When encamped near Smithfield in March, the brigade had numbered 493 men, but now counted only about 350. Their horses had been reduced to one quart of cornmeal a day, and mules subsisted on only a

12 Jones, *Historical Sketch of the Chatham Artillery*, 221-222; OR 47/1:1061.

13 Arnett, *Guns Were Stacked*, 124-125; OR 47/3:862. Beauregard commanded the able and stout coastal defense of Georgia and South Carolina from late 1862 to early 1864, including a couple of sieges at Charleston.

14 Schenck Reminiscences, 42, SHC/UNC; OR 47/3:861.

handful of "long forage." Groups of dazed men wandered off into the woods as the Confederacy melted away. But the stunned soldiers who remained did not know what to do or where to go. These men, unable to come to grips with their emotions, were causing problems.[15]

General Schofield, accompanied by XXIII Corps commander Maj. Gen. Jacob D. Cox, headed to Greensboro to oversee the last of the surrender operations. Escorted by the 104th Ohio, the generals boarded a train in Raleigh. At a stop in Durham, the generals received a dispatch from the paroling officer, Bvt. Brig. Gen. William Hartsuff, who told them he was almost finished issuing paroles, but also that the Rebels still in Greensboro were "dissolving and raising the devil." Hartsuff was especially concerned about ammunition getting into their hands and suggested sending two regiments to keep order. Cox telegraphed back to Raleigh and ordered the 9th New Jersey forward with haste. Arriving in Hillsborough, Union soldiers peered nervously from the train and watched R. H. Anderson's intoxicated cavalrymen dividing up Confederate government property. For William Bently and other Union soldiers the spectacle made the situation tense: "It looked a little squally for us for awhile, as a great many of them were drunk and inclined to be imprudent."[16]

At the depot, Confederate Mag. Gen. William Hardee stepped aboard the train and shook hands with Schofield and Cox. As they chugged down the track toward Greensboro, Cox nervously realized how deep he was venturing into his former enemy's lines, but Hardee relieved his fears. Cox admired Hardee, noting he had the "bearing [of] a good type of the brilliant soldier and gentleman." Like many other soldiers, both blue and gray, who encountered their enemies up close, the generals passed the time by reviewing the war.[17]

Schofield and Cox asked Hardee how he thought it would have turned out and when he realized the South's chances of victory were hopeless. At the outset of the war Hardee claimed to believe any Southern soldier could whip three of his Northern counterparts. He admitted, however, that the first year of the war sobered them: "[E]ver since that time we military men have generally seen that it was only a question [of] how long it would take to wear our army out and destroy it. We have seen that there was no real hope of success, except by some extraordinary

---

15 Hagood, *Memoirs*, 367, 372.

16 *OR* 47/3:376, 864-865; Bently, Smith, and Baker, *Burning Rails as We Pleased*, 152.

17 Jacob D. Cox, *Military Reminiscences of The Civil War*, 2 Vols. (New York, 1900), 2:525.

accident of fortune, and we have also seen that the politicians would never give up till the army was gone."[18]

What Hardee did not reveal was the great sadness he felt, not only over the defeat but for the loss of his young son Willie at the battle of Bentonville. Willie had tried for over a year to join the 8th Texas Cavalry, but his father refused. Only after constant pestering did Hardee relent and allow his son to join the Texans. When Union forces threatened Johnston's headquarters during the final day of the battle, the Texans repelled the attack. Willie was mortally wounded and died two days later in Hillsboro at the age of sixteen.[19]

The generals' train rolled into Greensboro around 4:00 p.m. and the Union officers stepped off into a sea of former enemies. Riding through the crowded streets, Schofield set up his headquarters in "Blandwood," the mansion of former Governor John M. Morehead. The two generals then rode to Joe Johnston's headquarters. After exchanging greetings, Schofield and Cox sat down and talked with the general. Johnston was reserved and grave as he submitted a list of his headquarters staff to Schofield, and parole slips were filled out with the names of each officer.[20]

Seeing what little remained of their once-formidable foe, Union soldiers sensed how hurt the defeated Confederates were. The ragged state of the Rebels shocked them, for their "appearance and equipment plainly show [their] exhausted and impoverished condition." One remembered the Rebels as "a sore set of people," while another, Morris Runyan, noted the sorry state of a group of parolees lining the road, "lying too sick and weak, by reason of disease or want of food, to travel." After talking with the Southerners, Runyon was shocked at the terrifying crimes they confessed to. "Stories were told us by them They told stories 'too shocking for belief, of raids on dwellings on farmhouses, assault, arson, and even murder."[21]

It did not take long for tempers to flare between the former enemies. "One Federal soldier taunted a Confederate about being whipped" wrote officer James

---

18 Cox, *Reminiscences*, 526.

19 Bradley, *Bentonville*, 394-395.

20 Cox, Reminiscences, 528-529.

21 Gaskill, *Footprints Through Dixie: Everyday Life of the Man Under a Musket, on the Firing Line and in the Trenches, 1862-1865* (Alliance, OH, 1919), 179; Morris C. Runyan, *Eight Days with the Confederates and the Capture of Their Archives, Flags, &c. by Company "G" Ninth New Jersey Vol.* (Princeton, NJ, 1896), 15.

Cole, the Rebel "leaped up and told the Yank that if they had whipped the South by having five to one he couldn't whip him, and at it they went—and down went the Blue Jacket and Gray on top." He recorded a more violent encounter between six Federal soldiers who attacked "one emaciated, drunken Confederate and beat his head against the ground barbarously after admitting he had killed many men in battle." One soldier described the demoralized state of the Confederates, "Drunkenness and disorder generally have been the order of the day."[22]

The Rebel soldiers' anger boiled over with nightfall. Union soldier Nelson Pinney wrote that, with "the restraint of military discipline" removed, "thousands of them had hid their weapons and were now 'raising Cain' in town and in their camps, some of them less than half mile away." Federals in Greensboro spent a nervous night in camp listening to the Confederate army collapse around them. "All night they made the region about us resound with their drunken brawls, and the vicinity extremely dangerous with their wild and reckless firing, as they sauntered through town and country, committing crimes and revages [sic] of the most horrible nature." While Schofield believed everything was progressing satisfactorily, he did note that "[t]he country is a good deal disturbed by the returned soldiers from Lee's and Johnston's armies."[23]

Given these circumstances, Cox believed he needed more men. He ordered two divisions to proceed to Greensboro by foot and a third by rail with the utmost haste. A 1,000-man detachment was dispatched, and another 1,500 were expected the following day, but it would take five days for all of the reinforcements to arrive in the city. Cox also tried to maintain order statewide with General Order No. 35, which authorized troops to be sent to every North Carolina county in order to organize citizen police forces.[24]

Fear continued to roil the minds of Greensboro's citizens. Federal authorities pressed Rev. Jacob Henry Smith to hold a service at the First Presbyterian Church to restore some normalcy. On the way to the church, Smith and his wife noticed the sheer number of Union soldiers in Greensboro: "every street, store, doorway, and corner [was] crowded with Federal troops. The whole world looked blue in unison with our feelings that bitter morning." Union officers, their heads bowed in prayer, saw evidence of the church's recent past: deep umber stains on the floor marked the blood of wounded soldiers. Traumatized by the anarchy days earlier, Smith's

22 Arnett, *Guns Were Stacked*, 92; Dunkerly, *Confederate Surrender*, 151.

23 Pinney, *History of the 104th Regiment Ohio*, 86; OR 47/3:384, 394.

24 OR 47/3:376, 396.

wife was even more vexed by enemy occupation. The fear of Union reprisals brought her to uncontrollable tears during the service. She "sat throughout . . . in blinding tears, not only because of our humiliation, but, lest in sermon or prayer some word might escape from the turbulent heart of the speaker to cause his arrest." Smith and other troubled civilians faced other, more blatant reminders of their conquered state. Like Sherman had done in Raleigh, Cox ordered a grand review of his troops in Greensboro, complete with a bandstand constructed for the occasion. Senator John A. Gilmer's wife expressed to repulsion of many citizens when she "flatly told her husband that she refused to add one more spectator to the pageant, for it was an enemy's bullet that had maimed her only son for life."[25]

To support the XXIII Corps in Greensboro, Kilpatrick's cavalry rode west. With them was a recruit named Henry Anderson, who was arrested for the murder of a civilian outside Chapel Hill. Caught, court-martialed, and condemned, Kilpatrick's command paused in Lexington for Anderson's execution. Freedman George Moses Horton witnessed the death, and it moved him to write a poem. Horton found the execution especially jarring because his new friend and benefactor, Capt. W. H. S. Banks, commanded the firing squad. His verse described Sherman's apathetic veterans who witnessed the scene as: "Gazing spectators seemed completely dumb." Horton deemed the punishment just, but sad considering the arrival of peace, and he blamed alcohol as the culprit for Anderson's crimes. After a month of living with the Michigan soldiers he understood, and perhaps witnessed, soldiers' behavior after seeking solace at the bottom of a bottle. Horton noted this destructive vice in a poetic verse, "Imbibing nectar from the bowels of hell! Inspiring depredations all the night."[26]

The extended service for Union soldiers remaining in North Carolina was difficult, dangerous, and disheartening. One regiment, the 128th Indiana, demonstrated how its experiences fighting in the Atlanta campaign and at Franklin and Nashville had twisted them. Increasingly demoralized with garrison duty, their discipline broke down, and the men took out their frustrations and anger on the citizens. Over a hundred townspeople attested to such outrages. An officer sent by departmental commander Brig. Gen. Thomas Ruger to assess the situation described the men's behavior as "disgraceful." Drunken soldiers cursing their officers in the streets was common, while "[r]obbing and stealing are nightly

25 Arnett, *Guns Were Stacked*, 90, 108.

26 Stevens Papers, UM.

pastimes." Months later, the Hoosiers would continue to rampage through the town.[27]

Charles Becker, deeply embittered by the war and left with a lifelong hatred of Confederates, was one of these men. "Those damn rebels. We should have killed them all," Becker frequently declared. His horrific duties at North Carolina's Salisbury Prison had helped shape this attitude. During the war, Confederate guards had buried the emaciated bodies of Union prisoners in hastily dug mass graves. When it rained, bones protruded from the earth. Becker and others in the 128th Indiana were charged with reinterring the rotting bodies, an experience that haunted him for the rest of his life. Another soldier in that regiment, William H. Guile, also suffered from his wartime experience for years afterward, and he grew violent and unable to take care of himself. Guile was especially incensed by the thought of former Confederates and made threats to kill any he encountered, proclaiming he would be happy to do it and "do it quickly."[28]

Jacob Bartmess of the 39th Indiana was another of those who remained on garrison duty. Like other soldiers, sadness cut through the joy of victory for him. The highs and lows he felt while still far away from home burdened his mind for months after the war. Bartmess found himself still in North Carolina celebrating the Fourth of July with a heavy heart. The patriotic celebration stirred a deep grief in Bartmess that measured the holiday against the war's suffering: "Many hearts, this day, in the cities and towns of the north will beat with heroic pride, while many more will swell with patriotic pride." But as the thrill of victory faded, Bartmess considered the cost of war too great. "But alas for poor me, the day has a vastly different meaning; and produces a vastly different effect upon my heart.... [T]o me it is a sad memorial of wrongs, of privations, of afflictions of mind allmost unedurable [sic]."[29]

May 3

Cornelia Phillips Spencer walked Chapel Hill's streets and contemplated the panoply of her experience with war. She passed paroled men as they meandered down the town's tree-lined streets and watched her neighbors weep for men who

27 Mark Bradley, *Bluecoats and Tar Heels: Soldiers and Civilians in Reconstruction North Carolina* (Lexington, KY, 2009), 92-93.

28 *The Wall Street Journal*, May 28, 2004; Dean, *Shook Over Hell*, 137.

29 "Jacob W. Bartmess Civil War Letters," *Indiana Magazine of History* (1956), 52:185.

never came home. Her mind raced as she struggled to make sense of what she had been through and the toll it took on her mind. She admitted to her diary how turbulent the final weeks had been, "the most remarkable three weeks in the history of this place. Three weeks of such excitement, as a century may fail to reproduce." The war left people hurt and confused, and defeat fostered great uncertainty. Spencer looked to God for answers and resigned herself to divine province to make sense of the war. "Oh our God! What sins we must have been guilty of that we should be so humbled by them now. . . . Peace is come—but what a peace! How different from what our hopes have so fondly pictured. . . . I cannot think two consecutive thoughts—I can only feel."[30]

Though scarred and deeply affected, Spencer managed the war's strain, but Allen W. Wooten did not. A wealthy planter and state legislator from Lenoir County, Wooten had amassed a fortune as one of North Carolina's eastern elites, but the deaths of his two oldest sons, James Bryan and Allen Whitefield, in Virginia in 1864 had brought on serious emotional problems. The loss of his plantation at the hands of Union soldiers and the Confederacy's defeat caused a mental breakdown. In early April, overwhelmed by grief and despair, he became homicidal. He was carried from his home to the shaded grounds of the North Carolina Insane Asylum in Raleigh, where he was admitted on May 4. Suffering from the affliction doctors simply identified as "the war," Wooten's mental condition declined rapidly, and he refused to eat. He died a month later on June 20, 1865.[31]

After minister Anthony T. Porter's emotional interview with General Johnston in Raleigh, he returned home to Columbia, dodging Union soldiers, Confederate deserters, and other rogues along the route. Porter arrived home a destitute and emotionally shattered man. "When the excitement was over, I was somewhat mentally broken down," he admitted. But at least his fear had provided a distraction from the heart-wrenching grief that filled his home. As it had in so many Southern homes, sorrow took the place of loved ones taken by war. The death of Porter's son "had been gnawing" at his heart, but the chaos of the war's final days had momentarily distracted him from his grief. Peace, however, restored his sadness. His family's destitution compounded the stress he felt, and Porter "was

30 Notebook, Vol. 3, Cornelia Phillips Spencer Collection, SHC/UNC; Robert Kenzer, *Kinship and Neighborhood in a Southern Community: Orange County, North Carolina, 1849-1881* (Chapel Hill, NC, 1987), 94.

31 North Carolina Insane Asylum registration books, NCDAH; Greg Mast, *North Carolina Troops and Volunteers* (Raleigh, NC, 1995), 174.

overcome." A house stripped of clothes, money, and food was his new reality, and this exacted a heavy toll on the minister, who wrote that "[t]here was nothing but blank despair; and my heart failed me." In addition to weakening his body and heart, war had shaken Porter's faith. "The question of right was after all a mere question of might, and such a God could not command my love or obedience. The thought that a cause in which Robert E. Lee and Stonewall Jackson, such men, such eminent Christian men, had drawn their swords, should fail, made life worthless, and I folded my hands and wished to die."[32]

Walking the miles of winding roads home allowed veterans time to reflect on the great changes they witness among the people they encountered. Riding through South Carolina, Brig. Gen. Josiah Gorgas observed the Confederacy's final collapse and took note of his own inability to comprehend what was happening. The people displayed "a strong disposition to possess themselves of all property of the Conf[ederate] Gov[ernment]." Gorgas struggled to understand this transformation and the new world that swirled around him. "The calamity which has fallen upon us in the total destruction of our government is of a character so overwhelming that I am as yet unable to comprehend it. I am as one walking in a dream, and expecting to awake." Like Cornelia Spencer, the Confederacy's demise left him stunned, unable to concentrate, and despondent. "I cannot see its consequences nor shape my own course, but am just moving along until I can see my way at some future day." A shaken man, Gorgas marveled at the drastic turn of events: from a country with an army to nothing, almost in the blink of an eye. Gorgas wondered about his life. Would it be one devoid of hope, "and that we live, breathe, move, talk as before—will it be so when the soul leaves the body behind it?"[33]

Those men who remained in Greensboro were the most traumatized, and were left stupefied by defeat. Colonel Frank Waring arrived in Greensboro to collect paroles for his men and noted the sad situation. "All was chaos, food was scarce," and the blue Federal uniforms "certainly unpleasant to look at," he declared. He described rowdy mobs of recently paroled Confederates on the verge of erupting into violence. But what most surprised Waring were the revelations the soldiers shared about how they had fought their war, and "all the deviltries they used to commit. I confess, I was appalled at the utter want of principle displayed in their

---

32 Porter, *Led On!*, 188.

33 Frank E. Vandiver, ed., *The Civil War Diary of General Josiah Gorgas* (Tuscaloosa, AL, 1947), 184.

confessions. Stealing was the regular occupation of those boys. I don't believe they know right from wrong."[34]

Even those defiant souls who confessed undying devotion to the Confederate cause could not abide the increasing reality of defeat. Joseph Wheeler and his cavalry never caught up to Jefferson Davis, realizing after days of chasing him that their errand was in vain. Trooper David Sadler saw reality setting in on his tired companions, and watched them slowly peel off as they rode through South Carolina and into Georgia: "Men were going in every direction; some paroled, some were not, but each was making for home. Everybody inquired of everybody for news, and we were fairly well posted as to movements, etc." At Washington, Georgia, Wheeler decided to end his pursuit of Davis and sadly told his men they "no longer owed allegiance to the Confederacy; that we were free to go and shift for ourselves; that our cause for the present was lost." Men sat and filled out their paroles, then shook hands for a final time. With Wheeler's last words of advice ("Look for the worst, but hope for the best.") still in their ears, they said farewell and left by themselves or in small squads. In total, 27,749 paroles were issued to the Army of Tennessee, and across Johnston's Department of South Carolina, Georgia, and Florida another 61,471 men were surrendered.[35]

Heading south from Greensboro, William J. Worsham of the 19th Tennessee encountered a group of women in Thomasville waving handkerchiefs from the windows of an academy as the column passed. "They received only a faint response," Worsham admitted. "We felt sad. We were but part of the funeral procession going home from the burial of the dead Confederacy." Reaching Salisbury, the Tennesseans formed for a last farewell from Maj. Gen. Frank Cheatham. The general walked down the line shaking the hand of each man as "great big tears rolled down his cheeks." Between sobs Cheatham could only utter "good-by." Emotion overwhelmed the soldiers. The crushing feeling of defeat interspersed with the joy of surviving made them weep, Worsham remembered. "There was not an eye but was suffused with tears; yea, they were fountains of tears." Worsham swore he would never forget the scene.[36]

Johnson Hagood had kept most of his brigade together throughout the chaotic surrender, but the time to go home was finally at hand. Around 8:00 a.m., 3,350 of

34 Waring Diary, May 2, 1865, SHC/UNC.

35 *New Orleans Picayune*, November 9, 1902; *CV* (1906), 14:309; Dunkerly, *Confederate Surrender*, 136.

36 Worsham, *The Old Nineteenth*, 177.

his men formed without arms or accoutrements and started their long march. As they left camp the ragged column halted at Maj. Gen. Robert F. Hoke's headquarters to bid him a final farewell. "He and his staff seemed to feel the occasion deeply," wrote one Confederate officer, "and their expressions of regard and good will were very grateful to us all. The last link that bound us to the army thus severed, we resumed our weary journey homeward." Marching south, the men scoured the barren countryside for food. During the day, they left the column and ranged widely for provisions, returning during the night. Starving animals began to eat the canvas wagon covers and gnaw trees as their only source of food. Hardee's men started for home that morning as well. The mob of what was once his command marched throughout the day, sadly plodding along, deep in thought. They stopped near Lexington, where Hardee took leave of them for the last time. Captain George Brewer of the 46th Alabama looked back at his emotions over the surrender with great sadness, and described his himself in the third person. "His voice at times choked so that the words could hardly be heard and tears ran down his cheeks and that of many of the men, as these sad, humiliating words were heard." Brewer's painful reckoning of the war's cost caused him pain, "We thought of the desolation of our land, the poverty of our people, the multitudes of widows and orphans of our comrades sleeping in the dust. Lives and families sacrificed, and for what?"[37]

Captain Samuel T. Foster likewise recorded his last thoughts of the Army of Tennessee. "After turning in our guns, and getting our paroles, we feel relieved. No more picket duty, no more guard duty, no more fighting, no more war. It is all over, and we are going home." The bittersweet relief of stress brought on by the surrender was soon spoiled by the reality of what peace truly meant.[38]

Traveling in the opposite direction toward Chapel Hill, Capt. Nicholas Schenck's first glimpse of the postwar South repulsed him. "We reached the rail road and train came a crowded in—among Yankee soldiers and Negroes and Negro wenches—a horrid crowd." Defeat brought the bitter realization to Schenck that the world he knew was gone. "The dawn of the 'dream of equality' was beginning to show itself—among the Negro—as taught by the soldiers—in word and act—we could do no better—so must bear the disgust."[39]

---

37 Hagood, *Memoirs*, 367, 372-373; Simmons, "The 12th Louisiana," 30; Dunkerly, *Confederate Surrender*, 108.

38 Daniel, *Soldiering in the Army of Tennessee*, 168.

39 Schenck Reminiscences, SHC/UNC, 45.

Georgian W. W. Gordon expressed a similar glum outlook for this new South. "If the Yankees desire to pacify and conciliate my people—of which I am not now able to judge—still their present course in freeing the negroes is an experiment of which time alone can show success." Reunification and freedom, he warned, "will try the health and happiness of all connected with or brought in contact with." Gordon began to worry about the legacy of the Confederacy; he instructed his wife to kiss their children and "never let them forget that the word 'rebel' means an unfortunate man whom success would have made a hero & patriot."[40]

May 4

As Joseph Johnston watched his army and his country drift into history, he began to build his justification for surrender. The general started collecting information to prove he had no other choice than capitulation because his small army lacked the material and arms to defeat Sherman. He also noted the lack of food "made it impossible to continue the war, except as robbers." Johnston had come to the painful assumption that the South was tired of war, and that continuing it meant "desolation and ruin" which would only cause "great suffering of women and children." This prolonging the war would necessarily endanger his army as well, those "brave and true men committed to me." He claimed these factors brought him to the negotiating table, and he wanted the Confederacy to know he only had its best interests in mind. Within a few days, "thinking it necessary to explain to the Southern people the state of things which compelled me to put an end to the war," Johnston contacted Maj. Gen. Lafayette McLaws in Georgia and shared the details of the agreement signed at the Bennett farm, including his written explanation. He asked McLaws to "have it published as widely in Georgia as you can."[41]

Johnston prepared to leave Greensboro for Salisbury and Charlotte in order to provide some guidance to the commanders trying to keep order in those cities. Before he departed, he paid a farewell visit to former governor John M. Morehead and his family. To his hosts it was obvious that Johnston's emotions reflected deep grief and sadness over the loss of his army and the dishonor he faced. "Never can I forget the scene," Morehead's daughter remembered, "when the brave and grand

40 W. W. Gordon to wife, May 16, 1865, Gordon Collection, SHC/UNC.

41 OR 47/3:873-874.

Joseph E. Johnston called to say farewell, with the tears running down his brown cheeks."[42]

Others leaving Greensboro saw scenes that revealed the depths of the trauma felt by the defeated army; images that haunted forever. William F. Allison of the 3rd Confederate Cavalry waited almost 30 years to share what he witnessed that day. In 1893, the first issue of *Confederate Veteran* magazine contained an article by Allison entitled, "Vivid War Incident," in which he bore his soul about an encounter that occurred as he walked away from war.

On the morning of May 4, as he trudged along with other paroled men toward Salisbury. Allison noticed splotches of blood on the road and thought they were from a wounded horse. On the roadside ahead, he noticed a man in a red floral-patterned shirt sitting on a pile of railroad ties. Upon drawing closer, Allison realized his shirt was white and splattered with blood. Many in the passing crowd walked silently by, ignoring the bloody man, but a few stopped and began talking to him. Allison remembered him as a fine looking individual about 30 years old. Joining the small crowd, he recognized the soldier as a high-ranking officer in a uniform of fine English cloth. The wounded man exclaimed in a clear voice, "No, there is no use trying to do any thing, for I am dying. But you can take that coat," which lay six or eight feet from him, "to my wife in Augusta, Ga. She is the daughter of Gen. Rains." But what struck Allison about the scene was that "[d]uring his talk he put his hand in the gaping wound, which had been made, as we supposed, by himself, and got out the blood and rubbed [it] all over his arms." The other soldiers simply walked away. Allison joined them and left the officer to his fate. The memory would trouble him for the rest of his life, always reminding him of war's power to tear asunder the hearts of those fight.[43]

42 Bradley, *This Astounding Close*, 243.

43 W. F. Allison, "Vivid War Incident," *CV* (May 1893), 1:133.

"It wrings my heart"

Despite the chill and overcast October sky, Reuben Oscar Everett stood beneath his towering sculpture and felt proud. He spent three difficult years campaigning on the monument's behalf and now it was finally ready for unveiling. The sculpture consisted of two twenty-foot tall granite columns supporting a pediment engraved with the word "Unity." It commemorated the site of Johnston's surrender to Sherman in the home of James Bennett. A progressive lawyer and legislator, Everett, joined other business leaders who saw the surrender as the event that propelled Durham into a booming business capital of the New South. But Everett's monument met opposition from those who still felt the War and regarded the monument as salt in old wounds.

The ladies of the Durham chapter of the United Daughters of the Confederacy detested the monument and deemed its public unveiling as highly inappropriate. They felt a monument at the Bennett farm would be a painful reminder of the surrender of one of "Lee's armies." Since their formation in 1894, the Daughters saw it as their mission was to wipe away the stain of Confederate surrender and redeem its defenders. In 1902, speakers at the UDC's national convention in Wilmington, North Carolina expressed their purpose, "What lies before us is not only loyalty to memories," but "loyalty to principles; not only building of monuments, but the vindication of the men of the Confederacy." Everett's monument undermined their efforts and represented an event and time that didn't align with the memory they were laboring to construct. Together with the aging former soldiers of the United Confederate Veterans, the Daughters launched a public campaign to quell support for the monstrosity.

Many locals seemed dubious of the monument and its meaning. On September 14, 1923, the *Durham Morning Herald* featured an editorial written by "A Son of the Confederacy" who did "not want to throw cold water on the project" but bluntly expressed publicly what a great many people had discussed in private. The anonymous writer declared it to be in bad taste to "celebrate defeat and surrender of a Southern army," adding: "Quite a number of citizens have in private conversation expressed a similar opinion but refrained from make in public protest." Another writer questioned the effort by asking, "'What are they going to celebrate?' is a question that has been asked more than once in this city."

One writer acknowledged the surrender was of national importance but "from a strictly southern sentimental point of view, it marks one of the south's greatest tragedies" and suggested the monument would evoke bad memories of defeat, "[I]t does seem out of place for a southern community and a southern people to have to assume the entire responsibility for perpetuation of an unpleasant history and preserving the victory of a one-time enemy." Especially controversial was that enemy, William T. Sherman, whose name became synonymous for the Devil and the extent of his destruction being especially controversial. It seemed people in Durham didn't care or want to be reminded of the war nor the surrender.[1]

Other papers noted the lack of support from any former Union soldiers. "The Grand Army of the Republica[sic], composed of union veterans of the war between the states and which should be interested in the plans, not only has displayed no enthusiasm, but has through its officers, displayed an attitude that reveals a total lack of interest in it." It seems they too, took no interest in commemorating the site, the event, nor the campaign which ended in their victory.

But Everett and other progressive Durham leaders pointed to Sherman's and Johnston's meeting as an important chapter in the city's history that would attract tourists. Some monument supporters believed it furthered reconciliation between the sections and helped to close old wounds, a sentiment captured in one column, "At this plain old farmhouse fell the curtain upon the last act of the terrible drama, and the dark cloud that had so long hung over the heads of our people began to clear away, and a new era commenced to dawn upon the South."

After weeks of skirmishing in the papers, the issue came to a head. A meeting was planned between the factions so both sides could make their cases. Everett and other business leaders claimed the monument "was not intended to be a celebration of the surrender . . . [the] main purpose was to preserve the memory of

---

1 *Durham* [NC] *Morning Herald*, September 12, 14, 18, 19, 23.

The Unity Monument was designed in 1923 to represent the reunification of the North and the South and to draw people to the site of Johnston's surrender. But few cared to remember this chapter of the war, and those who did felt it was pouring salt in old wounds. *North Carolina Department of Archives and History*

a great historical event, and was to be a display of the new spirit which accepts the verdict of the real struggle between the states." But the old veterans and the U.D.C. were unmoved and refused to support the monument nor participate in its unveiling. They were still haunted by painful feelings from a horrible time. Despite the resistance and apathy, Everett unwrapped the monument on that cold October in 1923 and reminded visitors of the spot where history was made but also woke nightmares in others.

The Unity monument represented an obstacle to sixty years of Americans' efforts to shape a palatable memory of the painful experience. Both North and South had their reasons for letting the story of the war's end in North Carolina drift into obscurity. For Southerners, the Unity monument was a reminder of a time that people wanted to forget. Johnston's surrender found no place in the romanticized Lost Cause movement. By the time of the Unity monument, defeat had been redefined, old Rebels deified, their cause sanctified, and a "true" memory of the struggle written. This new memory removed many of the "blots and blurs" of the Confederate experience that Cornelia Spencer acknowledged in 1865. Forgotten were the looting, desertions, and murders by Southern soldiers. Even the man who had the love of his army, Joseph E. Johnston, took a backrow in the Pantheon of cherished Confederate generals. The old soldiers he commanded struggled to live up to their new status as the embodiment of loyalty, duty, and honor, a mythology created to rekindle honor and unify white Southerners. The South embraced this glorified past because it provided solace to generations of traumatized people. Pride replaced deep pain and helped them deal with the war's persisting wounds.

Talking about the end of the war in North Carolina for a victorious North required talking about an inglorious campaign that saw war made on civilians. A grateful public greeted returning Union soldiers with enthusiastic congratulations as defenders of the Republic and liberators of the slaves. But soldiers quickly realized their friends and loved ones were ignorant of the realities of war and the impact on those who fought it. Men discovered their families and communities could in no way relate to their experiences and recoiled at their stories from the battlefield. Instead the March to the Sea became a cultural cornerstone of the war's memory, complete with its own wildly popular theme song, *Marching Through Georgia*, and the highlight of the general's legacy. Sherman's mythology didn't include the more ferocious war waged in the Carolinas. It was a complicated campaign that embodied a morally questionable side of war that no jaunty tune could lighten. As the North crafted its memory of the war, they, too, built an image of noble warriors fighting gallantly for the life of the nation. Veterans fueled this perception and changed their version of the march to help make them relevant in a rapidly changing society that was turning away from the war. The campaign against civilians, the riotous burning of Columbia, and Sherman's embarrassing fumbling of the negotiations were memories that needed refurbishing, or gilding to make their war record appear less repulsive to a nation struggling to reunite.

Memory also morphed to vindicate the sacrifice of not only the dead but also those who returned bearing the chronic effects of their war. The inescapable proof of the war's impact on survivors was found in the in the debilitated physical, mental, and moral states that afflicted many veterans. Families both North and South tried to put their own lives back together, while helping old soldiers deal with their maladies such as heart failure, rheumatism, bowel issues, arthritis, and other problems related to digestion, cardiovascular, and muscular systems. Communities watched veterans also suffer from ailments of the mind that caused them to behave differently and sympathized with men whose lives seemed unbearable. Many people shook their heads in pity as they struggled to understand what war did to

Veteran Commits Suicide.

Clayton, Ala., April 9.—N. W. Vinson, a prominent farmer, horse dealer and a confederate veteran, committed suicide at his home in Clayton by shooting himself through the heart with a rifle. Death was almost instantaneous. No cause was assigned for the deed, but the supposition is that it was from depression over business, as he had been in a state bordering on melancholia for several weeks.

Notices for soldiers' suicides filled newspapers both North and South. N. W. Vinson fought with the Jeff Davis Cavalry outside Raleigh in April 1865. A week before shooting himself through the heart with a rifle in 1902, Vinson resigned as commander of his United Confederate Veterans camp in Clayton, Alabama. *The Tuscaloosa Gazette, April 1902*

these men. It would take 150 years to fully understand and recognize their suffering was due to unseen injuries in the brain. The symptoms observed in modern veterans diagnosed with PTSD mirror those seen in survivors of the Civil War as well as in combat veterans throughout time.

Soldiers and civilians dealt with their trauma in a wide spectrum of ways. Many soldiers successfully packed their memories away and restarted their lives, while others fought to keep their nightmares at bay. Sometimes the depth of problems was known soon after the war ended, like that of Colonel John M. Orr who enlisted in May 1862 in the 16th Indiana. In January 1863, an artillery shell severely wounded Orr during the battle of Arkansas Post which forced his resignation. Orr struggled to recover and reenlisted as commander of the 124th Indiana and fought in the Atlanta Campaign and the subsequent battles in Tennessee. Physically healed but not mentally mended, he suffered "periodic fits of partial insanity." His old wounds from Arkansas were suspected to be the cause of Orr's suicide when he shot himself in the head only six months after the war's end on September 27, 1865 at age 35.[2]

It took only a few months before Confederate Samuel G. McCreight revealed the extent of his war wounds. He enlisted as a musician in the 9th Tennessee but found himself in the heat of battle. One of his surviving letters described a battle whose vicious hand-to-hand fighting that left piles of bodies, and blood that "was thick all about over the ground for several hundred yards." It was an experience and scene that shocked him. McCreight desperately wanted out of war and hired a substitute. His relief did not last long and he was forced to return to service and was captured at Perryville, 1862. After a stint in a prison camp, he returned to the ranks again but went absent without leave in early 1863. Yet again, McCreight returned to the army just in time to be wounded at the battle of Chickamauga. After healing,

2 *Fort Wayne* [IN] *Daily Gazette*, October 3, 1865.

McCreight was sent back into the ranks for a fourth time to fight at Bentonville. McCreight saw the very worst of war and walked away from Greensboro an emotionally disturbed man. Three months later, on July 21, 1865, friends helped him during "an attack of a low nervous fever." Soon afterward, he retired to his room and blew his brains out with a pistol. *The Memphis Argus* newspaper related no reason for his suicide besides the fact he was thought to be "mentally deranged at the time."[3]

Sometimes men broke after years of managing their issues. Calvin Carson had joined the war in 1861 as a private and rose to Captain in the 16th Alabama. He received wounds at Murfreesboro and again in the fighting around Atlanta on July 22, 1864. He resigned his command on February 20, 1865 because his company had only two men left. Carson walked home to Florence, Alabama from the surrender in North Carolina a troubled man. But he successfully overcame the war and worked for a time as a sheriff and court clerk, but the war finally caught up to him. Despondent over an inability to work and unable to provide for his crippled granddaughter, much like he failed to protect the men in his company, Carson snapped. On December 29, 1902 he killed his granddaughter with a glass of carbolic acid and then slit his throat.[4]

On the twentieth anniversary of the start of the final campaign in North Carolina, John Wesley Rabb killed himself. He had enlisted in August 1861 and joined the 8th Texas Cavalry; he tried to go on with life after the war by gold mining, trying to patent new farm equipment, and fathering eight children. But the war was always with him. It was believed he suffered the lingering effects of a gunshot wound received in November, 1863, which "had robbed him of his reason" and filled his imagination with enemies who were constantly after him. His family and neighbors knew he was a troubled man. While seeking medical attention in San Antonio, Rabb experienced a "momentary mental aberration [sic]" and took his life on April 10, 1885. Writing to one another his saddened family expressed what many others across the South who dealt with troubled veterans, "I hope, I trust, I pray that he is now at rest."[5]

3 Selected Records of the War Department Relating to Confederate Prisoners of War, 1861-1865, M598-88; James R. Fleming, *The Confederate Ninth Tennessee Infantry*. (Gretna, LA, 2006), 173-74.

4 *The Montgomery* [AL] *Advertiser*, Dec. 30, 1902; Compiled Services Records, Roll 0252. NARA.

5 Thomas W. Cutrer, "We are Stern and Resolved": The Civil War Letters of John Wesley Rabb, Terry's Texas Rangers. *The Southwestern Historical Quarterly* (October, 1987), 91:225-26;

The wave of post-war suicides provided the most shocking insights into how the war hurt soldiers, both North and South. In 1868, The *Tennessean* newspaper in Nashville included an article from the *New York Sun* that expressed worry over the wave of suicides by old soldiers and tried to understand the cause of their pain, "The prevalence of suicide is very remarkable." The paper speculated on the deaths of old soldiers by their own hands, "It is undoubtedly due in a great measure to the familiarity with death arising from the war, as well as the hardships of which it was the cause."[6]

Suicides represented the extreme impact of the war. Many more veterans returned home with psychological issues that left them troubled. Across the country, Johnston's and Sherman's former soldiers crowded the nation's hospitals, soldier's homes, prisons, and asylums. Francis Cook's behavior typified soldiers whose mental facilities were destroyed by toxic stress endured during the war. Cook enlisted in the 104th Illinois in 1862 and received a head wound a year later during the Battle of Chickamauga. He stayed with his regiment as it marched across North Carolina. Cook returned home a seemingly happy man but by fall, Cook's demeanor changed. He became "irritable and vicious" and "would make threats of violence and act in a violent manner." A family doctor examined Cook and pronounced him "not right in his mind." He suffered "periodic attacks of lunacy." His condition grew worse until he was finally, in 1883, he was committed to the Illinois State Asylum after attacking and trying to kill his father. Still, Cook's mental state declined, forcing the asylum to transfer him to St. Elizabeth's Hospital. There doctors described his condition as a "Nervous prostration with partial derangement of mind . . . insane, delusions numerous and decided." He remained in the hospital until his death in 1914, one of the 1,300 veterans who became patients in St. Elizabeth's from 1865 to 1890. Ten of these men were admitted the week after the Grand Review of the Union armies in Washington D.C.[7]

Some veterans struggled to fight the effects of PTSD with alcohol and drugs. Alcohol consumed men during the last months and this dependence carried over

---

Groesbeck [TX] Journal, December 9, 1909; John W. Rabb headstone, Old La Grange City Cemetery, La Grange, Texas. Rabb could have been the same soldier described by Tom Burney in 1909 who executed a Union prisoner outside of Atlanta in 1864. Burney noted the prisoner was executed by a cavalryman with at least 60 notes in his pistol grip noting every man he'd killed. He also noted this man committed suicide in Texas.

6 Silkenet, *Moments of Despair*, 25; The [Nashville] *Tennessean*, July 25, 1865.

7 Dillon Carroll, "Scourge of War: Mental Illness and Civil War Veterans," Ph.D. dissertation, University of Georgia, 2016, 126-28; Jordan, *Marching Home*, 39.

into peace time. Self-medicating veterans became the terror of families who struggled to deal with wild and violent fathers, brothers, and husbands. The introduction to opiates during the war, and the explosion of opium-based tonics and elixirs afterward, enabled many more troubled men the ability to self-medicate in search of relief. Robert S. Saffold, of the 46th Alabama, surrendered with Johnston and became an admitted "doper" in the post-war years. Saffold spent almost a decade in a sanitarium suffering with his addiction. After entering a soldiers' home in 1906, he attacked the superintendent with brass knuckles and tried to choke him. Addiction to patent medicines promised to ease different complaints and diseases that were a result of wartime service but only served to turn the aging soldiers into addicts. In 1904, a report investigating Georgia's Confederate Soldiers' homes labeled addiction among veterans as a severe problem. In 1913, another survey of South Carolina veterans in various homes came to the same dire conclusion about opiate's stranglehold on the old soldiers. Doctors regarded the condition of addicts as a product of heredity or weak morals. Today doctors can explain addiction among PTSD diagnosed veterans. This endorphin compensation theory suggest, stimulants, like alcohol and opiates, replicates the numbing effect that is created with the release of natural endorphins that help individuals deal with trauma.[8]

Besides the mental and physical injuries, veterans were further haunted by the moral wounds suffered during the war's finale. By 1865, the stress of campaigns and combat made men into hardened veterans and brought them into conflict with their long-held beliefs of duty, propriety, and faith. This process was the result of stress that influenced the brain's inability to make clear judgements, feel compassion, and manage anger. In short, the intensity of stress eroded moral boundaries. For soldiers like Confederate John Claiborne war caused a lapse in morality that made his crimes seem to be a justified action of war. There were other soldiers who retained their moral compass and questioned their own morals and the morals of those around them. With peace, and a return to civilian society, men realized how far war had pushed them and caused guilt and shame, that left them deeply conflicted. These men suffered PTSD-like symptoms of depression, addiction, or madness. John Cundiff's role in the firing squad that killed a

---

8 Marten, *Sing Not War*, 102-103; R. B. Rosenburg. *Living Monuments: Confederate Soldiers' Homes in the New South* (Chapel Hill, NC, 1993), 105-13. Volpicelli, Balaraman, Hahn, Wallace, and Bux, "PTSD and Alcohol Addiction," 260.

Confederate prisoner inflicted a moral wound that haunted him for the rest of his life.[9]

Trauma and the moral trespass it caused lies at the heart of why post-war America shied away from the story of the war's end in the Carolinas. But looking back, some of Sherman's men tried to understand what war made them do. Former Union army Maj. Gen. Carl Shurz, pressed Sherman years later about the warfare he unleashed in the Carolinas. Sherman bluntly admitted he let discipline go to dangerous levels but insisted that was the way the war had to be fought. "Human nature is human nature," Sherman noted, "You take the best lot of young men, all church members, if you please, and put them into an army, and let them invade the enemy's country, and live upon it for any length of time, and they will gradually lose all principle. It always has been and always will be so."[10]

One soldier, Albion Tourgée, wrestled with the aftermath of Sherman's war. Tourgée came to North Carolina and served as a local representative to the state's constitutional convention and as a superior court judge from 1868–74. He saw first-hand the lasting physical and mental problems of civilians traumatized by Sherman's men. He believed there are "bad, rough spirits in every army" but admitted "the conduct of our army in the respect cannot be justified or excused." Tourgée blamed not soldiers in the ranks but complicit officers who encouraged or allowed their behavior. He believed bad leadership was the true culprit for the lawlessness of the campaign. Besides the soldiers being "let loose" in the Southern interior, Tourgée could justify the undisciplined march if the commanders would have assumed the responsibility for what happened. However, leaders tacit approval of lawlessness opened the door for, what he considered, "the only thing in the history of the war for the Union which is really regrettable."[11]

The same stress damage that subverted morality on the battlefield kept men from recovering their moral compass in the civilian world. Sherman's Bummers earned a postwar reputation that epitomized civilian's image of the immoral and dangerous veteran who had little regard for property and social norms. Civilians feared returning veterans and justified their alarm by pointing to prisons filled with former soldiers unable to recover their morality in peacetime. Officials in

9 Roger E. Meagher and Douglas A. Pryor, eds., *War and Moral Injury: A Reader* (Eugene, OR, 2018), 2.

10 Frederic Bancroft and William A. Dunning, eds., *Reminiscences of Carl Shurz, 1863-1869.* 3 vols. (New York, 908), 3:133.

11 Tourgée, *The Story of a Thousand*, 355, 366.

Massachusetts, Pennsylvania, Illinois, and Wisconsin believed 50–90 percent of their incarcerated population to be former Union soldiers. One warden directly attributed their condition to the "demoralization by apprenticeship to the trade of war." It led one Northern writer to declare, "the moralization of the soldier is the demoralization of the man."[12]

Confederate veterans also had their moral issues in the war's final days. The intensity of the stress stoked the PTSD among Confederates that encouraged the robbing of Southern civilians, sacking of government facilities, and extreme violence against Union soldiers and African Americans. But the moral transgression that would cause the most duress in later years was soldiers' dereliction of duty by desertion in the Confederacy's final hours. For Southern memory makers this wartime demoralization was an inconvenient fact. Lost Cause memory evolved to the detriment of the truth about how the war ended and who remained dedicated to the cause. For Johnston's veterans the questioning of their moral fortitude took on a new reality when it jeopardized their veneration by Southern society and access to long-term care.

Former Rebels suffering from their wartime service looked to the states for the relief. Many states established soldier's homes starting in the 1880s to provide support for Confederate veterans who were considered an embodiment of Old South values of duty, honor, and self-sacrifice. Many of these homes prescribed by-laws that restricted admission to soldiers who served "honorably" and maintained an "unimpeachable" war record, a requirement that many of Johnston's soldiers could not meet. Speaking in 1885 at the opening of a soldier's home in Richmond, Johnston's adjutant, Col. Archer Anderson, praised the "supreme manliness" of the "devoted" Confederate soldier who had achieved "moral perfection." A high bar set for Confederate veterans and a surprising admission by an officer who watched his army disintegrate in 1865. Archer admitted some did not achieve this goal but assured the audience all "strove to attain it." But the war record of many men, especially those who served under Johnston, knew their service did not fit the mold set by society. Many men remained silent about their roles in the final days in order to protect the benefits they needed to deal with the war's lasting legacy.[13]

As the 19th century ended, America began to celebrate and commemorate those redeeming aspects of the great conflict. The nation's celebration served

12 Jordan, *Marching Home*. 5-6; Marten, *Sing Not War*, 51, 57, 222.

13 Rosenburg, *Living Monuments*, 3-12.

several purposes, promoting sectional reconciliation, reinforcing racial hegemony, and helping veterans find their place in the nation's constructed memory of their war. For some veterans, their families, and those who lived through the war, the appearance of monuments, relics, and organizations, triggered painful memories of the war's last days. Mary W. Smith expressed her feelings about her experience in Greensboro in April 1865, "Nothing recalls more eloquently the pain and pathos of [the past] eventful days than the haunting strains of the old war songs, as they came floating in on many a sleepless and sorrowful night, sung by the soldiers in passing. Their mission by campfire and field is ended, but in many a veteran's heart they will echo on forever." Mrs. L.A. Walker reluctantly gave a private lecture to the Greensboro chapter of the United Daughters of the Confederacy and professed that the invitation to speak, and the memories it evoked, were a "strain on memory and nerves." Walker admitted she had taken those memories and "banished [them] to the silent vaults of memory, the door closed, and keys lost." Robert Phillip Howell penned his memoirs in 1900 and agonized as he talked about the surrender, "Never shall I forget my feelings at that moment. I wept like a child and said I was sorry I had not been killed in the war. After a lapse of thirty-five years it wrings my heart to write about it."[14]

In the close of his memoir one of Sherman's former soldiers, Charles Willison, boasted he had been in good health during his service, but since then, the impact of army life on the growing body of a young nineteen-year-old came back to haunt him. But the sights of the battlefield remained vivid for Willison who spent his life searching for meaning in his wartime experiences, "[My] [m]ind seems to cling them more vividly as the years go by, and, what is peculiar, the most fearful and trying have made the deepest impression." The experiences of the battlefield and the war's end were the most impactful, but could not be shared with those who did not experience that war. It was clear that war forever changed those who lived through it. After 75 years one observer of the old Confederate veterans concluded the pain they still struggled with dwarfed their service. "The aftermath of a great war often seems worse than the war itself."[15]

14 Jordan, *Coming Home*, 68; Arnett, *Confederate Guns Were Stacked*, 131; L.A. Walker, *The Surrender in Greensboro*, 1898, GHM; Silkenet, *Moments of Despair*, 29, 114; Robert Phillip Howell Memoirs, SHC/UNC.

15 Charles A. Willison, *Reminiscences of a Boy's Service with the 76th Ohio in the Fifteenth Army Corps, Under General Sherman, During the Civil War, by that "Boy" at Three Score* (Huntington, WV, 1995), 124; Augustus W. Long, *Son of Carolina* (Durham, 1939), 38,155.

The Civil War made a sublime impact on the nation and those who fought it. The completeness of this change has taken over a century and a half to unlock, providing a window into the human experience in war. Utilizing modern understandings, the brain's and body's reaction to war provides a new insight into how war is made and the shaping of its memory. Considering PTSD and other diagnoses may not precisely underlay the experience of Civil War veterans, but it provides a timeless explanation of how war changes the hearts, bodies, and souls of those who fight it. Recognizing the impact of chronic physical, mental, and moral stress on the survivors reveals how they remembered, or forgot, the war's concluding chapter in North Carolina.

"Lincoln is Dead"
by George Moses Horton

M**ajor** William C. Stevens described the freedman George Moses Horton in a letter to his mother on May 23, 1865:

I do not think I have ever mentioned an odd character we have in our camp in the form of an old negro who has considerable poetical talent. He joined us at Chapel Hill and is now with Capt. Banks of our Regt. under whose direction he is writing a book. He has already written more than one hundred pieces of poetry upon difficult subjects. All that is necessary is to give him the subject and an idea of what you wish to portray in the piece, and he will do the rest. He is upwards of sixty years old and has always been a slave and has no education except what he has been able to get himself, he having learned to read without the knowledge of his master. The Book will be published in a few days in pamphlet form and I will send you a copy. I will enclose a copy of one of his pieces entitled "Lincoln is dead."

The text of the poem Stevens included in his letter, which is on the following page, is an early unpublished version. Scrawled in pencil vertically on one side of the paper is "Chappel Hill," which suggests it was originally written when Horton joined the Union troopers.

Lincoln is Dead

He is gone to the strong base of the nation,
The dove to his covet has fled,
Ye heroes' lament his privation
For Lincoln immortal is dead.

He is gone down the sun of the Union
Like Phoebus that sets in the west,
The planet of peace and commotion
Forever has gone to his rest.

He is gone from a world of commotion,
No Equal succeeds in his stead,
His wonders extend with the ocean
Where waves murmur "Lincoln is dead."

He is gone and can [ne'er] be forgotten
Whose great deeds eternal shall bloom,
Where gold, pearls and diamonds are rotten
His deeds will break fresh from the tomb.

He is gone out of glory to glory,
A smile with the tear may be shed;
Oh, then let us tell the sweet story
Triumphantly, Lincoln is dead.

Source: WCS to Mother, May 23, 1865, William Collins Stevens Collection, BL-UMI.

Poem Composed by George Moses Horton
"Execution of Private Henry Anderson,
Co. D, 9th Mich. Cav. Vols.,
Lexington, North Carolina, May 13, 1865."

This verse is plain, that all may understand,
The scene is solemn and expressly grand;
The must'ring concourse form'd in grand array,
Betrayed the fate of the expiring day;
Gazing spectators seemed completely dumb,
Beneath the sound of bugle and the drum.
The fun'ral march attracted every eye,
To see the trembling malefactor die;
O, memorable eve, not soon forgot,
We never can the scene portray,
The ghastly aspect of the fatal day.

We've heard of martyrs at the cruel stake,
From which an adamantine heart would break;
We've heard of victims on the fun'ral pyre,
Containing sacrifice and set on fire,
When victims died beneath the ruthless flame,
The brutal torture of eternal shame.

This case seems to bear the mark, tho' justly done,
A case that every sober man may shun;
'Twas for the deed of open homicide,
This guilty malefactor fell and died.
See well arrayed the attentive squadrons stand,
Thus to discharge their guns at one command;
'Till pointing at one mark the shaft of death,
He breaths at once his last decisive breath.

It is, indeed, a sad infernal crime
To one's own self, thus hurried out of time;
He introduces first the murderous strife,
By his own hand he spurns away his life!
How many creatures thus have fell,
Imbibing nectar from the bowels of hell!

Inspiring depredations all the night,
And thus betrayed the death at morning light;
Thus flies the deadly shaft without control–
He fell upon his coffin, O, my soul!
Let all that live the scene appall–
He dies! No more to live at all, at all!

Source: George Moses Horton, Naked Genius, Raleigh, NC: William B. Smith & Co., 1865, 51-52.

Manuscript Sources

Alabama Division of Archives and History, Montgomery, AL
Bolling Hall. Family papers
  Civil War Unit File
    51st Alabama Cavalry
  Hall, James. Letters
  Kennedy, Ed. Letters
Atlanta Historical Society, Atlanta, GA
  Lawson, George. Diary
Auburn Special Collections and Archives, Auburn, AL
    Smith, Jabez N. Papers
Author's Collection
    Martin, H. Page. Letter
Bennett Place State Historic Site, Durham, NC
  Allen, Moses. Diary
  Sparkman, Jesse. Diary
Bentley Historical Library, University of Michigan, Detroit, MI
  Nina Ness Collection
    North, Solomon Jack. Letters
    Washburn, Washington. Letters
  Stevens, William C. Papers
Betsey B. Creekmore Special Collections and University Archives, University of
  Tennessee, Knoxville, TN
  Pippitt, Henry. Diary

Department of Archives and Special Collections, University of Mississippi, Oxford, MS
> Charles Roberts Collection

Georgia Department of Archives and History, Morrow, GA
> Talley, William R. Memoirs

Gilder Lehrman Institute of American History Collection, New York, NY
> Wheeler, Lysander. Papers

Greensboro Historical Museum, Greensboro, NC
> Dantzler, Daniel D. Diary
> Foust, Mana D. Letter

Illinois State Historical Library, Springfield, IL
> William Brown Collection

Indiana Historic Society, Indianapolis, IN
> Chamberlain, Joseph and Orville. Papers
> Ward, Williamson D. Letters

Iowa State University Archives, Des Moines, IA
> Hostetter, John L. Papers

Michigan State University, East Lansing, MI
> Howe, Simeon H. Letter

North Carolina Division of Archives and History, Raleigh, NC
> Crabtree Jones Collection
> James Crozer Collection
> Dorothea Dix State Hospital Records
> Lavender, Alston. Papers
> Taylor, John D. Papers
> Vance, Zebulon. Governor's Papers

National Archives and Records Administration, Washington, DC
> Selected Records of the War Department Relating to Confederate Prisoners of War, 1861-1865
> United States Civil War Service Records of Confederate Soldiers, 1861-1865
> United States Civil War Soldier Pension Files

South Caroliniana Library, University of South Carolina, Columbia, SC
> Coleman, John Kennedy. Diary

Southern Historical Collection, University of North Carolina, Chapel Hill, NC
> Battle Family Papers
> Bean, Jesse S. Diary
> Buford, Munson M. Papers
> Collins, Anne Cameron. Papers

Dean, Henderson. Reminisces
Mily Gordon Collection
    Gordon, W. W. Diary
    Grimes Family Papers
    Grimes, William. Recollection
    Hargis, O. P. Reminiscences
    Hinton, Jane Constance. Reminiscences
    Laurens Hinton Collection
        Howell, Robert Philip. Memoir
        Charles W. Hutson Collection
        Lacy, Drury. Papers
    Mallett, Charles P. Diary
    Miller, George Knox. Papers
        Schenck, Nicholas. Reminiscences
    Cornelia Phillips Spencer Collection
    John L. Swain Collection
        Waring, Joseph Frank. Diary
        Webb, Henry Louis. Papers
Special Collections, Duke University, Durham, NC
    Anderson, Z. W. Notebook
    Aumack, Ellen. Papers
    Brent, George William. Papers
    Charles S. Brown Collection
    Eltinge-Lord Collection
        Powell, Young J. Diary
    Jenkins, Gertrude. Papers
    Jenkins, Robert Alexander. Reminiscences
    Metz, George P. Papers
    Otey, John M. Papers
    Stetson, Joseph M. Papers
Special Collections, Knox College, Galesburg, IL
    Burkhalter, Savina Karl. Papers
Special Collections, University of Tennessee, Knoxville, TN
    Henry Pippitt Collection
State Historical Society of Wisconsin, Madison, WI
    Charles S. Spencer Collection
St. Bonaventure University Archives, St. Bonaventure, NY
    Pettit, Joshua. Diary

St. Mary's School, Raleigh, NC
    Cain, Bessie. Diary
Tennessee State Library and Archives, Nashville, TN
    Sullivan, Thomas L. Account Book
United States Army Military History Institute, Carlisle Barracks, PA
    Ellis, Orrin L. Diary
    Kittinger, Joseph. Diary
University of Alabama, Tuscaloosa, AL
    Huston Family Papers
University of Arkansas, Fayetteville, AL
    Reynolds, Daniel H. Papers
University of Georgia Libraries, Athens, GA
    Platter, Cornelius C. Diary
University of Iowa, Iowa City, IA
    Allspaugh, Jacob. Diary
    Culver, Joseph Franklin. Papers
    Emmons, W. B. Diary
    Palmer, David James. Papers
University of Maine,
    Mendenhal, Delphina E. letters, Orono, ME
University of Texas Archives, Austin, TX
    Stanton, William E. Letters
Virginia Military Institute, Lexington, VA
    Crowther, John. Diary
Virginia Museum of History and Culture, Richmond, VA
    Tucker, St. George Mason. Diary
Wright State University, Dayton, OH
    Overholser, James F. Diary
Z. Smith Reynolds Library Wake Forrest University, Winston-Salem, NC
    Mt. Pisgah Baptist Church Records

Newspapers

Buffalo Commercial, November 1897
[Salisbury, North] *Carolina Watchman*, February 1863
Charlotte Democrat, March 1885
The [Raleigh] *Confederate*, March 1865
Daily Confederate [Raleigh], December 1864

Daily Conservative [Raleigh], March 1865
Daily Standard [Raleigh], April, December, 1865; 1868
Daily State Journal [Raleigh], February 1865
Durham Morning Herald, September 1923
Evening Bulletin [Charlotte], December 1862
Fayetteville Weekly Observer, February 1863
Fort Wayne [IN] *Daily Gazette*, 1865
Greensboro [NC] *Patriot*, March, September, 1864; 1865
Groesbeck [TX] *Journal*, January 1910
Maysville [OH] *Tribune*, May 1865
Montgomery [AL] *Advertiser*, December 1902
Morning Post [Raleigh], August 1905
National Tribune, July 1903
New York Herald, February–May, 1865
New York Times, May 1865
Philadelphia Inquirer, April 1865
Raleigh Daily Progress, February, April, 1865
The Tennessean [Nashville], July 1865
The Times [Philadelphia], May 1887
Wall Street Journal, May 2004
Weekly North Carolina Standard [Raleigh], March1865
Weekly Standard [Raleigh], April 1865

Government Sources

The War of the Rebellion: A Compilation of the Official Records of the Union and Confederate Armies. 128 volumes in 3 series. Washington, DC: United States Government Printing Office, 1880-1901.

Report on Epidemic Cholera and Yellow Fever in the Army of the United States, During the Year 1867. Washington, DC: United States Government Printing Office, 1868.

Born in Slavery: Slave Narratives from the Federal Writers' Project, 1936-1938. 17 Vols. Washington, DC: Library of Congress, 2001.

Published Primary Sources

"Address of General Sherman." *Report of the Proceedings of the Society of the Army of the Tennessee,* Vol. 1. Cincinnati: The Society of the Army of the Tennessee, 1877.

Albright, James W. *Greensboro 1808-1904: Facts, Figures, and Reminiscences.* Greensboro, NC: Joseph J. Stone Co., 1904.

Allen, Stacy Dale, ed. *On the Skirmish Line Behind a Friendly Tree: The Civil War Memoirs of William Royal Oake, 26th Iowa Volunteers.* Helena, MT: Farcountry Press, 2006.

Allison, W. F. "Vivid War Incident." *Confederate Veteran,* Vol. 1 (May 1893), 133.

Amis, Moses N. *Historical Raleigh from its Foundation in 1792; Descriptive, Biographical, Educational, Industrial, Religious; Reminiscences Reviewed and Carefully Compiled.* Raleigh: Edwards and Broughton, 1902.

Andersen, Mary Ann, ed. *The Civil War Diary of Allen Morgan Geer.* Tappan, NY: R. C. Appleman, 1977.

Anderson, William Martin, ed. *We are Sherman's Men: The Civil War Letters of Henry Orendorff.* Chicago: J. F. Leaming & Co, 1904.

Andrews, William Hill and McMurry, Richard M. *Footprints of a Regiment: A Recollection of the 1st Georgia Regulars, 1861-1865.* Marietta, GA: Longstreet Press, 1992.

Arbuckle, John C. *Civil War Experiences of a Foot Soldier Who Marched with Sherman.* Columbus, OH: No publisher, 1930.

Armstrong, Robert. *Civil War Diary of Robert Armstrong, Sergeant, 66th Indiana Infantry, 1862-1865.* Fort Wayne, IN: Allen County Public Library, 1960.

Aten, Henry J. *History of the Eighty-fifth Regiment, Illinois Volunteer Infantry.* Hiawatha, KS: Eighty-Fifth Regiment Illinois Volunteer Association, 1901.

Bancroft, Frederic and Dunning, William A. *The Reminiscences of Carl Schurz, 1863-1869.* 3 Vols. New York: Doubleday, Page & Co., 1917.

Barber, Lucius W. *Army Memoirs of Lucius W. Barber, Company "D," 15th Illinois Volunteer Infantry.* Chicago: J. M. W. Jones Stationery and Printing Co., 1894.

Barnwell, Joseph W. "Capt. Thomas Pinckney." *Confederate Veteran,* Vol. 24 (1916), 342-344.

Battle, Kemp Plummer. *Memories of an Old Time Tarheel.* Chapel Hill: University of North Carolina Press, 1945.

Beasecker, Robert, ed. *"I Hope to Do My Country Service": The Civil War Letters of John Bennitt, M.D., Surgeon, 19th Michigan Infantry.* Detroit: Wayne State University Press, 2005.

Betts, A. D. *Experience of a Confederate Chaplain, 1861-1865.* No publisher, no date.

Belknap, William Worth. *History of the Fifteenth Regiment Iowa Veteran Volunteer Infantry.* Keokuk, IA: R. B. Ogden & Son Pub., 1887.

Bohrnstedt, Jennifer Cain, ed. *Soldiering with Sherman: The Civil War Letters of George F. Cram.* DeKalb, IL: Northern Illinois University Press, 2000.

Bradley, George S. *The Star Corps: or, Notes of an Army Chaplain, During Sherman's Famous March to the Sea.* Milwaukee: Jermain & Brightman Printers, 1865.

Brant, Jefferson E. *History of the Eighty-fifth Indiana Volunteer Infantry*. Bloomington, IN: Cravens Brothers, 1902.

Brooks, Ulysses R. *Butler and His Cavalry in the War of Secession, 1861-1865*. Germantown, TN: Guild Bindery Press, 1994.

Brooks, U. R. and Rea, D. B., eds. *Stories of the Confederacy*. Columbia, SC: The State Company, 1912.

Brown, Alonzo L. *History of the Fourth Regiment of Minnesota Infantry Volunteers During the Great Rebellion, 1861-1865*. St Paul, MN: Pioneer Press, 1892.

Brown, Norman, ed. *One of Cleburne's Command: The Civil War Reminiscences and Diary of Capt. Samuel T. Foster, Granbury's Texas Brigade, CSA*. Austin: University of Texas Press, 1980.

Bryant, Edwin E. *History of the Third Regiment of Wisconsin Veteran Volunteer Infantry, 1861-1865*. Madison, WI: Veterans Association of the Regiment, 1891.

Burton Elijah P. *Diary of Elijah P. Burton*. Des Moines, IA: Historical Records Survey, 1939.

Bull, Rice C. *Soldiering: The Civil War Diary of Rice C. Bull, 123rd New York Volunteer Infantry*. San Rafael, CA: Presidio Press, 1977.

Byrne, Frank L., ed. *The View from Headquarters: Civil War Letters of Harvey Reid*. Madison: State Historical Society of Wisconsin, 1965.

Calkins, William W. *The History of the One Hundred and Fourth Regiment of Illinois Volunteer Infantry, War of the Great Rebellion, 1862-1865*. Chicago: Donahue & Henneberry, 1895.

Carmony, Donald F. "Jacob W. Bartmess Civil War Letters." *Indiana Magazine of History*, Vol. 52 (June 1956), 157-186.

Claiborne, John M. "Secret Service for General Hood." Confederate Veteran, Vol. 9 (1901), 31.

Chamberlin, William H. *History of the Eighty-first Regiment Ohio Infantry Volunteers, During the War of the Rebellion*. Cincinnati: Gazette Steam Printing House, 1865.

Clark, Olynthus B., ed. *Downing's Civil War Diary*. Des Moines: Iowa State Department of History and Archives, 1916.

Clark, Walter. *Histories of the Several Regiments and Battalions from North Carolina in the Great War 1861-65*. 4 Vols. Goldsboro, NC: Nash Brothers, 1901.

Collins, Robert M. *Chapters from the Unwritten History of the War Between the States, or, The Incidents in the Life of a Confederate Soldier in Camp, on the March, in the Great Battles, and in Prison*. St. Louis: Nixon-Jones Print Co., 1893.

Crow, Terrell Armistead and Barde, Mary Moulton, eds. *Live Your Own Life: The Family Papers of Mary Bayard Clarke, 1854-1886*. Columbia, SC: University of South Carolina Press, 2003.

Cox, Jacob D. "The Sherman-Johnston Convention." *Scribner's Magazine*, Vol. 28 (1900), 489-505.

_____. *Sherman's March to the Sea*. Boston: Da Capo Press, 1994.

_____. *Military Reminiscences of The Civil War*. 2 Vols. New York: C. Scribner's Sons, 1900.

Crews, C. Daniel and Bailey, Lisa D., eds. *Records of the Moravians in North Carolina*. 13 Vols. Raleigh, NC: Division of Archives and History, 1922-2006.

Cruikshank, Robert. Letters. Ohio State University: www.ehistory. osu.edu/exhibitions/letters/cruikshank/index, accessed May 14, 2010.

Culver, Mary, Dunlap, Leslie Whittaker, and Bearss, Edwin C., eds. *"Your affectionate husband, J. F. Culver": Letters written during the Civil War*. Iowa City, IA: Friends of the University of Iowa Libraries, 1978.

Cumming, Joseph B. "How I Knew That the War Was Over." *Confederate Veteran*, Vol. 9 (1901), 18-19.

Cutrer, Thomas W. "We are Stern and Resolved": The Civil War Letters of John Wesley Rabb, Terry's Texas Rangers." *The Southwestern Historical Quarterly*, Vol. 91 (October 1987), 185-226.

Cuttino, George Peddy. *Saddle Bags and Spinning Wheels: Being the Civil War Letters of George W. Peddy, M.D., Surgeon, 56th Georgia Volunteer Regiment, C.S.A. and His Wife Kate Featherstone Peddy*. Macon, GA.: Mercer University Press, 2008.

Davis, Jefferson. *The Rise and Fall of the Confederate Government*. 2 Vols. New York: Collier Books, 1961.

Dawson, George Francis. *The Life and Services of John A. Logan*. New York: Belford, Clarke & Company, 1887.

DeCosta, J. M. "On Irritable Heart: A Clinical Study of a Form of Functional Cardiac Disorder and Its Consequences." *The American Journal of Medical Sciences*, edited by Isaac Hays, Vol. 61 (January 1871),17-52.

Devereux, Margaret. *Plantation Sketches*. Cambridge, MA: The Riverside Press, 1906.

Dickert, D. Augustus. *History of Kershaw's Brigade, with Complete Roll of Companies, Biographical Sketches, Incidents, Anecdotes, etc*. Newberry, SC: E. H. Aull Company, 1899.

Dodson, William C., ed. *Campaigns of Wheeler and his Cavalry, 1862-1865*. Atlanta: Hudgins Publishing Co., 1899.

Dunbar, Aaron and Trimble, Harvey Marion. History of the Ninety-third Regiment, Illinois Volunteer Infantry, From Organization to Muster Out. Chicago: The Blakeley Printing Company, 1898.

Eaton, Clement. "Diary of an Officer in Sherman's Army Marching Through the Carolinas." *Journal of Southern History*, Vol. 9 (May 1943), 238-254.

Elliott, Colleen M. Elliott and Moxley, Louise A. *Tennessee Veterans Questionnaire.* Easley, SC: Southern Historical Press, 1985.

Evans, J. W. "With Hampton's Scouts." *Confederate Veteran*, Vol. 32 (December 1924), 470.

Fleharty, S. F., *Our Regiment: A History of the 102d Illinois Infantry Volunteers with Sketches of the Atlanta Campaign, the Georgia Raid and the Campaign of the Carolinas.* Chicago: Brewster & Hanscom printers, 1865.

Ford, Arthur P. and Ford, Marion Johnstone. *Life in the Confederate Army: Being Personal Experiences of a Private Soldier in the Confederate Army and some Experiences and Sketches of Southern Life.* New York: The Neale Publishing Company, 1905.

Fox, William F. *Regimental Losses in the American Civil War, 1861-1865.* Albany, NY: Albany Publishing Company, 1889.

Garber, Michael C. "Reminiscences of the Burning of Columbia, South Carolina," *Indiana History Magazine*, Vol. 11 (December1915), 11:285-300.

Gage, Moses D. *From Vicksburg to Raleigh; or, A Complete History of the Twelfth Regiment Indiana Volunteer Infantry and the Campaigns of Grant and Sherman, with an Outline of the Great Rebellion.* Chicago: Clarke & Co. Pub., 1865.

Gaskill, J. W. *Footprints Through Dixie: Everyday Life of The Man Under A Musket, On The Firing Line And In The Trenches, 1862-1865.* Alliance, OH: Bradshaw Printing Co., 1919.

Girardi, Robert I., ed. *Campaigning with Uncle Billy: The Civil War Memoirs of Sgt. Lyman S. Widney, 34th Illinois Volunteer Infantry.* Bloomington, IN: Trafford Publishing Co., 2008.

Gorgas, Josiah. *The Civil War Diary of General Josiah Gorgas.* Tuscaloosa: University of Alabama Press, 1947.

Gould, David and Kennedy, James B., eds. *Memoirs of a Dutch Mudsill: The "War Memories" of John Henry Otto.* Kent, OH: Kent State University Press, 2004.

Grant, Ulysses S. *Personal Memoirs of U.S. Grant.* 2 Vols. New York: Charles L. Webster & Company, 1886.

Guild, George B. *A Brief Narrative of the Fourth Tennessee Cavalry Regiment, Wheeler's Corps, Army of Tennessee.* Nashville: No publisher, 1913.

Hagood, Johnson. *Memoirs of the War of Secession: From the Original Manuscripts of Johnson Hagood.* Columbia, SC: The State Co., 1910.

Halliburton, Lloyd, ed. *Saddle Soldiers: The Civil War Correspondence of General William Stokes of the 4th South Carolina Cavalry.* Orangeburg, SC: Sandlapper Publishing Co., 1993.

Harris, James S. *Historical Sketches of the 7th North Carolina Troops, 1861-1865.* Mooresville, NC: Mooresville Pub. Co., 1893.

Harwell, Richard Barksdale and Racine, Philip N, eds. *The Fiery Trail: A Union Officer's Account of Sherman's Last Campaign.* Knoxville: University of Tennessee Press, 1986.

Hatcher, Edmund N. *The Last Four Weeks of the War.* Columbus, OH: Edmund N. Hatcher Publisher, 1891.

Herriot, Robert. "At Greensboro, N.C., In April, 1865," *Confederate Veteran*, Vol. 30 (1922), 101-102.

Hight, John J. and Stormont, G. S. *History of the 58th Regiment of Indiana Volunteer Infantry.* Princeton, IN: Press of The Clarion, 1895.

Hinkley, Julian W. *A Narrative of Service with the 3rd Wisconsin Infantry.* Madison, WI: Wisconsin Historical Commission, 1912.

Hopkins, Vivian C, ed. "Soldiers of the 92nd Illinois: Letters of William H. Brown and His Fiancée, Emma Jane Frazen." *Bulletin of the New York Public Library*, Vol. 73 (February 1969), 114-136

Howard, Oliver Otis. *Autobiography of Oliver Otis Howard, Major-general, United States Army.* New York: Baker & Taylor, 1908.

Howard, Wiley C. *Sketch of Cobb Legion Cavalry and Some Incidents and Scenes Remembered.* Atlanta: Privately published, 1901.

Howe, M. A. DeWolfe, ed. *Marching With Sherman: Passages from the Letters and Campaign Diaries of Henry Hitchcock, Major and Assistant Adjutant General of Volunteers, November 1864-May 1865.* New Haven, CT: Yale University Press, 1927.

Jackson, David P., ed. *The Colonel's Diary: Journals kept Before and During the Civil War by the Late Colonel Oscar L. Jackson, Sometime Commander of the 63rd regiment O. V. I.* Sharon, PA: Privately published, 1922.

Jamison, Matthew H. *Recollections of Pioneer and Army Life.* Kansas City: Hudson Press, 1911.

Johnson, Robert Underwood and Buel, Clarence Clough, eds. *Battles and leaders of the Civil War. 4 Vols.* New York: The Century Company, 1884-88.

Johnston, Joseph E. *Narrative of Military Operations Directed, in the Late War Between the States.* New York: D. Appleton and Co., 1874.

_____. "My Negotiations with General Sherman," *The North American Review*, Vol. 143 (August 1886), 183-197.

Jones, Charles Colcock. *Historical Sketch of the Chatham Artillery During the Confederate Struggle for Independence.* Albany, GA: Joel Munsell Pub., 1867.

Jones, J. Keith. *The Boys of Diamond Hill: The Lives and Civil War Letters of the Boyd Family of Abbeville County, South Carolina.* Jefferson, NC: McFarland & Company, Inc., 2011.

Jones, John W. *Christ in the Camp: or, Religion in the Confederate Army.* Atlanta: Martin & Hoyt Co., 1904.

Jordan, Francis Marion. *Life and Labors of Elder F. M. Jordan.* Raleigh: Edwards & Broughton, 1899.

Kennedy, Edward. "The Last Work of Wheeler's Special Confederate Scouts." *Confederate Veteran*, Vol. 32 (1924), 60-61.

Kirwin, Thomas and Splaine, Henry, eds. *Memorial History of the Seventeenth Regiment, Massachusetts Volunteer Infantry (old or new organizations) in the Civil War from 1861-1865.* Salem, MA: The Committee on History by the Salem Press Co., 1911.

Kohl, Joyce, ed. "Civil War Letters of William Samuel Craig." Ohio State University: www.ehistory.osu.edu/exhibitions/letters/craig/default, accessed May 14, 2010.

Latta, Morgan London. *The History of My Life and Work.* Raleigh: M. L. Latta, 1903.

Lee, Laura Elizabeth. *Forget-Me-Nots of The Civil War: A Romance, Containing Reminiscences and Original Letters of Two Confederate Soldiers.* St. Louis: A. R. Fleming Press, 1998.

Lindsley, John B., ed. *The Military Annals of Tennessee.* Nashville: J. M. Lindsley Co., 1886.

Long, Augustus W. *Son of Carolina.* Durham, NC: Duke University Press, 1939.

McAdams, Francis Marion. *Every-day Soldier life, or a History of the Hundred and Thirteen Ohio Volunteer Infantry.* Columbus, OH: Charles. M. Cott & Co., Publishers, 1884.

McBride, John Randolph. *History of the Thirty-third Indiana Veteran Volunteer Infantry During the Four Years of Civil War.* Indianapolis: William B. Buford, Printer, 1900.

Mallory, Stephen R. "Last Days of the Confederate Government." *McClure's Magazine*, Vol. 16 (December 1900), 239-248.

McCaleb, Walter F., ed. *Memoirs, with Special Reference to Secession and the Civil War.* New York: Neale Publishing Co., 1906.

Merrill, Samuel. *The Seventieth Indiana Volunteer Infantry in the War of the Rebellion.* Indianapolis: Bowen-Merrill Co., 1900.

Morhous, Henry C. *Reminiscences of the 123rd Regiment, N.Y.S.V., Giving a Complete History of Its Three Years' Service in the War.* Greenwich, NY: People's Journal Book and Job Office, 1879.

Morse, Loren J., ed. *Civil War Diaries of Bliss Morse.* Pittsburg, KS: Pittcraft Inc., 1964.

Mowris, James A. *A History of the One Hundred and Seventeenth Regiment, N.Y. Volunteers, (Fourth Oneida,) from the Date of Its Organization, August 1862, Till that of Its Muster Out, June, 1865.* Hartford: Case, Lockwood and Co., 1866.

Nichols, George Ward. *The Story of the Great March from the Diary of a Staff Officer.* New York: Harper & Brothers, 1865.

Olive, Johnson. *One of the Wonders of the Age; or The Life and Times of Rev. Johnson Olive.* Raleigh: Edwards, Broughton & Co., 1886.

Paxson, Lewis C. *Diary of Lewis C. Paxson, 1862-1865.* Bismarck, ND: State Historical Society of North Dakota, 1908.

Peak, Samuel. Scrapbook. Internet Archive: www.archive.org/stream/SamPeakMemoir/Peak%20Memoir-reduced_djvu.txt, accessed November 11, 2018.

Pepper, George W. *Personal Recollections of Sherman's Campaigns in Georgia and the Carolinas.* Lexington, KY: Lost Cause Press, 1968.

Perry, Henry F. *History of the Thirty-eighth Regiment Indiana Volunteer Infantry.* Palo Alto, CA: F. A. Stuart, 1906.

Pinney, Nelson A. *History of the 104th Regiment Ohio Volunteer Infantry from 1862 to 1865.* Windham, OH: Werner & Lohmann, 1886.

Porter, Anthony T. *Led On! Step by Step, Scenes from Clerical, Military, Educational, and Plantation Life in the South, 1828-1898.* New York: G. P. Putnam's Sons, 1898.

Post, Lydia M., ed. *Soldiers' Letters, from Camp, Battle-field and Prison.* New York: Bunce & Huntington, Pub., 1865.

Quinlan, John, ed. *Armed Only with Faith: The Civil War Correspondence of Chaplain William Lyman Hyde, 112th New York Infantry.* Jefferson, NC: McFarland & Company Inc., 2015.

Report on the Proceedings of the Society of the Army of Tennessee. 45 vols. Cincinnati: F. W. Freeman Press.

Rennolds, Edwin Hansford. *A History of the Henry County Commands Which Served in the Confederate Army, Including Rosters of the Various Companies Enlisted in Henry County, Tennessee.* Jacksonville, FL: Sun Publishing Company, 1904.

Reynolds, Daniel Harris and Bender, Robert Patrick, eds. *Worthy of the Cause for Which They Fight: The Civil War Diary of Brigadier General Daniel Harris Reynolds, 1861-1865.* Fayetteville, AR: University of Arkansas Press, 2011.

Ridley, Broomfield L. *Battles and Sketches of the Army of Tennessee.* Mexico, MO: Missouri Printing and Publishing Co., 1906.

Rood, Hosea W. *The Story of the Service of Company E, and the Twelfth Wisconsin Regiment Veteran Volunteer Infantry in the War of the Rebellion.* Milwaukee: Swain & Tate Co., 1893.

Runyan, Morris C. *Eight Days with the Confederates and the Capture of Their Archives, Flags, &c. by Company "G" Ninth New Jersey Vol.* Princeton, NJ: Wm. C. C. Zapf, Printer, 1896.

Saunders, W. J. "Governor Z. B. Vance: Story of the Last Days of the Confederacy in North Carolina." *Southern Historical Society Papers.* 52 Vols. Richmond: Southern Historical Society, 1876-1959. Vol. 32 (1904), 164-168.

Saunier, Joseph A., ed. *A History of the Forty-seventh Regiment, Ohio Veteran Volunteer Infantry.* Hillsboro, OH: Lyle Printing Co., 1903.

Schofield, John McAllister. *Forty-six Years in the Army.* New York: The Century Company, 1897.

Schurz, Carl. *Intimate Letters of Carl Schurz, 1841-1869.* Madison: State Historical Society of Wisconsin, 1928.

Semmes, Raphael. *Memoirs of Service Afloat, During the War Between the States.* Baltimore: Kelly, Piet & Co., 1869.

Sherman, William T. *Memoirs of General William T. Sherman.* Boston: Da Capo Press, 1984.

_____. *Sherman's Civil War: Selected Correspondence of William T. Sherman, 1860-1865.* edited by Jean V. Berlin & Brooks D. Simpson, Chapel Hill, NC: University of North Carolina Press, 1999.

Smith, Barbara Bentley and Baker, Nina Bentley, eds. "Burning Rails as We Pleased": *The Civil War Letters of William Garrigues Bentley, 104th Ohio Volunteer Infantry.* Jefferson, NC: McFarland & Company, Inc., 2010.

Smith, Daniel E. Huger, Smith, Alice R. Huger, and Childs, Amy R., eds. *Mason Smith Family Letters, 1860-1868.* Columbia, SC: University of South Carolina Press, 1950.

Spencer, Cornelia P. *The Last Ninety Days of the War in North Carolina.* New York: Watchman Publishing Co., 1866.

Stauffer, Nelson and Tanis, Norman (ed.). *Civil War Diary.* Northridge, CA: California State University, Northridge Libraries, 1976.

Stearns, I. H. "A New Name for an old Veterans Disease." *Medical Summary,* Vol. 10 (May 1888), 49-50.

_____. "Neurokinesis." *The Medical Bulletin: A Monthly Journal of Medicine and Surgery* (July 1888), 216-217.

Stelle, Abel C. *Memoirs of the Civil War.* New Albany, IN: Abel C. Stelle, 1904.

Stockard, Sallie Walker. *The History of Guilford County, North Carolina.* Knoxville, TN: Gaut-Ogden Co., Printers, 1902.

Strong, Robert Hale and Halsey, Ashley (ed). *A Yankee Private's Civil War.* Chicago: Henry Regnery Co., 1961.

Sylvester, Lorna Lutes, ed. "Gone for a Soldier': The Civil War Letters of Charles Harding Cox." *Indiana Magazine of History,* Vol. 68, Issue 3 (September 1972), 181-239.

Tourgée, Albion W. *The Story of a Thousand.* Buffalo: S. McGerald & Son, 1896.

Thompson, Bradford F. *History of the 112th Regiment of Illinois Volunteer Infantry, In the Great War of the Rebellion, 1862-1865.* Toulon, IL: Stark County News Office, 1885.

Tappan, George H., ed. *The Civil War Journal of Lt. Russell M. Tuttle, New York Volunteer Infantry.* Jefferson, NC: McFarland & Co., Inc., 2006.

United Daughters of the Confederacy, South Carolina Division. *Recollections and Reminiscences 1861-1865 through World War I.* 12 Vols. South Carolina Division, United Daughters of the Confederacy, 1990.

Upson, Theodore. *With Sherman to the Sea.* Baton Rouge: Louisiana State University Press, 1943.

Vance, Zebulon B. *Life and Character of David L. Swain.* Durham, NC: W. T. Blackwell and Co., 1878.

Ward, Dallas T. *The Last Flag of Truce.* Franklinton, NC: Privately published, 1915.

Whitaker, R. H. *Whitaker's Reminiscences: Instances and Anecdotes.* Raleigh: Edwards and Broughton, 1905.

Wills, Charles Wright. *Army Life of an Illinois Soldier, Including a Day by Day Record of Sherman's March to the Sea; Letters and Diary of the Late Charles W. Wills, Private and Sergeant 8th Illinois Infantry; Lieutenant and Battalion Adjutant 7th Illinois Cavalry; Captain, Major and Lieutenant Colonel 103rd Illinois Infantry.* Washington DC: Globe Printing Company, 1906.

Willison, Charles A. *Reminiscences of a Boy's Service with the 76th Ohio in the Fifteenth Army Corps, Under General Sherman, During the Civil War, by that "Boy" at Three Score.* Huntington, WV: Blue Acorn Press, 1995.

Wise, John S. *The End of an Era.* New York: Houghton, Mifflin & Company, 1899.

Wood, A. "The Last Shots by Gen. Johnston's Army." *Confederate Veteran Magazine,* Vol. 16 (1908), 585.

Worsham, W. J. *The Old Nineteenth Tennessee Regiment, C.S.A.: June 1861–April 1865.* Knoxville, TN: Press of Paragon Printing Company, 1902.

Secondary Sources
Books

Angley, Wilson, Cross, Jerry L., and Hill, Michael. *Sherman's March through North Carolina: A Chronology.* Raleigh: North Carolina Department of Cultural Resources, 1995.

Arnett, Ethel Stephens. *Confederate Guns Were Stacked at Greensboro, North Carolina.* Greensboro, NC: Piedmont Press, 1965.

Barefoot, Daniel W. *General Robert F. Hoke: Lee's Modest Warrior.* Winston-Salem, NC: John F. Blair, Pub., 1996.

Barrett, John G. *Sherman's March through the Carolinas.* Chapel Hill, NC: University of North Carolina Press, 1956.

Barringer, Sheridan R., *Fighting for General Lee: Confederate General Rufus Barringer and the North Carolina Cavalry Brigade.* El Dorado Hills: CA: Savas Beatie, 2016.

Beck, Paul N. *Columns of Vengeance: Soldiers, Sioux, and the Punitive Expeditions, 1863-1864.* Norman, OK: University of Oklahoma Press, 2013.

Bradley, Mark L. *Bluecoats and Tar Heels: Soldiers and Civilians in Reconstruction North Carolina.* Lexington, KY: University Press of Kentucky, 2009.

Bradley, Mark L. *The Battle of Bentonville: Last Stand in the Carolinas.* Mason City, IA: Savas Publishing, Inc., 1996.

Bradley, Mark L. *This Astounding Close: The Road to Bennett Place.* Chapel Hill, NC: University of North Carolina Press, 2000.

Browning, Mary A. *Remembering Old Jamestown: A Look Back at the Other South.* Charleston, SC: The History Press, 2008.

Bynum, Victoria E. *Unruly Women: The Politics of Social and Sexual Control in the Old South.* Chapel Hill, NC: University of North Carolina Press, 1992.

Crocq, Marc-Antoine and Crocq, Louis. "Overview: Literature, History, and the DSM All Document PTSD." *Returning Soldiers and PTSD.* Edited by Barbara Krasner. New York: Greenhaven Pub., 2018.

Cunningham, H. H. "Edmund Burke Haywood and Raleigh's Confederate Hospitals." *North Carolina Historical Review,* Vol. 35 (April 1958), 153-166.

Daniel, Larry J. *Soldiering in the Army of Tennessee: A Portrait of Life in a Confederate Army.* Chapel Hill, NC: University of North Carolina, 1991.

Dean, Eric. *Shook Over Hell: Post-Traumatic Stress, Vietnam, and the Civil War.* Cambridge, MA: Harvard University Press, 1997.

Diagnostic and Statistical Manual of Mental Disorders, 5th edition. Washington, DC: American Psychiatric Association Publishing, 2013.

Dunkerly, Robert M. *The Confederate Surrender at Greensboro: The Final Days of the Army of Tennessee, April 1865.* Jefferson, NC: McFarland & Company, 2013.

Dunkleman, Mark H. *Marching with Sherman Through Georgia and the Carolinas with the 154th New York.* Baton Rouge: Louisiana State University Press, 2012.

Foley, Bradley R. and Whicker, Adrian L. *The Civil War Ends: Greensboro, April 1865.* Greensboro, NC: Guilford County Genealogical Society, 2008.

Fleming, James R. *The Confederate Ninth Tennessee Infantry.* Gretna, LA: Pelican Publishing, 2006.

Gibson, John M. *Those 163 Days.* New York: Branhall House, 1961.

Glatthaar, Joseph T. *The March to the Sea and Beyond: Sherman's Troops in the Savannah and Carolinas Campaigns.* New York: New York University Press, 1985.

Grimsley, Mark and Simpson, Brooks D. *The Collapse of the Confederacy.* Lincoln, NE: University of Nebraska Press, 2002.

Hall, Charles W. L. *Plowshares to Bayonets . . . in the Defense of the Heartland: A History of the 27th Regiment Mississippi Infantry, CSA.* Bloomington, IN: Trafford Publishing, 2012.

Hanson, Victor Davis. *The Soul of Battle: From Ancient Times to the Present Day, How Three Great Liberators Vanquished Tyranny.* New York: Free Press. 1999.

Hartley, Chris J. *Stoneman's Raid, 1865.* Winston-Salem: John F. Blair, Publisher, 2010.

Hamilton, Joseph Grégoire de Roulhac. *The Correspondence of Jonathan Worth.* 2 Vols. Raleigh: Edwards & Broughton Printing Co., 1909.

Jones, James P. *John A. Logan: Stalwart Republican from Illinois.* Carbondale, IL: Southern Illinois University Press, 1982.

Jones, Katharine M. *When Sherman Came: Southern Women and the "Great March."* Indianapolis: Bobbs-Merrill Co., Inc., 1964.

Jordan, Brian Matthew. *Marching Home: Union Veterans and Their Unending Civil War.* New York: Liveright Publishing Corporation, 2014.

Kenzer, Robert. *Kinship and Neighborhood in a Southern Community: Orange County, North Carolina, 1849-1881.* Chapel Hill, NC: University of North Carolina Press, 1987.

Linderman, Gerald E. *Embattled Courage: The Experience of Combat in the Civil War.* New York: The Free Press, 1989.

Loague, Larry and Blanck, Peter. *Heavily Laden: Union Veterans, Psychological Illness, and Suicide.* Cambridge, UK: Cambridge University Press, 2018.

Losson, Christopher. *Tennessee's Forgotten Warrior: Frank Cheatham and His Confederate Division.* Knoxville, TN: University of Tennessee Press, 1989.

Lowry, Thomas P. *Sexual Misbehavior in the Civil War: A Compendium.* Bloomington, IN: Xlibris Corporation, 2006.

_____. *The Story the Soldiers Wouldn't Tell: Sex in the Civil War.* Mechanicsburg, PA: Stackpole Books, 1994.

Lundberg, John R. *Granbury's Texas Brigade: Diehard Western Confederates.* Baton Rouge: Louisiana State University Press, 2012.

Marszalek, John F. *Sherman: A Soldier's Passion for Order.* New York: The Free Press, 1993.

Marlow, David H. "Modern War: The American Civil War." *Psychological and Psychosocial Consequences of Combat and Deployment with Special Emphasis on the Gulf War.* Santa Monica, CA: RAND Corporation, 2001.

Meagher, Roger E. and Pryor, Douglas A., eds. *War and Moral Injury: A Reader.* Eugene, OR: Cascade Books, 2018.

Moore, Mark A. *The North Carolina Civil War Atlas: The Old North State at War.* Edited by Jessica A. Bandel and Michael Hill. Raleigh: North Carolina Department of Cultural Resources, 2015.

Mast, Greg. *North Carolina Troops and Volunteers.* Raleigh: North Carolina Division of Archives and History, 1995.

Marten, James. *Sing Not War: The Lives of Union & Confederate Veterans in Gilded Age America.* Chapel Hill, NC: University of North Carolina Press, 2011.

McKean, Brenda. *Blood and War at My Doorstep: North Carolina Civilians in the War between the States.* 2 Vols. Bloomington, IN: Xlibris Corporation, 2011.

Murray, Elizabeth Reid. *Wake: Capital County of North Carolina*. Raleigh: Capital County Publishing Co., 1983.

Rosenburg, R. B. *Living Monuments: Confederate Soldiers' Homes in the New South*. Chapel Hill, NC: University of North Carolina Press, 1993.

Rowell, John W. *Yankee Cavalrymen: Through the Civil War with the Ninth Pennsylvania Cavalry*. Knoxville, TN: University of Tennessee Press, 1971.

Silkenat, David. Driven from Home: North Carolina's Civil War Refugee Crisis. Athens, GA:

University of Georgia Press, 2016,

_____. Moments of Despair: Suicide, Divorce, and Debt in Civil War Era North

Carolina. Chapel Hill, NC: University of North Carolina Press, 2014.

Smith, Andrew F. Starving the South: How the North Won the Civil War. New York: St.

Martin's Press, 2011.

Smith, Margaret Supplee and Wilson, Emily Herring. *North Carolina Women: Making History*. Chapel Hill, NC: University of North Carolina Press, 1999.

Sommerville, Diane Miller. *Aberration of Mind: Suicide and Suffering in the Civil War-Era South*. Chapel Hill, NC: University of North Carolina Press, 2018.

Symonds, Craig. *Joseph E. Johnston: A Civil War Biography*. New York: W. W. Norton & Co., 1992.

Trudeau, Noah Andre. *Out of the Storm: The End of the Civil War, April-June 1865*. Baton Rouge: Louisiana State University Press, 1995.

Warner, Ezra. *Generals in Gray: Lives of the Confederate Commanders*. Baton Rouge: Louisiana State University Press, 1959.

Secondary Sources
Articles

Achenbaum, W. A., Howell, J. D., and Parker, M. "Patterns of alcohol use and abuse among aging Civil War veterans, 1865-1920." *Bulletin of the New York Academy of Medicine*, Vol. 69 (January-February 1993), 69-85.

Abdul-Hamid, Walid Khalid and Hughes, Jamie Hacker. "Nothing New Under the Sun: Post-traumatic Stress Disorders in the Ancient World." *Early Science and Medicine Journal*, Vol. 19 (2014), 545-557.

Costa, Dora L., Yetter, Noelle, and DeSomer, Heather. "Intergenerational transmission of paternal trauma among US Civil War ex-POWs." *Proceedings of the National Academy of Sciences* (October 2018). United States Department of Veterans Affairs, www.pnas.org/content/115/44/11215accessed January 2, 2020.

Costa, Dora L.; DeSomer, Heather; Hanss, Eric; Roudiez, Christopher; Wilson, Sven E.; and Yetter, Noelle. "Union Army veterans, all grown up." *Historical Methods: A Journal of Quantitative and Interdisciplinary History*, Vol. 50, No. 2 (2017), 79-95.

Courtwright, David T. "The Hidden Epidemic: Opiate Addiction and Cocaine Use in the South, 1860-1920." *The Journal of Southern History*, Vol. 49, No. 1 (1983), 57-72.

Dettmer, Jonathan R., Kappes, Erika M., and Santiago, Patcho N. "Shame and Moral Injury in an Operation Iraqi Freedom Combat Veteran." Edited by Elspeth Cameron Ritchie. *Post-traumatic Stress Disorder and Related Diseases in Combat Veterans*. Cham, Switzerland: Springer International Publishing, 2015.

Di-Capua, Yoav. "Trauma and Other Historians: An Introduction." *Historical Reflections/Réflexions Historiques*, Vol. 41, Issue 3 (2015), 1-13.

Dwivedi, Manish. "Physiology and Anatomy of Stress." *Journal of Advanced Research in Ayurveda, Yoga, Unani, Siddha Homeopathy*, Vol. 2, No. 3 & 4 (2015), 23-26.

Fellman, Michael. "Inside Wars: The Cultural Crisis of Warfare and the Values of Ordinary People." *Australasian Journal of American Studies*, Vol. 10 (December 1991), 1-10.

Friedman, Matthew J., Schnurr, Paula P., and McDonagh-Coyle, Annmarie. "Post-Traumatic Stress Disorder in the Military Veteran." *Psychiatric Clinics of North America*, Vol. 17, Issue 2 (June 1994), 265-277.

Gallager, Gary and Meirer, Kathryn S. "Coming to Terms with Civil War Military History." *Journal of the Civil War Era*, No. 4, 487-508.

Horwitz, Tony. "Did Civil War Soldiers Have PTSD?" *Smithsonian Magazine* (January 2015), www.smithsonianmag.com/history/ptsd-civil-wars-hidden-legacy-180953 652/, accessed December 21, 2019.

Jones, Jonathan. "War Trauma and the American Civil War: A Roundtable Discussion." H-Net, networks.h-net.org/node/4113/discussions/3182603/sha-2018-report-war-trauma-and-american-civil-war-roundtable, accessed February 29, 2020.

Kruman, Marc W. "Dissent in the Confederacy: The North Carolina Experience." *Civil War History*, Vol. 27, No. 4 (December 1981), 293-313.

Lande, R. Gregory. "Felo De Se: Soldier Suicides in America's Civil War." *Military Medicine*, Vol. 176, No. 5 (May 2011), 531-536.

McNeill, William J. "A Survey of Confederate Soldier Morale During Sherman's Campaign Through Georgia and the Carolinas." *The Georgia Historical Quarterly*, Vol. 55, No. 1 (Spring 1971), 1-25.

Nelson, B. H. "Some Aspects of Negro Life in North Carolina During the Civil War." *North Carolina Historical Review*, Vol. 25, No. 2 (April 1948), 143-166.

Parker, Daisy. "John Milton, Governor of Florida: A Loyal Confederate." *The Florida Historical Quarterly*, Vol. 20, No. 4 (April 1942), 361.

Pizarro, J., Silver, Roxanne C., and Prause, JoAnn. "Physical and Mental Health Costs to Traumatic War Experiences Among Civil War Veterans." *Archives of General Psychiatry*, Vol. 63, No. 2 (February 2006), 193-200.

Rogers, Abbie. "Confederates and Quakers: The Shared Wartime Experience." *Quaker History*, Vol. 99, No. 2 (Fall 2010), 1-19.

Silkenat, David. "?In Good Hands, in a Safe Place': Female Academies in Confederate North Carolina." *North Carolina Historical Review*, Vol. 88, No. 1 (January 2011), 40-71.

Simmons, R. Hugh. "The 12th Louisiana in North Carolina, January-April, 1865." *Louisiana History: The Journal of Louisiana Historical Association*, Vol. 36, No. 1 (Winter 1995), 77-108.

Sommerville, Diane Miller. "'Will They Ever Be Able to Forget?' Confederate Soldiers and Mental Illness in the Defeated South." *Weirding the War: Stories from the Civil War's Ragged Edges*, edited by Stephen Berry. Athens, GA: University of Georgia Press, 2011.

Thomas, Cornelius W. "Post-traumatic stress disorder: review of DSM criteria and functional neuroanatomy." *Marshall Journal of Medicine*, Vol. 4, Issue 2 (2018), 29-45.

Volpicelli, Joseph; Balaraman, Geetha; Hahn, Julie; Wallace, Heather; and Bux, Donald. "The role of uncontrollable trauma in the development of PTSD and alcohol addiction." *Alcohol, Research, & Health*, Vol. 23, No. 4 (February 1999), 256-262.

Yates, Richard E. "Governor Vance and the End of the War in North Carolina." *North Carolina Historical Review*, Vol. 18 (October 1941), 315-338.

Theses and Dissertations

Lundberg, John R. "Granbury's Texas Brigade, C.S.A.: The Color Brigade of the Army." MA thesis, Texas Christian University, 2005.

McGee, David H. "On the Edge of the Crater: The Transformation of Raleigh, North Carolina, Households and Communities during the Civil War Era." Ph.D. dissertation, University of Georgia, 2000.

Index

Ernest A. Dollar Jr., a native of Durham, North Carolina, graduated from the University of North Carolina-Greensboro with B.A. in History, a B.F.A. in Design in 1993, and M.A. in Public History from North Carolina State in 2006. He served in the U.S. Army Reserve/North Carolina National Guard from 1993–1999. Ernest has worked in several historic parks in both North and South Carolina, including as executive director of the Orange County Historical Museum, Preservation Chapel Hill. He currently serves as the director of the City of Raleigh Museum and Dr. M. T. Pope House Museum. He lives in Durham with his wife, Suzie, and their sons Elijah and Kilby.